SPIRITUAL
PARENTING

Books by David L. Carroll

Living with Dying
When Your Loved One Has Alzheimer's
The Complete Book of Children's Allergies
The Home Medical Handbook
Complete Book of Natural Medicine
Complete Book of Natural Foods

SPIRITUAL
PARENTING

David L. Carroll

Marlowe & Company
NEW YORK

First edition, 1990

Published in the United States by

Marlowe & Company
632 Broadway, Seventh Floor
New York, New York 10012

A Paperback Original,
Designed by Virginia Norey

Library of Congress Cataloging-in-Publication Data

Carroll, David. 1942-
Spiritual parenting / David L. Carroll.—1st ed.
p.   cm.
ISBN 1-56924-959-8
1. Children—Religious life.   2. Parenting—Religious aspects.
3. Religious education of children.   I. Title.
BL625.5.C37   1990
291.4′4—dc20   90-32013
CIP

Manufactured in the United States of America

The paper used in this publication meets the minimum
requirements of American National Standard for Information
Sciences—Permanence of Paper for Printed Library Materials,
ANSI Z39.48-1984.

CONTENTS

SPIRITUAL
PARENTING

1.

Introduction to Spiritual Parenting

GOD'S GREATEST SECRET

A profound story from an ancient Hindu scripture begins on an endless desert where God and a sage named Narada are walking side by side, gazing out at the great emptiness. After some time Narada turns to God and asks: "O Greatest Lord, what is the secret behind the appearances of this world and of the life all creatures live within it?"

God smiles and remains silent.

They continue on. "Child," God says after some time, looking toward the horizon. "I've become thirsty from the heat of the sun. If you walk ahead a short way you will find a river. Follow it till you come to a town, then go to one of the houses there and fetch me a cup of cool water."

"Immediately," replies Narada, and he sets off.

After walking several minutes through the wilderness Narada indeed comes upon a river; beyond it is a busy settlement. Approaching a tidy-looking farmhouse, he knocks at its ancient wooden door. Immediately it is opened by a beautiful young woman. Her eyes are luminous and strange; they remind him of his Great Lord's eyes; the moment Narada looks into them he forgets God's command and the purpose of his visit.

The girl shows him in. Perhaps he would care for some refreshment? Inside, the girl's father and mother seem to be expecting the sage's arrival, and a selection of delicious food is waiting for him. No one asks why he has come or what he wants here. It is as if he is simply an old friend, away for many years and now returned.

Narada stays on with this kindly family for several days, enjoying their hospitality and secretly marveling at the young woman's beauty. A week goes by, then two. Narada begins to share in the daily farm chores, and soon the family invites him to remain as a permanent guest. He accepts happily, and more time passes. Finally, after many idyllic days, Narada asks for the girl's hand in marriage. The father is delighted. Everyone was hoping for just this, he exclaims.

Narada and the young woman marry joyously and settle down in her family's household. Before long she bears him a son, then a second, and finally a daughter. Narada opens a small shop in the village and it quickly prospers. When his wife's mother and father die he takes over as head of the family. More time passes and the villagers come to depend on Narada for financial guidance and then for personal advice; soon he is made a high official of the town council. Eventually his life becomes completely immersed in the natural joys and sorrows that existence in a small town brings. Life continues on in this way, meaningfully and prosperously, for many years.

Then one morning during monsoon season the skies darken and an unusually violent rainstorm erupts. Before long the river starts to overflow and the waters rise so high they threaten to destroy the town. Whole houses are being washed away.

By evening it seems certain that the storm will not abate and that there is no chance of saving the village. Narada warns the townspeople, then gathers his family and leads them into the dark night, hoping to find safety on higher ground. His wife and two sons cling tightly to his waist as they struggle against the roaring winds. He presses his young daughter to his breast.

But the winds blow so violently and the waters have risen so high that while Narada is fighting his way against the columns of rain he stumbles, and one of his sons is ripped from his arms by the angry elements. He reaches for the child and in so doing lets go of the second. A moment later a powerful wind tears his little daughter from his grasp, and then his beloved wife is washed away into the roaring darkness.

Narada wails helplessly and claws at the sky. But his cries are drowned by a towering wave that rises from the depths of the terrible night, knocking him down and unconscious. His body is tossed by the howling waters and thrown headlong into the river.

Many hours pass, perhaps even days. Slowly, painfully, Narada comes to his senses, only to discover that he has been washed onto a sandbank far down the river, almost naked and half dead. It is daytime now and the storm has passed. But there is no sign of his family anywhere—nor, for that matter, of any living creature.

For some moments Narada lays face-down on the hard sand, aching and alone, almost mad with sorrow and abandonment. Bits of wreckage float past him in the river and the smell of death is on the wind. Everything has been taken from him now; there is nothing left; all things dear and precious have disappeared into the swirling waters. There is little to do, it seems, but weep.

Then suddenly, Narada hears a voice. It makes the blood stop in his veins. "Child," it says. "Child. Where is my cup of cool water?"

Narada turns and sees God standing by his side. The river has vanished and once again they are alone in the midst of an endless desert. "Where is my water?" God asks again. "I have been waiting now almost a full five minutes."

Narada throws himself at his Lord's feet and begs His forgiveness. "I forgot!" Narada cries out again and again. "I
forgot, Great Lord,—forgive me!" God smiles and says:
"Now, Narada, now do you understand the secret behind the
appearances of this world?"[1]

WE COME TO LEARN

If you believe in the existence of a higher power, and if you
think that life has ultimate spiritual meaning, you probably
also subscribe to the somewhat unmodern belief that we
human beings—just like Narada—are sent to this world at this
time *to learn something.*

Instructions in life continue from womb to tomb, of course,
and in many ways the older we get the more demanding they
become. But the lessons we are taught as children have a
special quality all their own. They reside in a separate chamber of our minds and hearts, a chamber that cannot be opened
again once childhood is over but that can never be entirely
closed either.

These lessons are the most influential we will ever receive
in all our lives. Once planted, no one can entirely uproot
them. Once accepted, they can never be fully returned.
Drop by drop, day by day, for better and for worse, they
form our character and our fate. "As we become drunkards
by so many acts," said William James, "so may we become
saints."

This is a particularly ironic fact when you consider that
during this early period so critical to our formation we are,
paradoxically, given the *least* amount of say over our own
destinies. At an age when, ideally, we should be carefully
selecting the influences that will mold us as adults, nature
instead renders us as impotent as—well, as newborn babes.
Not only has God in His infinite wisdom taken the matters of
early personality formation out of our hands; he has as well
placed them in the hands of two perfect strangers: our parents.

THIS BOOK IS FOR YOU

If you are taking the time to read this book I will therefore assume that you are:

1) A parent, grandparent, perspective parent, step-parent, godparent, someday-to-be parent—or the friend or relative of someone who fits this description. And, or:

2) A person who is attracted to spiritual teachings.

3) A person who is interested in raising children in a spiritual way.

As a father myself, I discovered that there was something of my own involvement in all three of these categories. When my first child was born I also learned, to my disappointment, that few books have been written to accommodate those who share these concerns.

True, religious publishing houses of a number of persuasions distribute writings, some of them excellent, on child rearing as seen from their own particular perspective. And several top-notch books on parenting have been produced over the years by spiritually oriented educators, philosophers, and New Age professionals. But as yet few works have been written on child raising for those parents who may or may not practice a particular religion but who nonetheless desire to bring their children up with a definite *concept of the sacred.*

As a professional author, full-time parent, and sometime teacher I decided I would hazard the perilous job of filling this gap—with a little help from my friends. What follows is therefore an approach to the age-old question of child rearing, seen this time from a nondenominational yet wholeheartedly *religious* perspective—if by religious we agree to mean the desire of the human soul to know the Divine. It is hoped that a committed Christian, Jew, Muslim, Buddhist, or Hindu (among others) can read this book with much agreement and a minimum of objection. It is also hoped that spiritually minded persons who belong to no particular church or synagogue but who believe in a higher power, and wish their child to believe in it too, will find what they read here useful and appropriate.

SPIRITUAL VERSUS RELIGIOUS

I gave the manuscript of this book to some friends for a critical reading. Two of these friends are teachers, two work in the field of children's education; one is an editor, one a minister, one a child psychologist. Though most of them liked the project, several were put off by the book's insistence that the terms *spiritual* and *religious* be taken as synonymous. They protested that sacerdotal trappings—mantras, rosaries, statues of Christ or Buddha—have nothing to do with the real spiritual journey; that spirituality pertains to brotherly love and reverence for life, not to churchly "bells and smells"; and that all reference to organized religions should be swept from these pages as one purges idols from a temple.

I understand the thinking behind this sentiment. But I do not agree with it, and I hope that you will come not to agree with it either. In my opinion and, more importantly, in the opinion of many wise and kind advisers whose names will appear throughout these pages, the inner contemplative process and the outer religious form are *both* necessary if a child is to develop a sense of the sacred. "Without faith," one astute writer remarked, "ritual is dry and empty; but without ritual, faith is scattered and uncontained."

Today especially, there is much confusion concerning the difference between the religious and the spiritual, as evinced by my friends' critiques. One informed me "You must draw a distinction between the spiritual on one hand, and religiosity on the other." Another remarked that "We are on a spiritual quest in this book, we are seekers of reverence for life, of all life. Hail Marys are not worth much on this trip, nor are crosses, or Stars of David, or trips to the Kaaba in Mecca, for that matter."

Let's begin by agreeing that at the heart of this disagreement is a vague, half-defined notion on the part of my friends that everything of social or ethical benefit is also, ipso facto, spiritual as well. This is the school of thought which believes that if you are kind to your spouse and neighbor, eat vegetarian and do Oriental exercises, respect animals' rights, attend channeling sessions, practice natural medicine, and march for world peace you are automatically a "spiritual" person.

You are a social-minded person, most likely, if you practice such activities, and perhaps a righteous one too. But you are spiritual *only* if you also believe in a higher intelligence, and if you actively strive to know its holy name. Otherwise you practice what the Muslims call *shirk,* which means worshiping the signs of God as God Himself. To paraphrase the First Commandment, *thou art having other gods before Me.* In Zen Buddhism the same idea is expressed, if a bit more elliptically, in the venerable edict, "A finger is pointing toward the moon; but don't mistake the finger for the moon." Spiritual in this book, therefore, refers exclusively to belief in the *spiritus—* which means, in turn, the Breath of the Divine.

As for the outer trappings of religion, the crosses, rosaries, Stars of David, the gods with many arms, plus the many other sacred symbols which tend to so irritate the nonreligious and irreligious, these are nothing more than contemplative aids designed to remind worshipers of sacred principles and to serve as concentration supports during prayer and meditation. They also possess, it is thought by many esoterically minded people, an inherent transformative power of their own. Just to see these symbols, it is believed by some, to hear or touch them, is to receive spiritual benefits.

The fact that ritual and spirituality are part of the same sacred fabric was brought home clearly to the many intellectuals who read the works of D. T. Suzuki and Jack Kerouac in the 1950s and then fancied themselves practitioners of Zen Buddhism. Interpreting Zen as a free-flowing, non-rule-bound teaching which dispensed with ceremony and had no patience with conventional morality, many of these persons were shocked when confronted by in-the-flesh Zen masters who began arriving in the United States during the 1960s from Korea and Japan. These austere, enigmatic men brought with them a highly formalized teaching that de-

manded almost superhuman efforts on the part of its followers. Young people, attracted to the supposed "hang-loose"
quality of Zen, suddenly found themselves whacked by a
stick when they squirmed during meditation or forced to ad-
here to codes of moral behavior diametrically opposed to
their previous style of free living. Sexual abstinence was a
central part of the Zen experience, they learned to their
amazement. So was strict obedience to a teacher's commands. Likewise the worship of Divinity in the form of god
and goddess figures. Surprise!

A similar revelation took place among fans and followers of
Sufism. Fascinated by the beguiling Sufi stories Idries Shah
presented to an avid following during the 1960s and 1970s,
many readers took Shah at face value when he claimed that
the Sufis pay allegiance to no organized religion but are members of a free-floating, magical secret society that traces its
lineage back to Pythagoras. When more reliable information
became available on Sufism in the following years, however,
it was made quite clear that all great Sufi masters quite emphatically insist on the importance of formal Islamic practice—prayer, fasting, pilgrimage to the Kaaba in Mecca, and
readings from the Koran—and that today, in any authentic
Sufi school, East or West, the first prerequisite for becoming
a Sufi is that the newcomer be an orthodox Muslim.

WHAT IS SPIRITUAL PARENTING?

There will thus be no attempt in these pages to turn you
into a "believer" or to convince you that the best approach
to child rearing is the spiritual approach. It is assumed that
you are already somewhat sympathetic to this idea. At the very
least you are not entirely opposed to it.

It will also be taken for granted that you already have some
misgivings concerning the way children are raised in modern
society. That you do not agree, for example, with parents who
believe that satanic music, electronic death games, denatured
foods, explicit sex, and entertainments that depict the type of
hellish horror that most traditional societies do not even

speak of (let alone put proudly on display) should all be a natural part of any normal child's upbringing.

Presumed, too, is that you are uncomfortable with other parents who teach their young that our beautiful world is a dumb machine where blind accident is the only cause and mechanical reaction the only real effect; and that you believe that human beings are more than random mutations whose only purpose is to eat, reproduce, seek pleasure—and to look out for number one.

It is supposed, moreover, that since you worry about the negative influences your children are routinely exposed to, you mourn the lack of positive influences currently available to young minds today.

Finally, it is assumed you believe that children are innately good and that you think they are something very special. Theodore Geisel, better known as the children's author Dr. Seuss, has said it quite well: "A kid is a guy I never write down to. He's interested in what I say if I make it interesting. He is also the last container of a sense of humor, which disappears as he gets older, and he laughs only according to the way the others, society, politics, or race want him to. Then he becomes an adult. And an adult is an obsolete child."

Children, many people believe, arrive at birth fully equipped with the potential for higher states of consciousness. Yet due to the personal and social education foisted on them by the adults who surround them, they soon find themselves, like the sage Narada, lulled into a state of spiritual forgetfulness: of where they came from—their higher Self—and of where they must return—back to this higher Self. They are literally put to sleep by the world. "Truly," states a passage in the Koran, "man is most forgetful, most deluded."

The mechanics behind this process of spiritual sabotage is vividly described by the literary critic and spiritual philosopher, A. R. Orage. A close disciple of the mystical teacher George Gurdjieff, Orage spent many years studying the effect adult influences have on young minds, and the processes by which children are transformed from aware, receptive beings into closed, mechanically behaving adults.

The cause behind this process, Orage believes, can be boiled down to a single critical factor: suggestibility—children's tendency to believe what others tell them, provided they hear it said enough times. "We have been told as children," Orage writes, "that to be rich is a happier state than to be poor; that people are superior or inferior according to their station in life, or their possessions or charm, education or gifts. . . . We are taught to believe that natural greatness is a condition of individual happiness, that amusements amuse, that distinguished company is brilliant, that other people's praise is necessary and that their disapproval is debilitating, that books, pictures, and music are stimulating, that leisure without work is desirable, that it is possible to do to nothing, that fame, the possession of power, titles, success, have real value."[2]

The items described on Orage's list are, metaphorically speaking, synonymous with the young lady in the tale of Narada. This symbol of earthly materiality who, in fact, stands at everyone's door, is known by the Buddhists as Mara, She Who Tempts Persons into Forgetfulness, and by the Hindus as Maya, Illusion. Without God's help (or, perhaps more mysteriously, *because* of His plan) even the wisest sage is rendered helpless when he gazes into this goddess' laughing, lingering eyes. He, like all of us, forgets that "everything that is here passes away, and there remains but the Face of thy Lord."

From a symbolic point of view, moreover, the moment of each person's birth is a also reenactment of Narada's fall. "We tumble out of the Beyond into the ether," as a Hindu text describes it, then onto this hard planet through the gateway of our mother's womb, whether kicked out or volunteered we do not know. Intoxicated by this shimmering world, we quickly forget our sacred origins, just as Narada forgot his divine command, and we are obliged to begin at the beginning, as children, with the world as our schoolhouse and two strangers as our instructors. "Man is born drunk," a Japanese saying has it, "and dies asleep." But yet "No one can imagine what a mighty opportunity it is to be born a human being," a Tibetan saying puts it. Another story tells of a child in the womb who is about to be born. The child repeats to itself over and over: "I will remember who I am, I will remember who I am." But, alas, at the moment of birth the cry from the child's lips echoes the first cry of newborn children everywhere: "Oh, I have forgotten! I have forgotten!"

This book and any other book that dares speak of such lofty things as spiritual parenting is thus based on the premise that it is every parent's duty to help put children in touch with their own spiritual potential. This potential is present in each of us, waiting to be awakened up like the sleeping princess in the fairy tale, *calling* to us, even. Spiritual parents believe that children who are encouraged to express this inner impulse will at some point in their lives then ask the ultimate questions: "Who am I? Where have I come from? Where am I going?" Once these questions are seriously pondered, humankind has believed for eons, the search for the sacred will follow, as the Buddhist *Dharmapada* says, as "naturally as the cart follows the horse."

To some people child raising seems a small thing, something to be gotten over with posthaste so that parents can "get on" with their lives. But it is not a small thing. It is a big thing, a big opportunity. So big that you will want to start now, right away, while the iron is hot and the child willing. So that at some sad day in the future you will not have to go on record with the writer Christopher Morley and with innumerable other parents who nostalgically lament: "We've had bad luck with our kids—they've all grown up."

Onward. Upward.

PART · 1

THE SPIRITUAL EDUCATION OF CHILDREN

2.

Spiritual Education Begins at Birth

It is never too early to begin a child's spiritual education. The hour of its first breath is not too soon. In the religion of Islam the moment a new being emerges from the womb, before it is washed or the umbilical cord cut, the father whispers into its ear *La ilahu illa Allah* ("There is no god but God"). In certain Christian sects the Lord's Prayer is recited to the child before it is an hour old, while among the Laguna Pueblo Indian tribes of the American Southwest a newborn's parents bathe their child in yucca weed while prayers are said aloud; then, just before the sun has set, they paint its body with white clay and sprinkle ashes on top of the clay. These remind this new soul that it, too, will someday return to dust. The child's spiritual education has begun.

Oscar Wilde once remarked that contemporary wallpaper was so ugly that a person exposed to it from childhood could cite it in court as a justification for turning to a life of crime. Wilde is spinning a caricature, as usual. Yet, as with the satirist's exaggeration, there is truth to his joke. What we see and hear and taste and smell as newborns, many writers, religious thinkers, and even some scientists believe, remains imprinted on our psyches like a brand, producing psychic ripples that spread out in concentric circles over time, continuing to influence behavior through every stage of our life.

This process starts at hour one. Imagine how strange and enormous the looming walls of a room appear to infants as they focus on their new world, how gargantuan the family members who hover above the crib. How monumental and alive the cartoon figures on the wallpaper; or the ceiling with its miraculous rivers of meandering cracks, or the stuffed rabbits and bears grinning down like good-natured giants. No habits of perception are established yet, no right and wrong way of looking at things. All is new:

> *How like an angel came I down!*
>   *How bright are all things here!*
> *When first among His works I did appear*
>   *Oh, how their glory did me crown!*
> *The world resembled his eternity,*
>   *In which my soul did walk;*
> *And everything that I did see*
>   *Did with me talk. . . .*
>   *—Thomas Traherne, "Poems of Felicity"*

Carlos Casteneda, in *Tales of Power,* the fifth book in his famous Don Juan series, presents an amazingly vivid portrait of an infant's sensory world, recalled while reliving memories of his own infancy during his training as a Yaqui Indian *brujo,* or shaman. Whether drawn from Casteneda's literary imagination or from actual visionary experience we will probably never know. But surely this strange, almost psychedelic passage must rank as one of the most astonishing descriptions ever written of an infant's perception of the world. It is worth quoting in its entirety:

> *I looked around. I was still in a dream, or having a vision of some sort. . . . It took me a long moment to orient myself. I was*

actually lying on my stomach and what I was lying on was a most spectacular floor. As I examined it, I could not avoid a feeling of awe and wonder. I could not conceive what it was made of. Irregular slabs of some unknown substance had been placed in a most intricate yet simple fashion. They had been put together but were not stuck to the ground or to each other. They were elastic and gave when I attempted to pry them apart with my fingers, but once I released the tension they went right back to their original position.

I tried to get up and was seized by the most outlandish sensory distortion. I had no control over my body; in fact, my body did not seem to be my own. It was inert; I had no connection to any of its parts and when I tried to stand up I could not move my arms and I wobbled helplessly on my stomach, rolling on my side. The momentum of my wobbling almost made me do a complete turn onto my stomach again. My outstretched arms and legs prevented me from turning over and I came to rest on my back. In that position I caught a glimpse of two strangely shaped legs and the most distorted feet I had ever seen. It was my body! I tried to curve my back and look at my legs but I could only jerk my body. I was looking directly at a yellow sky, a deep, rich lemon-yellow sky. It had grooves or canals of a deeper yellow tone and an endless number of protuberances that hung like drops of water. The total effect of that incredible sky was staggering. I could not determine if the protuberances were clouds. There were also areas of shadows and areas of different tones of yellow which I discovered as I moved my head from side to side.

Then something else attracted my attention: a sun at the very zenith of the yellow sky, right over my head, a mild sun— judging by the fact that I could stare into it—that cast a soothing, uniform whitish light.

Before I had time to ponder upon all these unearthly sights, I was violently shaken; my head jerked and bobbed back and forth. I felt I was being lifted. I heard a shrill voice and giggling and I was confronted by a most amazing sight: a giant barefoot female. Her face was round and enormous. Her black hair was cut in pageboy fashion. Her arms and legs were gigantic. She

*picked me up and lifted me to her shoulder as if I were a doll.
My body hung limp. I was looking down her strong back. She
had a fine fuzz around her shoulders and down her spine.
Looking down from her shoulder, I saw the magnificent floor
again. I could hear it giving elastically under her enormous
weight and I could see the pressure marks that her feet left on
it.*

*She put me down on my stomach in front of a structure, some
sort of building. . . . The giant girl sat next to me and made
the floor squeak. She smelled like candy or strawberries. She
talked to me and I understood everything she said; pointing to
the structure, she told me that I was going to live there.*

*My prowess of observation seemed to increase as I got over
the initial shock of finding myself there. I noticed then that the
building had four exquisite dysfunctional columns. They did not
support anything; they were on top of the building. Their shape
was simplicity itself; they were long and graceful projections that
seemed to be reaching for that awesome, incredibly yellow sky.
The effect of those inverted columns was sheer beauty to me. I
had a seizure of aesthetic rapture.*

*The giant girl made me slide on my back into the structure.
The roof was black and flat and was covered with symmetric
holes that let the yellowish glare of the sky show through, creating the most intricate patterns. . . . My state of exultation was
so immense at that moment that I wanted to weep, or stay there
forever. But some force, or tension, or something undefinable
began to pull me. Suddenly I found myself out of the structure,
still lying on my back. The giant girl was there, but there was
another being with her, a woman so big that she reached to the
sky and eclipsed the sun. Compared to her the giant girl was just
a little girl. The big woman was angry; she grabbed the structure
by one of its columns, lifted it up, turned it upside down, and
set it on the floor. It was a chair!*

*That realization was like a catalyst; it triggered some over-
whelming perceptions. I went through a series of images that
were disconnected but could be made to stand as a sequence. In
successive flashes I saw or realized that the magnificent and
incomprehensible floor was a straw mat; the yellow sky was the*

ceiling of a room; the sun was a light bulb; the structure that had evoked such rapture in me was a chair that a child had turned upside down to play house.''[1]

PROTECT YOUR NEWBORN
FROM INTRUSIVE INFLUENCES

The philosophy of the remarkable educator/philosopher/ mystic Rudolf Steiner, gives support to Casteneda's primal vision. Born and educated in Austria, Steiner spent his youth formulating a theory of universal knowledge and his later years turning this theory into a "science of the spirit" which he termed Anthrosophy.

Besides contributing to metaphysics, dance, painting, medicine, architecture, and agriculture, Anthrosophy developed a method of spiritual education for children that is still taught today in Waldorf schools around the world. An essential part of its teaching is that children are, quite literally, pure vehicles of light at birth, and that they must be carefully sheltered in the first several years after birth if their faculties are to remain intact. Pediatrician Norbert Glas, speaking for Steiner's system, caution us that during infancy a child's soul is still finding its proper inclination within its body, and that overstimulating its sense organs may disturb this precarious blending:

A new-born child can be pictured in the following way. The little body, with its over-developed head . . . this little body is surrounded by the invisible soul and spirit. As the child grows these latter are to find their way, step by step, to physical expression. The soul must gradually enter the body. Those around the child, then, should take care that nothing is overhastened, nothing done by force, but all through real love.[2]

Doctor Glas suggests that a bed be procured during the child's early months to accommodate both parents and child. "One could even consider building some sort of little cradle into the big bed," he adds. "But if none of these alternatives is a possibility, the cradle or Moses basket should be placed as near as possible to the mother. She should always be able to listen to the delicate breathing of the baby."

Some parents even believe that father and mother should share their sleeping quarters with young ones throughout childhood, or at least during the early years. Deborah Jackson, a British journalist who has spent much time studying families and interviewing parents on the subject of early sleeping arrangements, presents convincing evidence that a shared parental bed produces a sense of fearlessness and peace in a child that can last throughout a lifetime.[3]

Many childhood difficulties, Jackson believes, result from sleeping alone. Even though parents may be lying in the next room, to the child's immature way of thinking he or she has been sent into dark, terrifying exile. Studies made of youngsters in third-world countries who sleep in the same bed with parents, Jackson describes, show that these children are often free of the kinds of childhood insecurities (nightmares, midnight waking, fear of the dark, insomnia, and the like) that we in the West have come to assume are an inevitable part of infancy. As to the sexual question—How, parents ask, can we make love if a child shares our bed?—there are several possibilities:

> Let children fall asleep in another room, then carry them into your room later, when you are finished.
> Let children sleep with you every night *except* on the nights you wish to make love.
> If possible, make love in the afternoon or at some time of day before bedtime.
> When the child is very young, simply place him or her in a curtained-off area of your room, and proceed as usual. At worst, the child will simply wake up and cry.

EVEN AT BIRTH

Harsh impressions leave their mark even during the birth process, some doctors believe. Dr. Frederick Leboyer, a

French physician whose pioneering obstetric work has opened the eyes of many parents and doctors alike, has long insisted that newborns are keenly aware of their environment, and that the first few hours after birth are perhaps the most important of a child's life. In his now-famous book, *Birth Without Violence,* Leboyer presents readers with a series of birthing techniques which are designed to welcome the child to the world instead of dragging it in by the heels. These techniques include:[4]

   • Set the scene in the delivery room. All extraneous observers (including the ubiquitous peeping medical students) are barred from the premises.
   • During the actual delivery bright lights and loud noises are extinguished the moment the child's head begins to crown. The child is brought into the world in a calm, unhurried, low-light environment. Most babies do not cry under these circumstances, Leboyer explains. Some smile.
   • The moment the child emerges from the womb it is placed on the mother's stomach with the umbilical cord still intact. This is done, Leboyer tells us, both to establish the postnatal bond between mother and child and to provide extra oxygen for the child's proper breathing. Only after the cord has ceased pulsating is it severed. "The infant has not been torn from its mother," Leboyer explains. "The two have merely been parted."
   • Anguished by no longer having soft, fleshy barriers to press up against, newborns must now be given assurance through the medium of touch, and are thus placed in certain secure positions so that their spine lengthens properly and their breathing is unrestricted. Direct skin-on-skin contact is highly significant during these moments, and the infant is lovingly cradled in the mother's hands. "The newborn baby's skin has an intelligence, a sensitivity that we can only begin to imagine," Leboyer explains. To accustom the child to

human touch, he suggests, the parents should rub the infant's back in wavelike motions, massaging, stroking, caressing, communicating security through the affectionate energy of the fingertips.

• After five or six minutes of stroking, the newborn is next placed into a prepared bath of warm water—ninety-eight to ninety-nine degrees—which Leboyer believes is an ideal transition medium from womb to world. Many children at this moment, he insists, open their eyes, reach out, even begin to play. Unlike the crying, crumpled child of operating-room birth, the smiling Leboyer baby has received loving signals from its environment since the moment it first appeared. It is no longer afraid.

• Finally, the child is wrapped snugly in prewarmed diapers and blankets and is allowed to rest. Here, in contrast to the noisy perpetual motion of the womb, "in silent astonishment—it tastes the unknown: stillness."

Studies of older children who have been birthed by the Leboyer method indicate that these youngsters are calmer, more content, and more socially adaptable than those born under the glare of the operating-room lamp. They have fewer problems eating and sleeping, reports indicate, and tend to develop excellent relationships with their parents as the years pass.[5]

Part of the benefit conferred by Leboyer's system is that mother and child are kept together after delivery and are allowed time to form an intimate unit. In the world of animals, when a newborn creature is separated from its mother immediately after birth the mother will not recognize her offspring when she sees it again and will often reject it entirely. Among humans the first few hours and days are of analogous importance, for it is at this time that the crucial process of *bonding* takes place. Joseph Chilton Pearce, in his well-known book on child development, *Magical Child,* defines bonding as a genetically based, hormonally activated event in which the mother and infant are psychically welded together during the first few days of life into a single symbiotic unit.

Such bonding, when it is properly carried out—when the mother continually nurses the child, caresses it, plays with it—can produce an almost supernatural communication between mother and child. Pearce points out how in Uganda doctors and anthropologists report that native babies do not wear diapers, yet never seem to soil themselves. When the mothers were asked why this is so they replied that whenever their babies feel the call of nature they take them immediately to the bushes. The question was then raised, how do you know when a newborn child feels such a call? How, the mothers replied, do *you* know when you have to go to the bathroom? You feel it. Being so well bonded that mother and child are like two persons in one body, the Ugandan mother literally *feels* the child's discomfort and quickly attends to it.[6]

Further support of newborn sensitivity comes from recent scientific studies. William Condon and Louis Sander of Boston University, using high-tech measuring devices and films, found that "as early as the first day of life, the human neonate moves in precise and sustained segments of movement that are synchronous with the articulated structure of adult speech." In more poetic terms, the child literally dances in synchronization to the rises and falls of its parents' voices.[7]

Other studies by A. Meltzoff and M. K. Moore show that children imitate the facial gestures of their parents almost at birth, and that they are quick to copy the mouth movements and head movements made by people who peer down at them in the crib.[8] Writes the well-known child educator Dorothy Corkille Briggs: "From their earliest moments, infants are sensitive to their environment. They know whether they are picked up with tender or tense arms. Long before they know language, infants are aware of whether tones and looks are friendly or kind, harsh or indifferent. Each infant is affected by the 'vibes' around him. And from those messages he forms generalized impressions as to how safe and trustworthy this new world is."[9]

Unlike the self-absorbed mannikin or blank slate posited by

modern psychology in the past, much recent evidence points
to the fact that the newborn is a responsive and intelligent
being who, if coaxed out gently, can relate to its parents with
joyous rapport from the start. "The baby has a miraculous
sureness in understanding us," Frederick Leboyer writes.
"The baby knows everything. *Feels* everything. The baby sees
into the bottom of our hearts, knows the color of our
thoughts. All without language. The newborn baby is a mirror
reflection in our image. It is for us to make its entrance into
a world of joy."

THE FIRST FEW WEEKS AFTER BIRTH
While both Leboyer and Joseph Pearce warn against the
careless exposure of children to negative influences, the positive side of the issue is that wholesome impressions can have
an equally strong effect for the good. The goal, as T. S. Eliot
reports his mother to have once said, is "to make the best of
every faculty."
As soon as newborns are brought home they should be
given an environment that affords protection, harmony, welcome, and silence. Make certain that the crib is positioned
away from drafts, bright lights, and noise. One New York-
based family placed its newborn in a room on the street side
of their apartment so that, the mother explained to me, "He
can get used to the traffic sounds early." But this kind of exposure is disturbing to many newborn children, believes Dr.
Wilhelm zur Linden. A partisan of the Rudolf Steiner philosophy, Linden believes that at birth the child's soul enters
every organ and limb of its body, and that every impression
it receives affects it to its very cells.
"It is therefore obvious," writes zur Linden, "that the quality of the impressions received by the baby is of the greatest
importance. Not only physical noise and bustle or garish
lights or cold but also emotional disturbances, anger, quarrel-
ing or hatred have direct effects on the development of the
child's body." General disharmony can "lead to acute illness
straight away or their effects may go unnoticed for decades

and appear much later in life as various organic weaknesses."
Equally, "healthy impressions, pleasant sounds and light, the
right warmth, love and harmony help the child to build and
transform his body in the right way."[10]

Here are some time-proved methods for shepherding the
newborn child through the potential hazards of its earliest
days.

Keep the Child's Stomach Protected

During the first few weeks of life keep the child warm and
well bundled and make especially sure that the stomach and
lower back are protected. In traditional Oriental medicine the
stomach is considered the storehouse of the life force, and
several acupuncture procedures are designed to draw this
energy (known as the *chi* or *qi*) up from the abdominal region
to nourish the other organs. Many Oriental mothers believe
that the child's stomach is the seat of its life—it is known as
the *hara* in Japan and the *Tan Tien* in China—and they go to
great lengths to keep this area well wrapped during the early
years, believing that if it is chilled the vital force will literally
"leak" out.

Later on, moreover, when children are older and attempt
to sit up, Oriental mothers steady them by placing one hand
across the abdomen and the other at the base of the spine.
Children everywhere respond to this pleasant position, many
parents have noted, as it seems to produce a sensation that is
at once psychologically reassuring and physically supportive.
Warm hands held snugly across a child's stomach and back is
also a wonderful method for calming a fearful child or for
helping it recover from a crying jag.

At a later age in Japan, parents will remind their children
of the importance of the stomach center, the *hara,* and the
latent power there. The concept of stomach power among
both young and old was and to a lesser degree still is central
to Japanese culture where it plays a part in every segment of
life from cooking to Zen Buddhism. Bad posture can damage
the *hara,* the Japanese mother informs her children. Children

are told to sit straight, not to slump "at the *hara,*" and this lesson is remembered by youngsters who may grow up to assume the meditation posture of the monk: knees together, resting on heels, back aligned to an invisible axis whose center of gravity is at the navel. Or the geisha, whose self-contained kneeling posture mirrors the balance of "the stillness in motion" as she arranges flowers or serves tea.

"From childhood the Japanese is taught the power of *Hara.*" The German scholar Karlfried Durckheim writes: "*Hara, Hara,* the father calls to the growing boy when he seems to fail in a task or when physical pain saps his morale and threatens to overpower him or when he loses his head with excitement. . . . All this is such a natural, basic and general knowledge for the Japanese that it is not at all easy for him if you ask him about his secret treasure to raise it to consciousness, let alone to explain it."[11]

Let There Be Light—Slowly

Children double in weight during the first three months of postnatal life and triple within the first year. From birth to six months they will grow at approximately two grams every twenty-four hours, a rate of increase significantly faster than it will ever be again.

Given such an extreme rate of acceleration, it is imperative that infants be looked after with special care during this time, as there is much evidence to show that those deprived of appropriate care during the first year (for example, children raised in institutions) grow up less socially adjusted and less physically robust than their well-tended counterparts.[12]

Part of this nurturance process calls for keeping newborns protected in a low-light environment during the first days and to introduce them to daylight in phases. Be careful not to open the blinds suddenly or to let sunlight stream directly onto the baby's face. Sudden exposure can hurt young eyes and even shock an infant's delicate nervous system, which in the early weeks is especially vulnerable. Some parents train a light directly on the newborn when they are changing the diapers, but this practice is to be discouraged. In one family a newborn's six-year-old brother had the habit of sneaking in at night while the baby was asleep and studying her with a flashlight. The newborn would almost always wake up during these examinations, with appropriate screams and quivers to follow.

Rudolf Steiner suggests that newborns be kept in a cradle with a small canopy above it to filter and soften the light. For babies who cry frequently, he advises that an orange-tinted swatch be stretched across the canopy. The quality of light that passes through, he claims, will have a quieting effect on the child.

Keep Them Warm

Since the child has been living for nine months inside its mother's womb, where the temperature is comfort-controlled, it is wise to continue this thermostatic effect for the first few days after birth. Check all drafts in the nursery area, keep the heat well turned up in winter, and even during the summer months wrap the newborn well. Especially important is to protect the head: "The head," warns Dr. Norbert Glas, should be kept covered for some time, and especially should the fontanelles [the so-called soft spot] be protected so that warmth shall not be lost through these openings in the skull bones. . . . Next to its skin, it should have a soft vest knitted of pure wool, and the head also should be covered with a little woolen bonnet. . . . Just as the rest of the body would quickly become cold if it were not covered, so is this true also of the head in the early months."[13]

Avoid Loud Noises

In the early days, both Glas and zur Linden agree, it is best to keep the newborn child well guarded from noise. After a few weeks regular garden-variety household sounds can be allowed without doing any harm, and, in fact, the hubbub of older brothers and sisters playing or parents chatting will make an excellent introduction to social life.

At the same time, zur Linden warns, raucous mechanical noises such as the vacuum cleaner should be discouraged as long as possible. "Sounds from radio and television, even music, are particularly harmful," he claims, "whereas live music, especially singing . . . is helpful for the child."[14]

Introducing Your Baby to the Outdoors

Some parents believe that newborns should be taken outside immediately, during the first week of life, to accustom them to the bustle of the world. But imagine how confusing this assault of impressions can be for a child, to be taken suddenly from the serenity of womb and cradle into the clanging, banging din of Main Street. A good rule of thumb is to wait two weeks before wheeling newborns out-of-doors, then to take them out only for short periods each day.

If you live in the suburbs or country, spend a few minutes introducing children to the nearby flowers and trees on your first outing. Show them the sky and the ground, the flowers and grass. Then return home. Next day come back to the same spot and look at the same flowers or trees. The day after that let children see more, and the next day a little more. Hold their little hands out to touch a twig or leaf. Talk to them. Babies are extremely receptive to impressions at this age. A little goes a long way now.

If you live in the city, follow the same routine but be sparing, as urban environments can quickly become enervating to infants. A nearby park or even a playground will make an ideal first visiting spot.

Prepare to See Individual Character Differences Early

Differences of temperament seem to manifest themselves at birth. Causes can be attributed to genetics, environment, nutrition—or, from a spiritual standpoint, to fate, karma, God's will, whatever one chooses to call it. One infant may cuddle serenely in its mother's arms. Another howls and kicks when picked up. Still another is able to sleep through the noise of a power generator.

What is the significance of these early differences? One study of 141 children done over a fourteen-year period at Northwestern University suggests that such characteristics are expressions of a child's inborn temperament and that every newborn brings with it behavioral tendencies that continue into adulthood. A physician who examined one of my own daughters several days after she was born noted that she had a noticeably serene disposition, even when poked and pinched. "She'll probably stay this way," the doctor remarked. "Quiet babies tend to remain quiet, you know. Noisy ones stay that way too." He thought for a moment, then added: "My own kid started out being a terror from day one— he's thirty-six now and he's *still* making everyone miserable!"

The psychologists A. Thomas, S. Chess, and H. G. Birch, observing that certain character tendencies seen to be innate, formulated the theory that newborns arrive ready-made in one of three basic temperament types which they term Easy, Difficult, and Slow to warm up. For example:

Easy infants are relaxed, cry little, smile easily, and are agreeably adaptable to their surroundings. Often they remain affable all through childhood and up to their teenage years.

Difficult infants can be feisty handfuls. They react violently to new people, to unusual situations, even to their parent's own cutchie-cooings. As they get older they may tend to be peevish and stubborn though also energetic, intelligent, and full of curiosity about the world around them.

Slow-to-warm-up kids are withdrawn, careful, gentle, and cautious in their response to the world. Unlike the difficult tantrum-throwers, they do not willingly express their feelings. Unlike the easy child, they are often lackadaisical. In later life, the authors found, children of this type temperament tend to have difficulty relating to others and dealing with competitive situations.[15]

Interestingly enough, these three infant types correspond

to an ancient system of classification used by Hindus to categorize not only children but also food, weather, disease, and just about anything else in the world you can think of. According to Hindu doctrine, three fundamental forces are at work in the universe: *sattva, rajas,* and *tamas.*

Sattva is the force of gentleness, equilibrium, balance, and benevolence. Because of it the sun shines, arguments are settled, and the molecular structure of matter maintains its coherence. "Sattvic" children, accordingly, are easy-going, extroverted, and happy, similar to children in the easy category.

Rajas, the second primal force, is the power of violence, autonomy, ego, heat, anger, energy. It causes storms and earthquakes, inspires great ideas and wars, sets all life into motion. "Rajasic" babies are fierce, bright, uncooperative, frequent criers and occasionally tend toward hyperactivity—similar to children in category two.

Tamas is the force of inertia, coldness, rest, and decay. On the cosmic plane it produces quiet, darkness, and entropy. On a human level "tamasic" children are gentle, diffident, slow to get moving. They can be lazy and hard to motivate, but also tenacious and determined once they get on a roll.

Whatever parallels exist between these nomenclatures (and here other systems could similarly be discussed such as the medieval system of "humors" whereby individuals are characterized as *sanguine* [easy], *choleric* [difficult and active], or *phlegmatic* [slow to respond], the purpose of such groupings is simply to help parents understand that their child springs into this world with "prepackaged" tendencies and that these tendencies often show themselves from the beginning, even in the cradle. So go with them. Get a feel for them early. They are the stuff you'll be working with for the next ten or twelve years as you chisel and polish your child's character.

The Importance of Mothering

During the first year of life children's physical and spiritual growth depends largely on their mother. In one study conducted over a six-month period, increases of from five to twenty points in intelligence scores were noted among children who were attentively mothered. In another study of children aged twelve months to twenty-four, quality maternal behavior was found to lead to an upgraded sophistication in the level of a child's play and in a youngster's ability to get along with others.[16]

"A growing body of literature now suggests that even from the first hours after the infant's birth," Alison Clarke-Stewart writes, "the amount and kind of interaction between mother and infant affects the subsequent course of their mutual attachment. . . . Cognitive development seems to be significantly shaped by the mother's behavior. Even at this early age (the first six months) maternal stimulation is highly related to measures of the infant's overall development and IQ . . . and to measures of specific aspects of the infant's perceptual responsiveness and cognitive development. . . . In general, cognitive development seems to be related to stimulating maternal behavior, particularly looking at, talking to, and playing with the baby."[17]

In certain religious traditions, especially the Hindu and Taoist, it is even believed that the umbilical cord connecting mother and child has an invisible counterpart constructed of etheric or "astral" substances. Unlike the physical one, the invisible cord is supposedly not severed at delivery but continues to keep mother and child attached for months and even years after birth. This cord is believed to remain intact over great distances, even thousands of miles, though it functions best when mother and child are together.

Many people have witnessed how newborns become sick or agitated if separated from their mothers, or how they seem to sense the mother's return, becoming suddenly animated or serene minutes before she actually walks into the room. At eight months of age one of my own daughters was left with a babysitter for four or five hours while my wife and I attended a wedding. On returning, the babysitter announced that the child had spent the greater part of the afternoon reaching for a photograph of my wife near the bed, and smelling my wife's nightgown. This binding force, many people believe, is more than psychological; it is the unseen spiritual energy that flows between the nourished and the nourisher and that is a kind of food for both.

In view of this notion (and it doesn't matter much if you accept the idea of an invisible umbilical cord as actual fact or helpful metaphor), mothers who give birth and who then return to their jobs several months later are missing a powerful opportunity both to provide the infant the utmost spiritual nourishment *and* to profit emotionally from the experience. Financial pressures often give parents no options, of course, and then one must acquiesce. But when a choice does exist, it is worth remembering how crucial these first years are in the child's development, how short the time taken off from the job is when seen from the spectrum of one's entire life, and how much there is to gain on both sides by devoting this time exclusively to the infant.

Touching Is Teaching

Skin-to-skin contact is the name of the game here. Babies especially savor the luscious sensation of a massage with warm oil or being soaped up in a warm bath. Stroke your child's neck, glide your palm up and down its back. Use a little baby oil for lubrication. Concentrate on sending your energy into the child's organs as you rub and stroke.

Scientific studies have demonstrated that infants who are frequently fondled and talked to in loving, intelligent tones are healthier and more alert than those who are seldom touched. Dr. Margaret Ribble cites a study made of newborns who, due to a sickness at home, were kept in the hospital for weeks after birth and who were afforded a minimum of affectionate handling during this time. Though the babies were well cared for by the nurses, she notes, a disproportionately large number soon developed weight loss, enlargement of the head and liver, apathy, and severe energy depletion. These symptoms, Dr. Ribble reports, almost all disappeared as soon as the children were taken home and provided with loving physical contact.[18]

The noted anthropologist Ashley Montagu points out in his extraordinarily well-documented work on the social and psychological significance of human touch, *Touching,* that during the first half-hour after birth skin contact between mother and child is a prerequisite if the child's later development is to run smoothly:

> *It is clear that the mother needs her baby immediately after birth quite as much as the baby needs her. Each is primed to develop their own potentialities—the maternal role in the one case, that of developing human in the other. The crucial timing within this sensitive period is the first thirty minutes after birth. Any interruption in the physical contact between mother and infant at this time detrimentally affects both. Physiologically, the physical interaction activates and enhances those essential hormonal and other changes in each which contribute to their optimum functioning. Psychologically, the involvement in each other is profoundly deepened.* "[19]

According to Montagu, a summary of eight clinical studies conducted to determine the effect of touching in infancy reveals that infants who are frequently fondled by their mothers cry less and smile and giggle more than children from control groups who receive a minimum of tactile stimulation. This finding agrees with the work of Dr. Myron Hofer at the Department of Psychiatry at Albert Einstein College of Medicine in New York. According to Hofer, a mother's touch actually provokes positive physiological changes in a child. It serves, for example, to reduce levels of excitability and to keep physiological functions, heartbeat and metabolism, in proper rhythm. Dr. Hofer believes that the effect of early separation from the mother, with its consequent deprivation of tactile stimulation and, equally important, loss of mother's milk, is equivalent to depriving the child of highly important biological information. Hofer suggests that at the early developmental stage it is possible that the child's central nervous system is "informed" of the amount of nutrient in its gut by its mother's milk, and that the cardiac rate becomes regulated accordingly.[20]

Montagu speculates further that lack of physical contact between infant and parent may be responsible for many of the physical ailments and neurotic needs that develop in adult life. Deprivation of loving contact, Montagu suggests, may manifest later on as an "itch to be loved," which translates itself literally in an outbreak of eczema. The popularity of twin beds among married couples, he suggests wryly, correlates to Western child-rearing habits in which the child is made to sleep alone, away from the warm touch of a nurturant figure. "Can it be," he muses, "that dances like the Twist and later ones of the same rock variety, together with rock music, represent at least in part, reactions to a lack of early tactile stimulation, to a deprivation suffered in the antiseptic, dehumanized environment created by obstetricians and hospitals?"[21]

Surround Your Child with Good Thoughts

Although force of mind cannot be gauged on a Richter scale, many parents know instinctively that the quality of their thoughts and feelings affects the atmosphere of the household and that this atmosphere, in turn, affects children, making them gleeful, peevish, or melancholy, in turn.

One mother I know makes a point every morning and evening of sitting by her infant's cradle for ten-minute periods and imagining that she is sending a ball of light, warmth, and love out of her heart into her child's heart. She imagines that the ball surrounds the child, enfolds it, infuses it. She visualizes the child taking this light into itself, transforming it into energy and right determination. She imagines the child playing with the ball, having a catch with angels; she imagines the ball streaking through the air, leaving a glittering silver trail behind that fills the entire room; she pictures the child bathed in the glorious light, laughing and rolling and smiling in joy.

Here are three suggestions from other parents on the same theme:

1. Try not to think angry or careless thoughts when near a very young child. (Some parents try never to argue or disagree in a child's presence.)
2. Maintain a mental image of the child becoming healthy and strong, especially when the child is sick or colicky.
3. Make a point of remembering to say silent prayers for the infant's welfare. (Some parents pray that when the child grows up he or she may become reverent and devout.)

Polly Berrien Berends writes in *Whole Child/Whole Parent*: "The most freeing contributions we can make to our children are mental ones. By constantly calling to mind the child's ideal self, his essential perfection, we keep him free to pursue true freedom."[22] To this Norbert Glas adds: "[I]t is clear that a child should live in an atmosphere of right thoughts. If an untruth is spoken in the world around it, the child takes in harmful thought forces through its sense of thought perception. Loving thoughts in the minds of its mother will make the child jump for joy. They are as blessed a food for his soul as pure milk for his body."[23]

MASSAGING THE INFANT

Though massaging infants is a relatively new procedure in the West, it has been practiced from time immemorial in India and the Orient. Designed to relax the child, clean it, protect its sensitive skin, and stimulate its organs—and most of all, to send it warm, pulsing feelings of love—both mother and father can participate in this luxurious, satisfying act; no training is required. Using warmed mustard or olive oil, begin by rubbing the child's shoulders,

back, and chest. Employ slow, circular motions with
the palms and fingers. Repeat each movement three
times. Knead the flesh on the child's arms and legs,
moving gent'y up and down the arms from fingers
to shoulders. On the legs knead the flesh from the
thighs down to the toes. Then rub the abdominal
area with deep, firm circular movements. After a
little practice your own hands will find the best
way.

Encourage Play

Play is an impulse that comes early for most children, sometimes in the first weeks of life, and it seems to be as highly
developed a childhood instinct as hunger or the desire to
stand. Encourage it, even at this early age. Later on it will help
the grown person develop that most excellent of character
traits, a sense of fun.

Generally speaking, store-bought commercial toys are unnecessary for infants under a year old. Children at this stage
will derive a good deal more entertainment from simple interaction with their parents and siblings: bouncing, patting,
peek-a-boo. For play objects, safe, humble items from nature's toy chest are best now: leaves, flowers, sponges, lamb's
wool swatches. These are gentle and, moreover, will subtly
introduce the child to the building blocks of the natural
world: water, fire, air, and earth.

Water

Water will quickly be discovered and enjoyed in the bath.
Splashing and cupping are great entertainments for infants
during the early months. When they get older and can sit up
on their own, wooden bowls full of water kept on the floor in
a controlled environment provide long periods of amusement. Give the child a wooden mixing spoon and a cup to
further the fun.

Fire

While fire is clearly not a toy for people of any age, parents can introduce their children to this elemental force during the colder months by letting them sit near a fireplace and directing their gaze to the flames. At first fire proves fascinating for most infants, then restful, finally narcotic. Try it. It is no accident that one of the basic yogic meditations is candle-gazing and that this practice has been recommended for centuries as a means of calming the nerves and centering the spirit. Some parents burn candles in an infant's room at night, allowing children to fall asleep by its warm shadows and blending rays. Needless to say, **every safety precaution should be taken if this is done.**

Air

Many infants enjoy having parents blow on their hands and feet. The sensation produces a curious tickling sensation on the skin and prepares infants for the more serious business of windy days to come. After a while toys like pinwheels and kites and hand fans introduce children to the mysteries of wind. One father would regularly take his young daughter out for a stroll on windy days, and as they walked he would ask her if she could tell what the wind's voice was trying to tell her.

Earth

One family I know keeps their infant daughter outside much of the time in a large backyard during the summer months. Since the child can not yet sit up, they make a cozy blanket-and-comforter bed for her on the earth and allow her to lie quietly, gazing up at the sky and trees while the family gardens nearby. Lying on the earth, well protected, allows the subtle ground vibrations to penetrate the child's body as the scents of grass and soil communicate their silent messages. Later, when the child is sitting up and begins to manipulate objects, sand, rattles made from gourds, and pieces of clay will further introduce the element earth.

Introducing New Babies to New People

Be sparing when allowing other people to handle your child, especially strangers or casual acquaintances. At this early age children are like photographic plates, claims the Sufi master Hazrat Inayat Khan: Whatever impressions fall on these plates remain imprinted on them forever. A spiritual teacher in India for many years and a proponent of a form of Sufism heavily influenced by Hinduism, Inayat Khan's writings have done much to introduce Sufi teaching to the Western world. His work continues to be carried on by his son, Pir Vilayat Khan.

In Volume III of his *The Sufi Message*, Inayat Khan produced one of the few true classics ever written on the subject of spiritual parenting. Read it!

Speaking specifically on the matter of a child's early socialization, Khan tells us:

> *In the Orient there is a superstition that an undesirable person must not be allowed to come near an infant. If the parents or relatives see that a certain person should not be in the presence of an infant, that person is avoided for the very reason that the infant is like a photographic plate. The soul is negative, fully responsive, and susceptible to every influence; and the first impression that falls on a soul takes root in it. . . . In the same way a photographic plate is first negative; afterwards, when it has undergone a certain processs, it becomes positive. And that is the process through which the soul passes in its infancy. All that it has brought from the higher spheres and from its family becomes developed, becomes positive or solid, in other words it becomes condensed; because that is the time when the spirit is being formed and is becoming positive. If an undesirable impression has fallen upon an infant at that time, no matter what education is given later that first impression remains concrete and solid. Nothing can erase it because infancy is the moment when the soul is becoming positive.* [24]

The Importance of Rhythm

According to Hindism, all phenomonal existence is a divine dance with God Himself the galactic choreographer, creating and destroying world upon world over vast cycles of time by means of His own primal rhythmic energy. "The Cosmos is His theatre," writes Ananda Coomaraswamy; "there are many different steps in His repertory, He Himself is actor and audience." Infants are a particularly sensitive part of this rhythmic movement and thus respond readily to cadences, to beats and claps and movements, rattles and measured sounds.

When, for instance, children cry from pain or anger, rhythmic rocking will calm their spirit. "The rocking of babies is the custom wherever people's natural instincts have not yet been overlaid by civilization," writes Wilhelm zur Linden. "There is no question of spoiling the child, for only a few minutes of rocking are needed to send him to sleep. The right speed can be found with the help of a lullaby." The gentle to and fro, zur Linden points out, resembles breathing in and out. The repeated slight jolt between every swing helps detach the consciousness from the nervous system and sends the baby to sleep.[25]

Inayat Khan suggests that capturing the attention of a crying child by shaking a rattle or clapping parents can slow the infant's inner speed and bring it into sync with their own. "However excited the infant may be," Khan writes, "begin by making some noise in its rhythm, and then bring it to a normal rhythm. For instance, if a rattle or something similar is first moved with the infant's rhythm, and then moved gradually in a slower rhythm, the infant will come naturally to that rhythm. The excitement will abate; the whole condition of the infant's mind, the blood circulation, the movements, the expression, everything will change to a normal rhythm."[26]

Other rhythmic sounds children respond to include:
- Gently playing a drum or tambourine
- Steadily tapping one's feet or fingers
- Singing soft, repeating melodies.
- Reciting simple metric rhymes. Some parents re-

cite Mother Goose or poetry to crying infants, or read
to them from a selection of sacred writings: Confucius,
the Bible, the Buddhist canon, the *Bhagavad Gita,* the
Koran.

And Finally, Remember . . .
All in all, the most important spiritual messages you can
give to infants during the first year of life is that they can trust
the people around them; that their environment is a safe,
benevolent one; that their parents, especially the mother, are
close by and attentive; and that they are deeply loved. This,
plus a repeat of the reminder: it is never too early to begin a
child's spiritual education. Khan writes: "Most often what
happens is that the parents never think of education at all in
infancy. They think that is the age when the child is a doll, a
toy; that everyone can handle it and play with it. They do not
think that it is the most important moment in the soul's life;
that never again will that opportunity come for a soul to
develop."[27]

3.

Teaching Toddlers

By the time children approach the walking age they are mature enough to learn spiritual fundamentals. Principally, that we live in a world of constant opposites—hot and cold, strong and weak, yes and no—and that the best of all paths through this labyrinth is the middle way, the golden mean between extremes.

Many methods can be used to teach this profound lesson, but undoubtedly one of the best is to use the vehicle of bodily movement itself. Why? Because toddlers take in information concerning the world primarily through the five senses. They study their environment quite scrupulously, yes. But they do so with their fingers and their tongues, their skin and ears and the bottoms of their elbows. The Swiss psychologist Jean Piaget refers to this stage as the sensorimotor period, a time when primary education is received through touchy-feelie impressions rather than the intellect.

Some time ago in New York City I was tending a young child in a large playground when I noticed a mother and her toddler son in a corner playing what at first seemed an odd game. The woman had placed a narrow board about five feet long on the ground in front of her child. At one end of the board the prints of two small feet had been blocked out; a stuffed toy tiger with open arms was secured at the other. A thin, straight line painted directly down the center of board connected the two ends.

The woman was obviously using the invention as a training device to help her child walk a straight line. The idea seemed contrived and farfetched, yet the more I observed the more sense it made. I watched the mother grip her child's hand and coax him down the center line. She patiently guided his aim as he wobbled comically from one side to the other, using the line as a balance coordinate. While they walked, the mother called his attention to the smiling tiger that waited patiently at the end of the board with outstretched paws. The child seemed to be having a whopping good time with all this, and I could have sworn that after a few minutes he was already walking with increased confidence.

MAKE WALKING A SPIRITUAL LESSON

If toddlers are encouraged to develop a sense of physical and mental balance when taking their first steps, this experience of equilibrium will root itself in their psyches as well as their bodies, showing up later (hopefully) in such characteristics as poise, gracefulness, and trust. Why? Because the physical experiences children undergo at a very early age are assimilated in the form of symbols as well as sensations, and these symbols are, in turn, transformed into psychological behavior as well as muscular habits. Dr. Norbert Glas again: "It is possible, through the activity of the sense organs in childhood, to attain later to a quietude of soul so great that one can, as Steiner puts it, feel oneself as a spiritual being. He who was able, as a child, to develop the sense of balance in the right way, may achieve a human quality that can be considered as a climax of individual development: the ability to experience an inner peace and quietness, the working of the spirit."[1]

In turn, if the early experience of walking is a joyous one for children the recollection of finding the magic balance point may (again hopefully) be used later in the quest to find one's own *spiritual center*. Conversely, if the early experience of walking is conflicted, the child may become awkward and tentative as an adult, both physically and emotionally.

Is it pushing the point to suggest that many such metaphors silently guide our lives? Certainly a number of people of spiritual understanding have taken just this point of view. Hazrat Inayat Khan: "The moment when the infant stands up and walks is a moment which should be guarded with the greatest interest and keenness. This is the moment when the powers are being manifested. . . . Now there is a symbolism in the actions of a child. If the child goes straight towards something, that shows the straightness of his nature. If the child is wobbly, then it shows lack of will power. . . . If the child runs and reaches a certain place, it is impulsive and venturesome; it will jump into something when it is grown up. But if an infant as soon as it begins to walk adopts a proper rhythm and reaches a desired spot, that infant is very promising. It shows singleness of purpose and balance by the rhythm of its walk."[2]

Parents can practice their own brand of balance during the toddler's walking lessons, which must be maintained at a point halfway between detachment and overprotectiveness. I watched as Joan, a twelve-month-old, struggled mightily to get to her feet. Her parents were members of a meditation group to which I also belonged, and they believed firmly that their child should accomplish this task alone. No matter how often they were tempted to interfere, they refrained from lifting their daughter or propping her up. "If she starts learning the law that effort counts," Joan's mother told me, "she'll already be on her way."

At the same time, Joan's parents made a point of encouraging their daughter's progress with inspiring words and imagery: "There, there, that's right," I overheard them say one August afternoon in their apartment as Joan took her first steps. "You're as straight as a tree now. That's it—you're standing up tall and reaching to heaven. Up, up you go, touching the sky. That's a girl! You're going to walk across the stars pretty soon! What a big giant step! What a big giant step toward the light you take!"

I talked with Joan's parents afterward concerning their methods of instruction. While Joan could not comprehend all her parents told her, they both agreed, she could recognize basic words: *stop, go, good.* More important, she could intuitively translate her parents' voice tones, and these exerted a powerful guiding force as she tottered and swayed her way to success. Another teaching tool the same parents used was to verbally mirror back Joan's actions to her at the moment they occurred. This, they believed, gives a child a simultaneous sense of succeeding on its own, plus the assurance that the parents' attention is constantly focused on him or her alone: "There, you've fallen down, Joan. Boom! Try again. Now you're getting up again. Now you're on your feet. That's right. Joan's stepping up. That's a tall, straight girl."

When your toddler takes his or her first steps provide encouragement by kneeling down, opening your arms, and exhorting a forward march. In this way you can catch the child who falls *or* be there at the other end with an embrace when the goal is reached. The result in either case is an emotional reward.

Another technique, this one suggested by Inayat Khan, is to encourage toddlers to take their first steps in the direction of something spiritually precious. This something can be the parents themselves. Or it can be an object with religious significance. In Thailand, for example, babies are encouraged to take their first steps toward a statue of the Buddha. If the child responds readily the family celebrates this as an auspicious sign and an indication that the Lord Buddha has favored the child. You can, of course, use whatever inspirational objects you wish: a picture of your spiritual teacher, a sacred book, a meditation diagram—whatever. In this way you provide toddlers with a luminous message as well as an incentive: Wherever you walk in your life you will be walking toward the light.

As a parent you'll realize that your child will hit the floor often and sometimes with a noisy *thwak!* and that trial and error and harmless pratfalls are still the best of all instructors. It is amazing how undaunted children are even after their hundredth fall.

If during the walking process the child does reach out to you in a particularly fearful or needful way, offer help quickly and without argument. The idea is to keep the experience of walking as free from conflict as possible. *Never* tease your child during these moments. I know of one father who made his child walk the length of the room by standing in the youngster's path, encouraging her to come forward for a hug—then, at the last moment, as she was about to tumble into his arms, stepping back several paces and continuing to urge her on with promises of affection. Don't do this to your child. These false promises can break trust. Symbolically they say to the child that mother or father is not to be believed and that the security they offer has strings attached to it, that it is not true security. Therefore—symbolically—God offers no security either. I will live my life in fear and distrust.

LEARNING GAMES FOR TODDLERS (AGES 1–4)

There are many ways for conveying spiritual information to toddlers. One of the best is through play. Child therapists know that children act out their deepest concerns during games and that when children are relaxed and having fun they are especially receptive to learning. While you will want to frame certain spiritual learning games to your child's own personality, these suggestions will get you started:

Let Toddler Toys Be Simple Toys

The English call toddlers runabout babies, and for good reason. Children at this age are explorers par excellence, and

experimenters and runners and knock-downers. Babyproof
your house accordingly, but also leave interesting (but harmless) objects around for the child to touch, fondle, drop, and
examine. Toys, as one child psychologist called them, are the
"textbooks of toddlerhood." Nifty toys for this age include:
 • Soft or hollow blocks
 • Crayons, colored pencils, water colors, finger-
paints, play dough (Stay away from anything that uses
glue; it's too soon.)
 • Swatches of material
 • Homemade dolls and stuffed animals
 • Climbing and swinging apparatus
 • Wooden kitchen utensils: mixing spoons, bowls,
cups
 • Beanbags
 • Hammering toys
 • Natural substances like sand, water, clay
 • Smooth-edged wooden pull toys
 • Simple musical instruments like maracas, small
xylophones, tin-can drums, tambourines, triangles,
whistles, simple flutes, metal pans for use as cymbals
or drums
Keep a toddler's toys earthy and uncomplicated at this age.
No need to stock up on commercial items. Toddlers will find
practically anything you give them amusing. In fact, in any
Montessori classroom you will see children well past toddler
age still playing contentedly with swatches of material, dishes
of walnuts, blocks of wood, and simple round-the-house items
like eggbeaters or coffee pots.
  You can even build child's toys yourself, and if you do
several advantages will come your way. First, it will be easier
on your pocketbook. Second, it will be fun and creative for
you and more special for the child (years after the store-
bought items are forgotten many grownups still own a doll or
boat or wooden pull toy made for them by their parents).
Third, you can tailor-make the toy to the child.
  If you do build toys, remember that they can serve as spiri-

tual reminders as well as entertainment. One father and mother I know, who attend meetings of a Sufi group in New York City and who are trying to bring their child up under the influence of Muslim ideals, procured a photograph of a whirling dervish. They copied the graceful design of the dervish's outspread arms, tall cap, and flowing robes onto a piece of inch-and-a-half-thick pine board and cut the figure out using a jigsaw. Then they drilled a two-inch-deep hole in the bottom of the figure and fitted a half-inch dowel into the hole, allowing about an inch of the dowel to protrude. After painting the figure with bright colors and decorating it with Islamic designs, they mounted it, dowel first, onto a round wooden base with a hole drilled in its center. When completed, the dervish could be spun on its dowel axis, round and round, in imitation of whirling-dervish dancers in Turkey. My friend's two-and-a-half-year-old son plays with it for hours and has even named it: "Spinhead."

In foreign countries one frequently sees children playing with toys that incorporate religious themes. In India a common pull toy is made in the shape of a chariot with the child god Krishna at the reins. Youngsters in the Philippines play house with Nativity figures. In the Buddhist countries of Indochina a small clay Buddha figure is the first plaything given to a child. Among the Pueblo Indians of the American Southwest, at birth all children, boys and girls, receive a katchina doll, believed to be modeled after the deities and spirits who live in the surrounding hills. The children are expected to keep this doll their entire lives and to establish a special rapport with its indwelling spirit.

For parents who do not belong to a particular religion but who want their child to develop a feeling for sacred objects, wooden figures can be decorated with universal symbols: crosses, squared circles, medicine wheels, six-pointed stars, arabesques. Figures of gods and goddesses from mythological tales can be made from wood or paper. One family that followed the teachings of Gurdjieff gave their child a stuffed animal with Gurdjieff's sacred sign, the enneagram, embroidered on the animal's stomach. Another family that belonged to a Tai Chi school made a wooden puzzle for their child using a yin–yang symbol as the design.

Books that provide parents with toy-making ideas and plans for children include:

Mario Dal Fabbro, *How to Make Children's Furniture and Play Equipment* (McGraw-Hill).

Ann Wiseman, *Making Things* (Little, Brown); *Making Things, Book 2* (Little, Brown); and *Making Musical Things* (Macmillan).

Steven Caney, *Invention Book, Toy Book,* and *Play Book* (Workman Press). Emphasizes hands-on toys and experimental games, especially for inquisitive minds.

Goldie Taub Chernoff, *Easy Costumes You Don't Have to Sew* (Macmillan).

Peggy Jenkins, *A Child of God* (Prentice-Hall: Spectrum Books). Emphasizes homemade spiritual toys and games.

Introduce the Concept of Yes and No

During the toddler stage children must learn the difference between yes and no. An interesting way of introducing this idea is to concretize the concept in the child's imagination with visual imagery, using a toy or a physical gadget.

For example: Your child probably owns that favorite toddler's item, a workbench. You match the right-sized block to the right-sized hole, then pound it through with a mallet. Watch as children hammer away. When they attempt to squeeze a round peg into a square hole shake your head seriously and say *"Nooooo!"* When a block and hole match and the young one proudly whacks it through, give a loud, smiling *"Yes!"* There can even be the slight hint of judgment to all this: The nos can be serious, the yeses lighthearted.

The yes-or-no tone of the voice can then be transferred from play objects to actual situations, the toddler's behavior in particular. From now on the young person will have a concrete visual image of what yes and no really mean. *Yes* fits. *No* gets stuck.

Keep Lessons Simple

Don't assume that toddlers of one or two years are capable of understanding complex ethical principles while at play. If they yank the dog's tail it's wise not to launch into philosophical explanations about cruelty to animals, about how much it hurts poor Spot, about how we should always try to be kind to God's creatures. That will come at a later point in their maturity; toddlers are too young to understand another being's pain. Instead, state what it is you wish to communicate in a terse imperative that tells it like it is: "Dear, that hurts the dog. Please don't do it any more." Let it be known in direct terms that the action causes pain and that it should not be repeated. Period.

Emphasize the Constructive

Stress the creative side of children's games and de-emphasize the destructive. Not long ago I watched a group of children enjoying various games in a nursery-school classroom. The teacher was a sensitive woman who informed me that she attempted to convey positive spiritual messages to her children with her presence and body language as well as through her words.

Particularly striking was the way this teacher played blocks with her youngsters. She began by encouraging them to build whatever they liked. As they built she merrily approved their placement of blocks, the choice of colors, the attempts to balance one block on top of the other, and so forth. When

the youngsters knocked the house down, as they inevitably did with screams of pleasure, the teacher would smile coolly. But she did not enter into the children's glee. In fact, she said nothing at all but simply looked quietly at the child, her passivity contrasting with her earlier enthusiasm. In this way she gently and subtly sent an important message to her youngsters: Building up is better than tearing down.

Share in Your Child's Games

Simple interactive games such as patty-cake are among the first ways children learn to give something back to their parents, and to the world. Any game that enhances this message is excellent. Try placing several colorful objects in front of children—shells, flowers, or pieces of colored paper—and have them choose one or two. Then hold out your hand and ask the child to place the object in your palm. Express your gratitude energetically. Then do it again.

Another toddler's game with teaching potential is this-little-piggy. The child has a body and will want to get to know it. Most thrilling is the shout of "Wee, wee, wee, all the way home," which speaks of return and of unexpected moments of glee. Or you can try giving the game a moral twist. The thumb piggy is kind to its friends—it goes to the market to buy them roast beef. The index piggy shares its food at home. The middle-finger piggy loves its brothers and sisters and shares the roast beef with them. The ring-finger piggy gives up all its roast beef to someone who needs it. And so forth.

THE DARK SIDE

A different lesson is contained in the simple game of peek-a-boo. Now the parent's laughing face is here, now it's gone. Disappearance: Life is gain, life is loss. Without stretching the point, peek-a-boo can even be seen as a kind of preliminary exercise in death education. Implicit in this happy little sport is a stark reality: All things pass. The lesson is not spoken or explained. The child's consciousness, in its own way and at its own speed, will get the point.

More spiritually oriented games for toddlers include:

Have children identify simple objects in a picture. Pictures can be chosen for their spiritual or religious content.

Show children a simple inspirational picture minus one or two or its crucial parts. Have them tell you what's missing (this game works best for children in their late twos and early threes).

Sing a song together. Songs can be simple and inspirational. Maintain a 4/4 beat as you sing—children are believed to learn the words of a song better when they sing in this meter.

Encourage children to dance. Expose them to a wide range of ethnic and religious music: Indian sitar music, East Europe folk dances, Chinese lute, Moroccan dervish chants, Irish jigs, Zen chants, Indonesian gamelan.

Montessori Games

Also of great interest for spiritually minded parents are the toddler games and activities devised by Maria Montessori. The first woman to earn a medical degree in Italy and a pioneer worker with mentally retarded children, Montessori's orientation was decidedly spiritual, as can be seen from her private writings. She was also, however, an eminently practical educator who developed a number of simple, to-the-point play techniques designed to awaken a young child's spontaneous interest in learning.

Several activities drawn from Montessori's large canon (and here put into form specifically for the home by the Montessori teacher Elizabeth Hainstock) will prove helpful for increasing the toddler's sensory abilities and expanding their world:

Game to develop the tactile sense. Set up a line of bottles or glasses filled with warm liquids, cold liquids, ice-cold liquids, lukewarm liquids, and so on. Have children touch each container. Explain to them that this container is warm, that one cold, and so forth, then have children identify the different temperatures on their own.

Game to teach color perception. Take a handful of buttons, some blue, some green, some black or brown or red. Separate the buttons by color into different dishes, announcing the name of each color as you sort them. Now have the children do the same. As youngsters begin to get the hang of grouping the colors, increase the number of different colored buttons.

Game to develop the tactile sense. Fill a basket with a variety of textured fabric swatches. Using touch to distinguish between them, have the child pick out the swatches that have approximately the same texture. Then blindfold the child and have him or her do it again.

Game to develop coordination and visual perception of dimensions. Take seven or eight colored blocks of graded size. On a table or floor, pile the blocks up towerlike, the largest blocks toward the bottom, the smallest at the top, in graduated sequence. Count the number of blocks in the tower and identify their colors, then have the child knock it down. Point out how the light blocks fall, the heavy ones stay in place. Let children construct the same tower on their own.

To teach muscle coordination and introduce children to household chores. Procure some dishwashing utensils: soap, towel, apron, sponge, drainer, and so forth. Put on your apron, fill the sink with water, add the soap, and wash several plates with the sponge. Then drain the water, wring out the sponge, and dry the plates. Now invite the child to do the same. After the task is completed encourage the child to put all the utensils away.

To develop control of the fingers. Take a cloth napkin and lay it on the table. Fold it several times into different shapes, then invite the child to try the same. As you fold identify each shape: square, rectangle, trapezoid, triangle.[3]

4.

Rules of the Game for Older Children

A child's inner education begins in earnest after he or she has learned to talk. The opportunities for spiritual growth now are legion and a family strategy will be required, one that prescribes both a philosophy and a blueprint of action for overseeing a child's daily activities.

Though devising a spiritual parenting plan for older children (ages five to ten) depends on the character of the child and the vision of the parents, the following axioms have a more or less universal application and can, with adaptations, be used as a basis for practically any long-term spiritual parenting program:

1. Children Learn Best When They Are Enjoying Themselves.

Punitive education in any subject (and, for that matter, at any age) is an extraordinarily inefficient way to teach. Although pointed out several decades ago by Rudolf Dreikurs, few psychologists today would dispute the fact that "Fear seems to set in motion protective devices in the autonomic nervous system so that neither digestive tract, nor circulation, nor mental process function effectively for an extended period of time. Fear always induces some inner state of tension or panic: this may produce the immediate obedience desired, but it does not bring about constructive learning, or growth in maturity. The child learns to fear and yield to brute force, and a little of his dignity, courage and self-reliance is destroyed with each blow."[1]

In a supportive atmosphere children absorb astonishing amounts of information in amazingly short periods of time. But the moment a scolding makes a child feel stupid or inadequate his or her psychological system shuts down and receptivity shrinks accordingly. Thus, the more upbeat the child's teaching environment is made the better. Vis-à-vis this point, bear in mind that:

2. Many Basic Lessons in Spiritual Parenting Can Be Passed on to Children in the Form of Games, Stories, Puzzles, Skits, Art, Jokes, and Fun.

Spiritual parenting need not—should not—be viewed as a superserious affair or as a formal classroom endeavor. Games, stories, goofing, and antics speak to the little one in the universal childhood language, and that language is *play.* In other words:

3. The Best Kind of Teaching Takes Place When Children Are Not Actively Aware That They Are Being Taught.

Young ones, by and large, are resistant to sitting still for solemn orations on "serious" matters—as parents who have witnessed the zombielike stares produced the moment the "religion speil" is trotted out can testify to. One trick for overcoming resistance is to avoid the "Ahem, I am now going to discourse on the following important spiritual subject" approach, and instead introduce spiritual ideas during moments of relaxed interaction, specifically during play, games, stories, and casual social exchange. The following four chapters will explore this technique through many doors.

A second, related method, and one that complements the first, is to integrate these lessons into the child's world on a day-to-day basis. This means you must:

4. Introduce Lessons into the Child's Consciousness at the Precisely Appropriate Moments, Taking Care to Fit the Right Lessons to the Right Time, Place, and Situation.

Don't, for example, start speaking with children about Divine Mercy when they are absorbed in a favorite TV program or while they are carrying on a serious game of house with their friends. Youngsters will not be receptive at this time and they will resent the intrusion.

On the other hand, certain opportunities lend themselves quite naturally to spiritual conversation. When six-year-old Danny and his grandfather were visiting the zoo and saw a mother lion caressing her young, Danny's grandfather seized the opportunity, pointing out the mother's lion's solicitousness and explaining that God takes care of us in the same way. Another time Danny came into his grandfather's bedroom dangling a dead mole, ready to ask the hard questions. Instead of dodging the issue with platitudes, Grandfather took advantage of the moment by bringing up matters of death and the afterlife, concepts that would otherwise be difficult to work into a conversation with the very young for whom the concept of personal mortality is as far away as the stars.

Whatever the lesson or the teaching situation, be aware that:

5. Incessant Repetition is Always Necessary When Teaching Children.

One trap many parents fall into is the illusion that after one time, or two, or six, or seventeen, a lesson *will* be learned. Unfortunately, it doesn't always work this way. Not that children are dense. They simply don't see any reason why they should go to church or temple every week or be kind to their baby sister or, for that matter, stop writing on the wall with Magic Markers or ripping out pages from your coffee-table editions. Civilized, kindly, reverent behavior must be learned.

The only sure way to get these lessons into the child's brain is s-l-o-w-l-y. Day after day after day after day is the way. No matter how much we wish it were not true, the differences between naughty and good, high and low, do not sink into the little one's noggin overnight. The hard fact is that sudden, dramatic lessons are *not* the fastest way to a child's learning center.

Not everyone shares this point of view, of course. Perhaps you have friends (usually childless) who believe it is their job to shortcut all this patience malarky and give your wee one the kind of shock you as parent are too afraid to administer. Such friends are well-meaning as a rule, and usually lecture you earnestly on how not to be intimidated by your own children. They harbor the old-fashioned "spare the rod" theory that with a couple of well-timed, physically painful lessons any child can be set straight.

Once, for instance, an impulsive young woman named Delia was baby-sitting for her girlfriend's son. The child was four years old, rambunctious, cute, with the unpleasant habit of hitting grownups. One day the child started practicing his technique on Delia's arm with enthusiasm. After warning him several times to cease and desist, Delia turned and punched *his* arm a good deal harder than she should have, shouting: "There, now you see how it feels!"

Her intent, of course, was to give the child a taste of his own medicine and to teach him that "others have feelings too." In fact, the child, being maturationally incapable of understanding anything as subtle as the Golden Rule, simply perceived this act as an unwarranted assault. He howled accordingly, and the young woman could never understood why from that day on the little boy avoided her.

"The first thing to recognize," writes child psychologist

Allan Fromme, "is that children are primarily dominated by their desires. They have little or no control over them, and it will take many, many, many years before control adequate for self-guidance is possible. It is a mistake for us to think that we can short-circuit the process of developing controls for them. We simply cannot expect to get them to accept the values of postponement, compromise, and denial in merely a few years, no matter what we do. Nor can we expect them to learn any lesson we teach them as a result of a single explanation or scolding."[2]

In other words, it is necessary to realize that:

6. Good Behavior and Spiritual Conduct Must Gradually Become a Habit Before It Is Fully Assimilated.

The purpose of all education, spiritual or otherwise, is to encourage right actions and discourage wrong ones. The easiest way to instill this is through the development or discouragement of habits.

Make daily toothbrushing, and telling the truth, and feeding the pets, and saying prayers, and giving a few pennies to charity each week, and helping with the dishes part of life's routine. Continually insist on certain acts, consistently discourage certain acts, until these behavior patterns become part of the woodwork, until they are as natural to the child's life as getting up in the morning and going to bed at night.

Instill these good habits at an appropriately early age—starting, say, at two-and-a half to three years of age, while the child is still flexible enough to accept and adapt. If you fail to do so now, the law of habit will turn against you later. "The chains of bad habit are too weak to be felt," remarked Dr. Johnson, "until they are too strong to be broken."

Psychologist William James believed that the establishment of habitual do's and don'ts during childhood is so important that he dedicated an entire chapter to the subject of habits in his great work, *The Principles of Psychology*. A few of his more interesting quotes make the point quite clearly:

The great thing, then, in all education, is to make our nervous system our ally instead of our enemy. For this we must make automatic and habitual, as early as possible, as many useful actions as we can, *and guard against the growing into ways that are likely to be disadvantageous to us.*

Could the young but realize how soon they will become mere walking bundles of habits, they would give more heed to their conduct while in the plastic state. Every smallest stroke of virtue or of vice leaves its ever so little scar.

Down among his nerve-cells and fibers the molecules are counting it, registering and storing it up to be used against him when the next temptation comes. Nothing we ever do is, in strict scientific literalness, wiped out.

Let no youth have any anxiety about the upshot of his education, whatever the line of it may be. If he keep faithfully busy each hour of the working day, he may safely leave the final result to itself. He can with perfect certainty count on waking up some fine morning, to find himself one of the competent ones.

William James understood quite well that in childhood:

7. The Process of Introducing Moral and Spiritual Concepts into the Life of a Child Is a Long-term Affair.

Do it on a steady, rhythmical basis, a little each day; so that after a while these ideas seem natural to the child and become a regular part of his or her routine. "How use doth breed a habit in a man!" to quote Shakespeare. At Robert's house Robert's mother and father make a point of saying, "Thanks be to God" in Robert's vicinity at least once a day, and they do it faithfully *every day.* After approximately a year of repeating this phase they found that Robert has started saying it, too. Just words perhaps, but words are ideas, and ideas have influence. Finally:

8. Be Inventive, Be Flexible, Be Sincere, and Don't Be Afraid of Making Mistakes.

The person who coined the witty saying that the road to hell is paved with good intentions is probably smoldering in hell right now. The road to *heaven* is paved with good intentions, not the road to hell, even if these intentions never bear positive fruit. Indeed, in many spiritual ways it is believed that God judges you not according to the success or failure of your actions (the ultimate outcome of such things is, after all, His department) but by the intention behind them.

In your enthusiasm to give your child the best possible moral and devotional upbringing, therefore, you will undoubtedly make mistakes, yes; and you will feel badly, sure; and you will do dumb things and feel like an imbecile—yes to all the above. But go easy on yourself. If one approach backfires, chalk it up to experience and take another. Just keep at it, and be consistent. Childhood is a long process, spiritual parenting is a difficult task, and there will be many opportunities along the way to make up for your mistakes. The important thing is to try, to make the effort, to have the intent. "If you take one step toward Me," God is quoted as saying by Muslims, "I will take ten toward you."

Now to the main question at hand: How can parents convey, both silently and in words, the spiritual messages they wish their children to understand?

5.

Conveying Spiritual Lessons Through Stories

Many parents look upon the traditional children's story merely as an exercise in entertainment or as a means of developing a child's imagination. Though myths, fairy stories, and folk tales will certainly accomplish both these tasks, the deeper purpose they have served throughout the centuries has largely been forgotten.

Many parents are not aware, for example, that certain stories were originally written not simply to teach moral lessons but as a means of introducing children to spiritual and esoteric truths. Having come down from the distant past at a time when religion was the center of all societal concern, many of these tales speak, in an oblique language perhaps, of things both magical and divine, as many psychologists and educators in our own time have come to realize. "It would not be too much to say," writes the famous explainer of traditional storytelling, Joseph Campbell, "myth is the secret opening through which the inexhaustible energies of the cosmos pour into human cultural manifestation. The wonder is that the characteristic efficacy to touch and inspire deep creative centers dwells in the smallest nursery fairy tale—as the flavor of the ocean is contained in a droplet or the whole mystery of life within the egg of a flea."[1]

On the other hand, parents can also get carried away looking for the hidden, higher meanings in ancient children's tales, for not all fairy stories perform such a lofty task. Several years ago while teaching a class on literature to a group of preteens I was struck by the way in which each student brought his and her own experience to the study of folklore. At one point in the semester I quoted a favorite proverb of mine: "Before you love, learn to run through snow leaving no tracks."

I asked the class what they thought this proverb really meant. A bright girl in the front row explained that for her it meant that the human heart is a delicate, gossamer thing that is easily bruised. Before persons attempt to love, she said, they should first become sensitive and unselfish, so that they leave no "tracks" on the other person's heart.

This explanation jibed with my own, and several other students agreed. Then from the back of the room a boy raised his hand. He had received, he said with a roguish smile, a somewhat different reading. For him the proverb meant that if you are going to have a girlfriend in the wintertime you'd first better learn to sneak in and out of her house so carefully that you don't leave tracks in the snow for her parents to see.

This interpretation, I had to admit, was as valid as the first. Myths, stories, proverbs, and the like work on a number of levels simultaneously, all of them legitimate and all speaking to the hearer at his or her own point of understanding. "It is because they are alive, potent to revive themselves, and capable of an ever-renewed, unpredictable yet self-consistent effectiveness in the range of human destiny," writes the Indologist and folklorist Heinrich Zimmer, "that the images of folklore and myth defy every attempt we make at systematization. They are not corpse-like, but imp-like. With a sudden and quick shift of place they mock the specialist who imagines he has got them pinned to his chart."

Chances are that you know the images Zimmer refers to from your own childhood readings of fairy tales and myths. Some of these have embedded symbolic spiritual meanings designed to reach the child's inner ear. Classic examples include:

· The *hero or heroine* who embarks on a sacred quest (representative of the human soul on its journey to the Divine; of the devotee's attempt to return to his or her higher Self)

· The *princess* locked in the tower or held prisoner by a wicked sorcerer (the individual soul imprisoned in matter)

· *Instant journeyings to mystical lands* (altered states of consciousness and mystical experiences)

· *Magical animals and luminous beings* who help the hero or heroine attain their goals (spirits, soul guardians, and angels)

· The *wise old mentor* figure (the spiritual teacher, the guru)

· The appearance of *fairies, giants, dwarfs, genies* (inhabitants of the invisible, astral world)

· *Magical words and incantations* (prayer and mantras); *magical wands, rings, swords, books, statues* (ceremonial religious objects, scriptures, and meditative supports)

· *Dragons, chimeras, monsters* (demons)

· *Evil kings, black magicians, wicked witches, powerful dark sorcerers* (the devil)

· *The good king, the all-forgiving father, the sun, the conquering lion* (God)

This, of course, is not the place to do a mystical analysis of children's literature, and parents interested in pursuing the subject would be well advised to read the books of Heinrich Zimmer, Joseph Campbell, Mircea Eliade, Ananda Coomarswamy, René Guenon, and Carl Jung (see the bibliography). The intent here is to call your attention to those tales that contain spiritual power and impact directly on the higher parts of a child's imagination in such a way that the child is reminded of sacred truths.

FINDING APPROPRIATE CHILDREN'S STORIES

You probably already know most of the good ones; they are many of the same stories you yourself heard as a child. But before we name names, what about the question of contemporary children's literature? Does it contain the same kind of magical imagery as traditional fairy tales and classics?

On the whole, no, but happily there are exceptions—more about this below. But, by and large, a great deal of what is being written today is at best empty, at worst subversive of the young person's spiritual understanding. Tales of rabbit families who compete on quiz shows, of planets populated by friendly robots, of deer who start fan clubs for a movie star—while these tales may seem cute and harmless, especially if skillfully illustrated, such stories perform, in essence, the same disservice as do the daily cartoon shows on TV, modeling trivia and superficial values, and encouraging love for creeping mechanization.

Contrast such pap with the classics young people have thrived on for centuries. Contrast it with the Greek and Nordic myths, with Grimm's fairy tales and the tales of Aesop and Perrault, with the Arthurian legends, the Ingolsby legends, the *Arabian Nights,* the Bible, with folktales from a hundred countries, with *Alice in Wonderland* and *Robinson Crusoe,* with animal stories from Uncle Remus or the *Pancha Tantra,* or with episodes from the Hindu *Ramayana,* and much more. How superficial so many modern works seem when compared to these classics, how formulaic and fatuous!

Support for the classics still comes from many places, happily, but perhaps none more unexpected than the president's

cabinet. William J. Bennett, U.S. Secretary of education under
Ronald Reagan, has made a number of astute statements on
the value of myth, lore, and classics for children:

> *Do we want them to know what courage means? [Bennett asked*
> *in a speech on values in education.] Then we might teach them*
> *about Joan of Arc, Horatius at the bridge, Harriet Tubman and*
> *the Underground Railroad.*
>
> *Do we want them to know about kindness and compassion*
> *and the opposite of these?* Then we should have them read A
> Christmas Carol *and* The Diary of Anne Frank *and,*
> *later,* King Lear.
>
> *Do we want them to know what honesty means? Then we*
> *might teach them about Abraham Lincoln walking three miles*
> *to return six cents and, conversely, about Aesop's shepherd boy*
> *who cried wolf.*
>
> *Do we want them to recognize vanity? Then we should tell*
> *them about King Midas.*
>
> *Do we want them to know that hard work pays off? Then we*
> *should teach them about the Wright brothers at Kitty Hawk and*
> *about Booker T. Washington learning to read. "*

Spend time sifting through the mound of contemporary
reading matter, ferreting out those recent books which are
wholesome, instructive, and (most important) inspiring. To
the extent that it is possible—and this is a principle to be
guided by throughout your parenting career—all books, pictures, and literature to which children are exposed should
have some kind of instructive *moral, social,* and/or *spiritual*
message behind them. Filling young people with stories that
say nothing and mean nothing, that dwell on nonsense or on
the horrific and trivial, without expanding the mind or warm-
ing the heart, is to leave a child bereft of ideals and is, therefore, to pave the way for a kind of nihilism and ennui in the
grown-up years.

HOW TO EVALUATE CHILDREN'S LITERATURE FROM A SPIRITUAL PERSPECTIVE

Eliminate the Following:

*Stories That Have No Significant Meaning or
Which Fail to Convey a Positive Life Message*

Especially beware of nonsense books and books with purposeless plots. Though children may enjoy these items for their silliness, they are confusing and distracting to small minds.

Stories That Give the Child Wrong Life Messages

These may include books about people taking advantage of one another or gaining revenge, of undue competition between characters, of jealousy, violence, of wrong social or moral values. Many comics and "young adult" books are culpable in this respect.

*Stories That Portray People As If They Were
Machines, or Machines As If They Were People*

Steer clear of books about kindly robots that befriend lonely children. The Machine Age, with its mechanization of just about everything, has its own particular form of PR. The strategy behind it (if I may be permitted such a paranoid word) is to focus on children via the media and to convince them that, while their parents may (or may not) love them, the computer, being so smart, invariably *understands* them. And that with its superior cosmic intelligence it will show them the *real* magic secrets of life. Implicit moral: The machine is God.

Stories That Overtax a Child's Emotional Capacity

These may include traditional as well as modern stories. If you feel certain that of the Grimm fairy stories are too dark or sad for your child's age or sensitivity, by all means follow your instincts. You know your child better than anyone else. My own daughter was shaken by Hans Christian Andersen's tale "The Little Match Girl," in which a starving child gives up her last matches (and her life) to conjure visions of her beloved dead grandmother. After one reading my daughter could not control her tears for hours. Clearly, this story overloaded her emotional circuits. So be careful: it's always wise to screen a story first, even the old favorites. Fairy tales can be strong stuff.

Stories That Are Especially Frightening or Macabre

These can become the stuff of nightmares fifty years later. As a child I was roundly terrified after a single listening to James Whitcomb Riley's poem "Little Orphan Annie." A slick and seemingly jovial piece of homespun, the story tells of a bratty child who "made fun of every one an' all her blood-an'-kin," and who that night, because of her waywardness, was snatched up through the ceiling by two black things, "fore she knowed what she's about." So be 'especial careful, kids, cause: "the Gobble-uns'ill git you

> *If You*
> *Don't*
> *Watch*
> *Out!"*

Stories Illustrated with Particularly Grotesque, Frightening, Suggestive, or Gaudy Artwork

Antispiritual messages can be contained in visual materials as effectively as in written.

Stories That Feature Violence for Its Own Sake or Glorify Angry Interactions Between Characters

The old Punch-and-Judy shows exemplified this motif par excellence. Be careful of books that feature aggressive behavior but do not point out the negative consequences that result from it. Never read to children books or stories that show characters getting away with a wrong act.

Seek Out the Following Kinds of Books:

Books That Demonstrate, Via the Deeds of Their Characters, the Positive Results to Be Gained from Virtuous Conduct and the Negative Results of Misbehavior

A majority of material that is worthy of small ears will conform in some way to this standard; indeed, the question of whether or not a story transmits morally elevated principles can be used as a measuring stick for most children's literature.

Aesop's Fables, filled with stories of foolish and clever animals is the prototype. Tales extracted for children from the Bible (such as the series published by Peter Haddock Limited in Great Britain, which includes such tales as those of Ruth and Naomi and Daniel) are excellent, as are Charles Lamb's *Tales from Shakespeare* and Kipling's *Just So Stories.*

Books That Tell an Ingenious, Fantastic, or Fascinating Story

Stories in this category help develop a child's powers of concentration and imagination, and can inspire a creative literary urge all its own. A few suggestions for good books of this type follow:

For Toddlers and Preschoolers:
Frog Went A-Courtin' (John Langstaff; Harcourt). A highly visual tale based on the folk song of the same name, about a gallant young frog who wins a lovely mouse for his bride.
Grandfather Twilight (Barbara Helen Berger; Philomel). About dusk, darkness, and how the moon comes out at night.
The Story of Babar (Jean de Brunhoff; Random

House). All-time French favorite about a noble or-
phaned elephant king who is adopted by a kind city-
dwelling little old lady.

*The Wedding Procession of the Rag Doll and the Broom
Handle and Who Was in It* (Carl Sandburg; Harcourt).
An excerpt from Sandburg's zany, oddly wise
Rootabaga Stories.

Where the Wild Things Are (Maurice Sendak; Harper).
The magical picture story of a boy who tames his own
demons, drawn by one of the great illustrators of the
century.

Harold and the Purple Crayon (Crockett Johnson;
Harper). A child who cannot sleep uses a crayon to
draw himself through a mystical land, then draws himself back to bed. A beloved fantasy favorite.

Gnomes (Wil Huygen; Abrams). A delightful picture
book for children of all ages. It starts from the whimsical premise that gnomes are, of course, a "biological"
species of quasi-magical beings who share the world
with the animal kingdom. It then proceeds to tell and
illustrate, down to the smallest detail, their natural
habits: gnome houses, gnome foods, how gnomes kiss
and dress, how they protect animals and fight trolls.
The whimsical and entirely believable illustrations by
Rein Poortvliet are among the best graphic renderings
for children produced in our time. If you explain the
pictures carefully even preschoolers will love it.

For Children Six Years and Older

For an older group the following works are all excellent:

Peter Pan (many editions)

The original Collodi version of *The Adventures of Pinocchio* (republished by Macmillan).

The Yearling (Marjorie Kinnan Rawlings; Macmillan).

Anne of Green Gables (L. Montgomery; Grosset & Dun-
lap).

Kenneth Grahame's *The Wind in the Willows* (many available editions).

Carl Sandburg's *Rootabaga Stories* and *Rootabaga Stories: Rootabaga Pigeons* (Harcourt).

All the books in P. L. Travers' Mary Poppins series: *Mary Poppins, Mary Poppins Comes Back, Mary Poppins in the Park, Mary Poppins Opens the Door* (Harcourt, Buccaneer Books, among others).

Frances Hodgson Burnett's *The Secret Garden* (many editions)

For preteens:

Little Women (many editions)

The Little Prince (Antoine de Saint-Exupéry; Harcourt). A modern classic of fantasy and feeling.

Works by Jules Verne and R. L. Stevenson.

Alice in Wonderland and *Through the Looking Glass* (many editions).

The above are typical of the time-tested quality literature children should be exposed to at some point in their reading and story-listening careers as a matter of course. Ditto the *Oz* books by Frank L. Baum and Baum's successors. This series, especially the early volumes by Baum, Jack Snow, and Ruth Plumley Thompson, chronicle the return of Dorothy to the land of Oz shortly after her original encounter with the Wizard. Each book transports the young reader to a wonderland populated by clever, whimsical peoples, and many implicit (and explicit) mystical adventures unfold. (Baum himself was a mystic of sorts.)

Traditional Folk Tales, Myths, and Fairy Stories

Most of the old standards are still absorbing for toddlers and preschoolers. Keep a copy of *Mother Goose* nearby, along with versions of "Little Red Riding Hood," "The Three Bears," "The Ugly Duckling," "The Three Little Pigs,"

"Henny Penny," "Three Billy Goats Gruff," "Cinderella," "Snow White," "Rumpelstiltskin," "Jack and the Beanstalk," "Puss in Boots," "Dick Wittington's Cat," and other familiar favorites. Anthologies containing these can be found in abundance at the children's section of any bookstore. Pantheon has published a definitive collection of the Grimm tales.

There are also a number of excellent retellings of traditional folk stories. Examples from this well-stocked larder include:

For Preschoolers:
How the Sun Was Brought Back to the Sky (Mirra Ginsberg; Macmillan). A delightful East European tale about five chicks, a duck, a rabbit, and a snail who go on a journey to wake up the sun.

Arab Folktales (Iner Bush; Pantheon). Supplies a typical sampling of spiritually oriented children's stories from the Middle East.

For the Early Grades:
Tibetan Fantasies (Li Gotami Govinda; Dharma Pub.). Lots of spiritual goodies about Tibet.

The Dragon Kite (Thomas P. Lewis; Holt). A Tibetan tale about a little boy whose love for kites leads him to become a Buddhist monk.

Why Mosquitos Buzz in People's Ears: A West African Tale (Verna Aardema; Dial). A beautifully illustrated folk tale about how a creature as small as a mosquito can stop the sun from rising.

The Nightingale and the Fool (Catherine Chase; Dandelion Books). A wise Indian tale of a hunter who captures a nightingale and misuses its sage advice.

The Enchanted Caribou (Elizabeth Cleaver; Atheneum). A traditional Canadian Indian story of sorcery and transformation.

Tales of Pan (Mordicai Gerstein; Harper). These tales of the nature god Pan offer a good early introduction to Greek mythology.

Paul Bunyan (Stephen Kellogg; Morrow). Retells the hyperbolic life and times of Bunyan the logger and his pal Babe, the blue ox. Always good fun.

The Stolen Appaloosa and Other Indian Stories (Paul Levitt, Elissa Guralnick; Bookmakers Guild). Presents little-known and spiritually charged children's tales from American Indian lore.

It Could Always Be Worse: A Yiddish Folk Tale (Margot Zemach; Farrar, Straus). A Jewish morality folktale about a man who goes to a rabbi for help but who (seemingly) receives calamity instead. An excellent illustration of the saying "I thought I was poor because I had no shoes—until I saw a man who had no feet."

For Children Eight to Preteen:

D'Aulaire's Norse Gods and Giants (Ingri and Edgar Parin d'Aulaire; Doubleday). A standard, solid collection of the sweeping Teutonic myths.

D'Aulaire's Book of Greek Myths (Ingri and Edgar Parin d'Aulaire; Doubleday). A readable collection of the best tales from Greek mythology. Good starter kit if your seven- or eight- or nine-year-old has yet to be introduced to the pleasures of Attic (Athenian) tales.

Fairy Tale Collections (Andrew Lang; Dover). A tried-and-true series of folk and fairy tales republished by Dover in several volumes (*The Blue Fairy Book, The Brown Fairy Book, The Green Fairy Book*). All of these feature translations of stories from across the world— Grimm tales, stories from Iceland, animal sagas from Africa, myths from the Australian tribes, Hungary, Russia, Japan, and many others. Lang's work, a standard for almost a hundred years, is still going strong.

Zlateh the Goat and Other Stories (Isaac Bashevis Singer; Harper). Collection of wise children's folk stories by a master Jewish storyteller. Illustrated by Maurice Sendak.

Seasons of Splendor (Madhur Jaffrey; Puffin). A power-

ful collection of Hindu myths. Good introduction to
Hinduism and Indian life in general.

*The Children's Homer: The Adventures of Odysseus and the
Tale of Troy* (Padraic Colum; Macmillan). Fabulous version of Homer by a master children's storyteller. This
volume, in paperback, is illustrated by the brilliant
work of Willy Pogany.

Babushka: An Old Russian Folktale (Charles Mikolay-
cak; Holiday). A poignant tale with many spiritual overtones about an old woman who turns down the opportunity to visit the baby Christ because she is too busy.
Since that time this woman has searched for the Christ
child endlessly.

The Dancing Granny (Ashley Bryan; Aladdin). Popular
African folktale about a battle of wits between a spider
and Granny Anika.

Fun and Instructive Children's Poems

Children do not listen to poetry as avidly as they did some
years ago. While the reasons for this change could be debated
endlessly, the fact is that if you start reading young children
poems written in easy rhymes and rhythms, they will soon be
requesting them (and sometimes writing them) on their own.

For Ages Three to Five:

Mother Goose is still perhaps the best collection to
begin with. Some of these seemingly nonsensical
verses, it has been suggested, have hidden spiritual
meanings. Consider, for instance, Little Boy Blue's
sheep and cows escaping into the wrong meadows.
Where is Little Boy Blue? Asleep.

Other collections of note for young children are R.
L. Stevenson's lovely *A Child's Garden of Verses* and A. A.
Milne's *When We Were Very Young*. William Blake's child-
like verses are nicely interpreted by Nancy Willard in
a contemporary volume, *A Visit to William Blake's Inn:
Poems for Innocent and Experienced Travelers* (Voyager).

Fine also for kids in the primary grades is a book whose title tells it all: *Poems Children Will Sit Still For* (Beatrice Schenk de Regniers, Eva Moore, Mary Michaels White; The Citation Press).

For Older Children:
A few poets new and not so new whose work is still music to children's ears include Carl Sandburg, Ogden Nash, A. A. Milne, Edward Lear, Shel Silverstein, Eugene Field, Walter de la Mare, Vachel Lindsay, Dr. Seuss, Christina Rossetti, Lewis Carroll, Rachael Field, and Elizabeth Madox Roberts.

Meaningful collections and anthologies of children's poems include *The Big Golden Book of Poetry* (Jane Werner; Golden Press), *The Oxford Book of Poetry for Children* (Edward Blishen; Oxford), *Over the Moon: A Book of Nursery Rhymes* (Charlotte Voake; Crown), *A Child's Treasury of Poems* (Mark Daniel; Dial), *Read-Aloud Rhymes for the Very Young* (Jack Prelutsky; Knopf), and for very, very young listeners, an introduction to poetic meter: *Finger Rhymes* (Marc Brown; Dutton).

Stories That Educate and Expand a Child's Understanding of the World

These Include Picture Books for Toddlers and Preschoolers Such As:
All Wet! All Wet! (James Skofield; Harper). Introduces a very young child to the world of rain and nature.

How Do I Put It On? (Shiego Watanabe; Philomel). Helps children understand the concept of doing things for themselves.

What Do People Do All Day? (Richard Scarry; Random House). Shows how people (actually pigs, ducks, cows, and worms) work with various tools at their various occupations.

Pat the Bunny (Dorothy Kunhardt; Golden Books/

Western). One of the early hands-on activity books and still going strong. Designed to teach toddlers about their senses: touch, sight—and even smell in later editions.

First Flight (David McPhail; Little, Brown). Sensitive and humorous introduction for young children who are about to take their first airplane trip.

The Cloud Book (Tomie de Paola; Holiday). Transports the child up over the earth into the clouds. Good book for developing an awareness of the environment.

The Little Duck (Judy Dunn; Random House). Part of a photographic series introducing children to friendly domestic animals.

Older Children Will Enjoy:

Up Goes the Skyscraper (Gail Gibbons; Four Winds). Children raised in big cities will find this tale of skyscraper construction absorbing.

Cathedral: The Story of Its Construction (David Macaulay; Houghton Mifflin). A kind of you-are-there saga about the construction of a great Gothic cathedral during the Middle Ages. Amazing for its wealth of information and for Macaulay's detailed drawings, this book will be especially interesting to children who enjoy building things and/or who attend a church built in traditional Gothic style. Other books by the same author—such as *City: A Story of Roman Planning and Construction, Pyramid,* and *Underground* (all Houghton Mifflin)—are equally instructive.

If You Are a Hunter of Fossils (Byrd Baylor; Scribner). Designed to interest youngsters in rock and fossil collecting and to awaken young sensitivities to the beauties of the natural world.

The Weaver's Gift (Kathryn Lasky; Warne). Interesting photographic essay about how wool gets from the sheared sheep to the woven blanket. Shows how animals serve humankind.

Stories That Emphasize and Encourage Family Values, or Which Help Children Come to Grips with Family Dilemmas

Don't think that such books will be a panacea for family problems. They won't. They can be useful, however, as a supplement to discussions on family and domestic problems such as divorce, the death of a pet, homesickness, and so on.

A Sampling for Children Aged Four to Seven:

The Accident (Carol Carrick; Clarion). How a young boy deals with the death of his beloved dog.

And My Mean Old Mother Will Be Sorry, Blackboard Bear (Martha Alexander; Dial). Deals with the universal problem of a child who has been severely scolded and who tries to run away.

A Visit to the Sesame Street Hospital (Deborah Hautzig; Random House). A gentle introduction, hosted by the Sesame Street gang, to what goes on inside a hospital. Especially good if your child must pay a visit to one.

Dinosaurs Divorce: A Guide for Changing Families (L. Krasny and Marc Brown; Little, Brown). A cartoon book that addresses the pain of divorce.

Ira Sleeps Over (Bernard Waber; Houghton Mifflin). All about the tribulations of the first night spent away from home. A kind of primer.

And for Older Readers:

Always, Always (Crescent Dragonwagon; Macmillan). Story of a girl from a broken home who has learned to accept the fact that she must spend part of her time with her mother, part with her father.

Here I Am, an Only Child (Marlene Fanta Shyer; Scribner's). All the pros and cons of growing up siblingless.

The Great Gilly Hopkins (Katherine Paterson; Crowell). Prize-winning novel for young readers about a savvy but sensitive young girl who, forced to go from one foster home to the next, finally finds her place in the sun.

Stories That Emphasize Harmonious Interaction Between Persons

A Friend Is Someone Who Likes You *(Joan Walsh Anglund; Harcourt Brace). An old standby in this genre. The Silver Anniversary Edition came out in 1983 and is still selling.*
Will I Have a Friend? *(Miriam Cohen; Macmillan). Helps children who have just entered kindergarden deal with the ubiquitous problems of being liked and accepted by their peers. This book can also help children think about other people's feelings.*
The Kid Next Door and Other Headaches: Stories About Adam Joshua *(Janice Lee Smith; Harper). Two best friends, Joshua and Nelson, work it out.* The Kid Next Door *by the same author is more of the same. Such stories emphasize the basic brotherly love that can lie beneath the squabbles of human personality struggles.*

Stories That Touch the Heart

Age Four to Seven:
Andersen's Fairy Tales are especially good in this regard—though a few, such as "The Little Match Girl" and "The Brave Tin Soldier," can be upsetting to some children and should not be read to the oversensitive. The Raggedy Ann tales are hard to improve on for plain goodness, as are A. A. Milne's Pooh stories. Try the Uncle Wiggly books by Howard Garris too.
Goodnight Moon (Margaret Wise Brown; Harper). One of the sweetest bedtime books ever written; recommended to help a child sleep peacefully. So is *Sleepy People* (M. Goffstein; Farrar, Straus).

Age Six Up:
   Stories from the Old Testament (such as the story of Joseph and his brothers, Noah's Ark, Daniel in the Lion's Den) are perennial heart-touchers. The Lyle Crocodile tales, such as *Lovable Lyle* (Bernard Waber; Houghton Mifflin), stars a courteous, kindly young crocodile named Lyle who lives with a family of humans on the Upper East Side of New York City and who always tries to help other people. *The Velveteen Rabbit* (Margery Williams; Doubleday), which makes adults cry as frequently as children, clearly states the point that it takes love to make a person real.

Wholesome Yarns of Adventure and Discovery,
Especially Those That Stress Sacrifice for a Higher Cause.

Mostly for Ages Eight and Over:
   Go for the classics here: *Robin Hood, The Knights of the Round Table, Ivanhoe, Kidnapped, Treasure Island, Little Women,* and especially the tales from *The Arabian Nights.* (A number of the stories in this series have been extracted into single volumes—see, for instance, *Sinbad's Seven Voyages* (retold by Gladys Davidson; Scholastic Book Services) and *Aladdin and the Wonderful Lamp* (retold by Andrew Lang; Viking).
   The Wonder Clock by the famous children's illustrator, Howard Pyle (Xerox University Microfilms) is a worthy collection of intricate stories for children. And don't overlook the power of Greek, Hindu, and Nordic myths to instruct and fascinate. Also, T. H. White's *The Sword in the Stone* (Dell) and *The Once and Future King* (Berkley). Also see E. B. White's *Charlotte's Web* (Harper), a deservedly popular tale about a kindly spider named Charlotte who makes great sacrifices out of love for her barnyard friends.
   Other recommended adventure books include the

justly famous wilderness series by Laura Ingalls Wilder that begins with *Little House in the Big Woods* and includes *Little House on the Prairie* (on which the TV show was based), *Little Town on the Prairie,* and *Long Winter,* all published by Harper. These works offer a model of writing for young people, stressing the right values and including just enough blood, thunder, and poignancy to keep everyone reading.

My Father's Dragon (Ruth Stiles Gannett; Knopf). A thrilling, heartwarming tale about a young boy (the author's father) who travels to a strange jungle, where he frees a captive baby dragon. Wonderful reading, though the follow-up *Elmer and the Dragon* and *Dragons of Blueland* fall far short of the original.

Little Tim and the Brave Sea Captain (Edward Ardizzone; Puffin). A beloved English story about a little boy who stows away on a steamer and of the harrowing—and instructive—adventures that befall him.

Beyond the Divide (Kathryn Lasky; Macmillan). An off-beat tale about a brave young girl and her father, raised in Amish country, who burn their bridges and head West on a wagon train.

Stories That Stress Courage and Fortitude in Times of Trial.

Mostly Ages Eight and Over:

Robinson Crusoe and *The Swiss Family Robinson* are wonderful examples of this genre. Ditto the tale of Joan of Arc. *The Little Engine That Could* (Watty Piper; Platt & Munk) is a standard for kids under seven. *Dogsong* (Gary Paulsen; Puffin) is an exciting and moral-laden adventure story for older children about an Eskimo boy who voluntarily roughs it on his own in the wilderness. Steinbeck's *The Pearl* (Penguin), mainly for preteens and older, has opened many a protected child's eyes about the dangers that await one in the big world. The tale of David and Goliath in the Old Testa-

ment is always welcomed by children, principally because they, like David, feel tiny and powerless against
the Goliath of the adult world.

*Animal Stories That Have a Solid Moral or That Introduce
Children to the Inner World and Workings of Nature.*

Mostly Six and Over:
   Kipling's *Jungle Book* for older children is perhaps
the greatest of this genre ever written. What a pity
more children have not made the acquaintance of
Mowgli, brought up by a mother wolf and taught the
language of the jungle by a mysterious black panther
and a lovable bear.
   Many children still love Hugh Lofting's perhaps
somewhat dated but heartwarming books about Doctor Doolittle, the kindly English veterinarian who talks
to animals and takes them on exotic adventures around
the world. While it may require fifty or so pages to get
children interested in the good doctor, once the hook
is set they'll be devotees for life.
   Black Beauty (Anna Sewell; numerous editions)
Though slow-moving and a bit turgidly written for
today's child, this classic still manages to capture the
hearts and imaginations of many young readers, especially animal lovers. Another favorite in this vein, *National Velvet* (Enid Bagnold; Morrow) also remains
rightly popular.
   The Story of Ferdinand (Munro Leaf; Viking). This
sweet tale of a prize bull who refuses to fight in the
bullring remains one of the best subliminal condemna-
tions of violence in all of children's literature.
   The Black Stallion books (Walter Farley; Random
House). Still among the most popular of all animal
books, about a boy who tames and befriends a beautiful runaway horse and their subsequent adventures on
the racetrack.
   The Red Pony (John Steinbeck; Viking). Another

child-loves-horse emotional tale with a bittersweet ending, mostly for preteens.

White Fang and *Call of the Wild* (Jack London; many editions) provide ingenious and thoroughly convincing windows into the minds and hearts of animals.

Stuart Little (E. B. White; Little, Brown). An adventure story of sorts; like many great children's books, it fits into a number of categories. Stuart is a winsome mouse brought up by humans who sets out to seek his fortune in a dangerous world.

The Incredible Journey (Sheila Burnford; Little, Brown). This immensely popular tale is based on a true story of two dogs and a cat who walk the length of a continent to find their lost owners. Faithfulness is the moral.

Books That Teach Arts and Handicrafts

There are many of these on the market. Indian Crafts and Lore *(W. Ben Hunt; Golden Press) is particularly impressive in the simple way it teaches Indian crafts.* Better Homes and Gardens' 167 Things to Make for Children *(Meredith) is excellent too. There are countless others in all fields of art and crafts.*

Books That Teach Manners and Consideration for Others

<u>For Six and Over:</u>
What Do You Say, Dear? What Do You Do, Dear? (Sesyle Joslin; Harper). A zany reissue of a classic on etiquette do's and don'ts illustrated by Maurice Sendak.

Always Room for One More (Sorche Nic Leodhas; Holt). A Scottish tale about a person so generous and hospitable that his house explodes from holding too many people. Good fun, and good sense.

Rotten Ralph (Jack Gantos; Houghton Mifflin). Ralph the cat's outrageous manners serve, by implication, as models for children *not* to follow. A clever way of getting the point across.

The Magician Who Lost His Magic (David McKee; Abelard-Schuman). Concerns a magician who uses his magic to do all the work for people so they don't have to make any efforts themselves. When he loses his magic everyone learns a few lessons about helping themselves.

The Giant Child (J. L. Garcia Sanchez and M. A. Pacheco; Methuen). Features a giant child who searches for his lost parents. Normal-sized (and otherwise "good") persons force him to work like a slave for his dinner until the children of the town get together to help him out. A good book for teaching tolerance and cooperation. This edition is one of several published in the United Nations' "The Rights of Children" series; other titles stress such important moral qualities as equal opportunity (*The Children and the Silly Kings,*) the rights of children everywhere to receive adequate food and housing (*The Child Who Cried in the Night,*) and protection from racial and religious bigotry (*Annie, the Invisible Girl.*)

Stories That Emphasize Lofty, Epic, and Spiritual Subject Matter

To my mind the most spiritual and, simultaneously, most entertaining books of our time for older children are the seven-volume *Narnia* series by C. S. Lewis (Macmillan). Though listed as a straight adventure series that chronicles the story of four British children who pass through a magical wardrobe into the kingdom of Narnia, it becomes apparent after reading the first volume (*The Lion, The Witch and the Wardrobe*) that the real theme here is the eternal struggle between good and evil, fall and redemption, God and the devil.

This fact is confirmed when the lion king, Aslan, Lewis' symbol for Christ, appears at the end of the first story (and in all that follow) to set the world spiritually right once again. The series maintains a remarkable balance between exciting story lines and high-level transcendental communication, producing the kind of narrative that goes directly to a young listener's inner consciousness. Recommended for readers of all religious persuasions, the Narnia stories are neither pious nor parochial, yet they succeed in conveying the kind of inspirational messages that many overtly religious works fail to deliver.

Other quality books with worthwhile spiritual messages include:

The Giving Tree (Shel Silverstein; Harper). A deceptively simple story about a boy and a tree who remain lifetime friends, thanks to the tree's unwavering loyalty. One of the sweetest short childrens' stories of our generation, it stresses sacrifice, generosity, and unqualified love.

The *Lord of the Rings* trilogy (J. R. R. Tolkein; Houghton Mifflin). Like the Narnia stories of C. S. Lewis, this now-famous trio for older children is a thinly disguised morality tale concerning the divine quest of the human soul in its battles against the powers of darkness. With a whimsical band of intrepid followers, Frodo sets out to return a magical ring to an alien country ruled over by a Satanlike personage. The many experiences he and his friends have along the way can be read as a Bunyanesque morality story as well as an edge-of-the-chair adventure. It is highly recommended for children over ten, as is Tolkein's warm-up volume to this saga, *The Hobbit.*

Also of value:

Stories from the Bible are excellent as usual, and younger children will enjoy them in "retold" versions. Look, too, for books published by the Bala Press in New York which offer retellings of Hindu scriptural tales, especially stories from the life of Krishna. Various versions of Bunyan's *Pilgrim's Progress* have been scaled down for children and make good reading for all ages.

Also:

The Spade Sage: Tales of the Buddha (Nazli Gellek, Annette Beven; Dharma Publishing). Tells the tale of a poor gardener who gives up his most beloved possession, his spade, to pursue Truth. Offers an excellent opportunity for younger children to learn about the Buddhist ideals of sacrifice and renunciation.

The Christmas Story from the Gospels of Matthew and Luke (Marguerite Northrup, ed.; The Metropolitan Museum of Art). The story of the Nativity as related in the Gospels. The tale is beautifully illustrated with icons and paintings from the Met's vast collection.

The Bronze Bow (Elizabeth Speare; Sandpiper). Especially for preteens—about a young boy in biblical times who vows revenge against those who killed his mother and father but who then meets a man whose teaching makes him re-evaluate his blood lust: Jesus.

The Selfish Giant and *The Happy Prince,* both by Oscar Wilde, are available in many editions. These moving though neglected religious parables should be heard by children everywhere. *The Selfish Giant* tells of a mean giant who excludes children from his wonderful garden until one day he is visited by a mysterious child who turns out to be the infant Jesus. *The Happy Prince* relates the poignant tale of a gilded statue who begs a friendly swallow to stay with him "just one more night," strip him of his valuable gold and jewels, and carry them to needy people throughout the city.

Ask Another Question: The Story and Meaning of Passover (Miriam Chaikin; Clarion). Full of wise ideas as well as religious explanations for Jewish children.

Holiday Tales of Sholom Aleichem (Scribner). Seven wonderful children's stories from the master to go with different Jewish holidays: Passover, Hanukkah, and so on.

The Clown of God (Tomie de Paola; Voyager). Poignant and radiant story about a clown so poor that the only gift he can give to Christ is a juggling show.

One Day in Paradise (Helme Heine; McElderry). Introduction to the story of Creation.

Story of Mohammad the Prophet (Bilkiz Alladin; Hemkunt Press). Simple and effective telling of the life story of the founder of Islam. For early schoolers.

Seasons of Splendor (Madhur Jaffrey; Atheneum). Moving Hindu tales for children.

The Child's Mahabharata (Santa Rameshwar Rad; Orient, Longman). An entertaining retelling of the greatest of Indian religious epics.

A Child's Bible (Jane Yolen; Paulist Press). Makes many of the best tales from the Bible comprehensible for young persons.

Yossi Tries to Help God (Miriam Chaikin; Harper). One of a series of books about a young Jewish boy trying to come to terms with his life problems.

The King in the Garden (Leon Garfield; Lothrop). Retellings of Old Testament tales.

THE DARK SIDE

Story, myth, and fairy tales are among the first ways in which children learn about the darker sides of things: death, evil, sickness, crime, and the rottenness that lurks in certain human hearts. Many of the books featured above deal with these themes in both a direct and indirect fashion. A few books that address such topics in a more frontal manner include: *The Devil's Storybook* (Natalie Babbitt; Farrar, Straus). A series of stories about the devil that subtly introduces children to the concept of the secret subversive character of evil.

The Mountains of Tibet (Mordicai Gerstein; Harper). A luminous adaptation of the Tibetan guide to the afterlife experience, the *Bardo Thodol* (also known as *Tibetan Book of the Dead*). The narrative takes the child into the various states that, Tibetans believe, a soul passes through after death. This book offers religious education, through story, at its very best.

Going Backwards (Norma Klein; Scholastic). A story

about a young boy who must deal with a grandmother suffering from Alzheimer's disease. Particularly helpful for children who are in contact with a
sick older relative.
The Tenth Good Thing About Barney (Judith Viorst;
Atheneum). Beloved tale about a child coming to
terms with the death of his cat—and with death
itself.
Bridge to Terabithia (Katherine Paterson; Crowell). A
heartbreaking novel for older children about dealing with the accidental death of one's best friend.
*I Had a Friend Named Peter: Talking to Children About
the Death of a Friend* (Janice Cohn; Morrow). A
book to help children work through the death of a
friend.

Naturally you will want to make your own amendments to
the lists above. Do choose carefully, critically, intuitively; if
you have any doubts whatsoever concerning a book's value,
opt for the conservative approach and put it back on the shelf.
Whatever choices you make, bear in mind that what goes into
young minds at this very receptive age will surely come out
later on, transformed now into the stuff of action, behavior,
and belief.

STORY HOUR: BEDTIME

The feelings youngsters experience before bedtime will
establish a certain presleep mood. These feelings can turn
into the tissue of childhood play fantasies the next day and in
some cases can become the stuff of dreams at night.

Many contemporary parents do not think of bedtime as
special but, traditionally, peoples across the world have considered it an especially fertile moment for the teaching of
spiritual ideals. Members of many American Indian groups
that honor the tribal ways, for instance, are convinced, like
their ancestors, that the information fed into children's minds

before sleep exerts a strong effect on their spiritual consciousness. "Before the youngster goes to sleep," reports the Crow
Indian, Henry Old Coyote, "the grandparents will sing some
songs and explain their meaning and significance; they'll also
tell legends that are meant to help build character, or tell a
story where somebody pulled a blunder. All of these things
work on the child when he is asleep. . . . Yes, the bedtime
stories encourage you to sleep and think about something
that will strengthen you. At the same time, we make a wish for
the child to have a dream; a good dream, not a bad one. This
parallels the expression of the non-Indians to have 'sweet
dreams.' "[2]

The emotional atmosphere created between parent and
child during the last moments before sleep is, thus, in its own
way as important as the content of the stories themselves. This
magical time of the day should be orchestrated accordingly.

First, let parents, grandparents, or an older sibling do the
reading or telling. If this is not possible, then other family
members or a trusted family friend can do the job. Now is a
time for affectionate serenity, for cozy physical closeness, for
a reaffirmation of familial love. Coming as it does during the
child's last waking hours, the story hour constitutes the final
impressions of the day. Best to keep them reflective, positive,
inspiring, and secure. Here are some tips that will help:

Set the Scene

During story hour some children enjoy having the lights
turned down or being read to by candlelight. Others prefer
the security of a blazing fire or sitting around the dining room
or kitchen table with other members of the family also listening to the yarn. Some children like to snuggle close to
mommy or daddy as the story unfolds and to look carefully
at each picture.

Tell It In Your Own Words

Reading stories from a book is fine. But telling it your own
words is better. Why? Because when parents tell a story from
memory they are not hemmed in by words on a page. Room

is left over for spontaneity and inventiveness and surprise. The teller's hands are free to make gestures. The faces are free to produce smiles and eyebrow raisings and grimaces in tune with the story. Bodies are free to stand up, sit down, fall down, lie down. The reader's creative energies are more easily passed into the child.

Telling a tale spontaneously also allows parents a chance to edit and improvise the narrative especially for the child's emotional or disciplinary requirements, adding or subtracting appropriate passages as the need arises. If children are having a problem facing up to bullies on the playground you can tell them the story of the Brave Little Tailor and emphasize how the tailor had courage when face-to-face with the nasty giants. If a child is having difficulty obeying you can tell the story of the Gingerbread Man and then add your own extra emphasis to the part where the gingerbread man is caught by the fox because he did not do what his parents told him.

While telling a children's story from memory may seem like a difficult task at first, realize that you have already have much more material on tap than you realize. Tales such as "Hansel and Gretel," "The Three Bears," "Pinocchio," "Little Red Riding Hood," "Jack and the Beanstalk," and many others remain imprinted on our brains forever, and kids are always happy to listen to these standbys a thousand times. For parents who can't recall the details, a few minutes brush-up an hour before bedtime will bring the images back, sometimes with a resounding rush. As far as new or unfamiliar tales go, parents can learn these in a reading or three. Once the story line is retained, it can then be retold to the child in your own words, this time stressing the parts you find spiritually meaningful.

Make it Zippy, Zappy, Zingy, and Zowie

Pizzazz is a must. Provide voices and funny sound effects for different characters. Act out passages as you go along. Sing, dance, holler, clown, let go, give in. You'll never have a better, more willing, less judgmental audience than now, so enjoy.

Play the part of the princess, and have your audience mimic the bashful frog. Or be Snow White and let the child act the awful witch. Throw your whole self into it. Have fun.

One mother introduces a new story to her daughter at the beginning of each week. On the first two days they read it from beginning to end. On the third and fourth days they tell the story back to each other from memory. On the fifth day they act out scenes from the story, and on the sixth they make paper puppets based on the story's major characters. On the last day of the week, following a festive Sunday-afternoon meal, mother and daughter present a puppet play in the living room for all family members to enjoy, using the cutout paper figures from the week's story as the performers.

Be funny. Humor, claims Marie L. Shedlock in her famous treatise on storytelling, *The Art of the Story-Teller* (Appleton, 1915), should help show children their real position in the universe and prevent them from developing an exaggerated idea of their own importance. Humor, claims Shedlock, "develops the logical faculty, and prevents hasty conclusions. It brings about a clear perception of all situations, enabling the child to get the point of view of another person. It is the first instilling of philosophy into the mind of a child and prevents much suffering later on when the blows of life fall upon him; for a sense of humor teaches us at an early age not to expect too much; and this philosophy can be developed without cynicism or pessimism, without destroying *joie de vivre.*"

Wring as much mileage as possible from your voice and your gestures. When describing pathetic passages use exaggeratedly sad expressions. During the exciting parts don't be afraid to ham it up. In the Children's Drama Theatre in New York City performers extract an extra bit of tension during peak moments by freezing for a second or two in the midst of a fight or a chase, then instantly resuming at full speed. This freeze-frame technique has a strangely heightening affect on the action.

Pause at appropriate moments, especially before an important denouement. Just as the red toad is about to reveal the hiding place of the magic slippers, just as Jack is about to snatch the golden goose—stop for a moment and stare intensely at the child. Then reveal the secret. The effect is assured.

Employ Vivid, Specific Language

Use simple, forceful words: present-tense verbs, specific (rather than general) nouns, and plenty of action adjectives. Don't just say:

> *Red Riding Hood walked up to the door and knocked.*

Instead, try:

> *Red Riding Hood* steals slowly *up to grandma's* old wooden door. *She knocks* hard *on it three times:* rap, rap, rap!.

Details help children see the action clearly in their own minds. They keep interest high and increase imaginative perception. Do not, however, overexplain the action as you go along, and especially avoid adding moral judgments concerning your characters. The sudden interjection of comments such as "Wasn't that mean of the witch to poison Snow White's apple?" or "See how nice Sir April was to his brother, even though his brother was so nasty?" may satisfy a parent's wish to instill moral lessons. But for a child these intrusions disrupt a story's rhythm and snap the precious suspension of disbelief.

Talk About It Afterward—Sometimes

Once a story is finished the evening's events do not necessarily have to end. Now is the time to discuss the meaning and moral implied by the tale. Ask your child how the story makes him or her feel:

Sad?
Happy?
Excited?

Peaceful?
Funny?
Anxious to seek adventure?
Eager to stay at home?

Ask about the characters:

Which ones does the child like and dislike?
Why?
Did the wolf do a bad thing?
Why?
What would you—or I—have done in the same situation?
Was the piper brave? What made him act that way?
Was the magician cruel? Why do you suppose some people behave so badly?

Ask leading questions but do *not* sermonize on the story's spiritual meaning. When you make comments, keep them short and to the point. If your child queries you on details, which is likely, especially on details that are dark or sad, keep your answers simple and succinct. Then ask the child for his or her feelings on the matter. On the other hand, if children are resistant to poststory discussions, by all means let the matter ride. They probably want to digest the story in their own way, and at their own tempo.

Illustrate
Some parents encourage children to illustrate bedtime stories with paint, crayon, or magic marker. When these drawings are finished parents staple the pages together into a special book with the child's name penned on the front page.

You can also ask children to draw the characters from a story, or to make a colored design that describes the way the story makes them feel.

A variation on this idea is to show children an interesting picture and have them tell you a story about it. Show them, for example, a reproduction of a Rembrandt self-portrait. Ask them to tell a story about this man: How does he feel right now, happy or sad? Where does he live? What is his life like? Is he a good man? What does he believe in?

Have the Child Tell the Story Back to You

Another interesting poststory game is to have children re-tell what they have just heard. You will be amazed at how many details they remember and how quickly they grasp prominent points. Some parents even encourage children to speak their stories into a tape recorder. Then they put these tapes away for posterity and listen to them years later, always with amazement and nostalgia. Perhaps your children's children will enjoy listening to these tapes someday. It will help them understand that even as a child Dad and Mom liked to tell stories.

Some parents also encourage children to make up their own tales, to free-associate, using whatever imagery comes to mind. Nine-year-old Jason's story, after listening to *Robinson Crusoe* from beginning to end, was about a boy who was ship-wrecked on a motorcycle driving through outer space and who managed to stay alive for seven years by eating "space mice" and drinking stars. Seven-year-old Lea's favorite story, told after having just gone through an appendicitis operation, was about Donald Duck's trip to the market in which Donald went around eating so much food off the shelves that he developed a terrible ache, could not control his bowels, and was forced to relieve himself in the aisles! Interesting.

A FEW TIPS FROM A MAGICIAN

Professional children's magicians, if they are worthy of their ancient craft, know how to tell a good tale along with the performance and how to give their presentation its greatest dramatic spin. The

professional magician Henning Nelms, in a volume
written for the use of other magicians, passes on a
few performing tips.

1. Give off a feeling of fun. Let the children know
that you are having a wonderful time.

2. Use props whenever you can: wands, rings,
magical spells. For the parent these items can be
added into the story. For instance, when telling *Jack
and the Beanstalk* get hold of some string beans, remove the seeds, and show them to the child at the
moment when Jack purchases them.

3. Create atmosphere. Turn the lights down. Or
up. Play appropriate music in the background.

4. Use red herrings. In magic this is done by
making the audience think the trick is going to
come out one way when it has an entirely different
outcome. Employ this same device when telling a
story—use surprises, dodges, or false leads.

5. All magical effects should be caused by something: a wand, a magical word, a spell. In stories, do
the same, and hence offer opportunities for participation. Have youngsters say the magic word with
you. Let them wave the fairy princess's wand or
read the magic scroll or put the ugly troll to flight.

6. Use running gags. These are always effective in
a magic show and can be used with equal force
when telling a story. For example, every time an
ugly troll appears in a story make a funny snorting sound. After a while the child will anticipate
this gurgle and will holler with laughter when it
occurs.[3]

THE DARK SIDE

Youngsters must face the shadowy side of things somewhere along the line, and fairy stories offer an excellent way
of easing them into it. But if you plan on featuring dark ideas
in your narratives be careful of hitting the nail too hard on the

head, and beware of grisly details. Bringing the dark side to a child can be done more efficiently, and a good deal more gently, via inference, symbolism, and suggestion.

For example, instead of terrorizing an impressionable tot with ferocious mind pictures like "The wolf had big white, bloody fangs, long pointed ears, a red prickly tongue, and a body covered with smelly hairs," say instead: "Picture the most ugly, smelly, angry creature you can imagine—and there you have our wolf."

Instead of telling how the giant fell off the beanstalk, hit the ground, and was smashed to bits, pretend you are watching the giant as he falls off the tree, down, down, down, to the ground, then make a huge sound when he hits and shake your head with a mock-sad expression on your face. Too bad, Mr. Giant! Better yet, act out the action yourself.

Remember, a good story is not meant to rouse interest in evil or to teach young ones to dwell on morbidity—which is exactly the kind of sentiments horror and ghost stories induce. Quite the opposite. Its purpose is to awaken the inner imaginative eye and to focus this eye on intuitions of mystery, sacredness, and awe.

6.

Communicating Spiritual Ideas During Daily Activities

The beauty of raising a child in a traditionally religious society (the type of society that, we are told, existed in the Christian West during the Middle Ages and still survives to some extent in Eastern countries) is that the child is surrounded from birth with a wide selection of verbal and visual spiritual reminders. Each of these reminders, small in itself, accumulates in the child's subconscious over the days, over the years, subtly implanting notions of a divine order and gradually forming the ground in which a child's spiritual realizations will later take root.

In religious societies spiritual messages come in a thousand shapes and sizes. Examples can be found in traditional styles of dress, which are patterned for modesty and ease of prayer rather than for fashionable display. Or on the covers of children's schoolbooks decorated with spiritual symbols. In the daily sound of church bells or the call to prayer heard from every child's bedroom window; or the smell of incense in the marketplace. Also in the celebration of religious processions through the streets of a town, traditional music broadcast over the radio, scriptural readings on television, a crucifix mounted over a work desk, a mezuzzah at the door. Commonplace items, yet deep symbols all.

In parts of the Muslim Middle East sayings such as "Blessings on it" or "God has made it so" are used so frequently in everyday speech that for most people they become mechanical. Yet such automatic habits transmit wholesome subliminal messages to listener and speaker alike. Indeed, few good Muslims would consider announcing that they will be visiting their friend next week, or that their vacation starts on Thursday, without first adding "Inshah Allah"—"God willing."

Similarly, the façades of many shops in India are painted with colorful spiritual symbols, while the windows of private homes are carved into a honeycomb of sacred designs. Children see them while playing in the streets or walking to school, and over time their symbolic messages become fixed and crystallized, helping to mold a spiritual worldview that will last a lifetime.

CREATING YOUR OWN
SACRED HOUSEHOLD SYMBOLS

In modern society children are rarely exposed to this kind of devotional input, and devout parents are forced to make up the spiritual deficit on their own. But how?

Everyone has a personal answer to this question, of course, though as a rule of thumb the best place to begin is at home, the best time during a family's ordinary daily activities. A starter list includes:

Establish the Habit of Giving Thanks at Meals

Dwell on gratefulness and on the fact that the food set before the family is provided by the generous earth, the generous plant, the generous farmer, the generous Creator.

Teach Children Morning and Evening Devotions

Let these prayers and meditations become as regular to the daily routine as washing hands or brushing teeth. Don't worry about the old rejoinder that the child will be saying prayers "by rote" or "like a wind-up doll." He or she *is* saying them by rote, but that's okay. If the prayers are real prayers they will have a power all their own. They will do the spiritualizing job, as it were, automatically. Trust in the process. It's an ancient one.

Begin Each Day by Introducing the Child to a Meditative Thought or Inspiring Pensée

Wake the child up with the announcement that "The stars and moon have gone to sleep, the sun and clouds are up and wide-awake in the sky. Why don't we join them?" Or "The birds are singing in the trees. Did you know that their songs are prayers? Can you hear what they are praying for?" Henry Old Coyote, a Crow Indian, discourses on the morning wake-up ritual among his tribe: "It's all right for a child to sleep because he needs the rest, but the moment of waking is a significant time. Come the early morning, my grandfather would always tell me, 'It's all right to sleep, but now you have had your rest. Sleep is not your ally; sleep is not your friend. Rise up early with the sun and face a new day. If you rise up early enough, you'll be lucky. Face that Old Man!' meaning the sun. 'He sees you and he's going to give you something. Face a new day—it's just like being born again!' These are some of the sayings he had. He would tell me."[1]

Cultivate Devout Verbal Expressions and Use Them Around the House

After a sneeze say "Bless you." After an escape from a difficult or dangerous situation say "God helped us." When things go well say "God is kind" or "It's karma." When they don't say "God knows best."

And so forth.

Celebrate Your Own Spiritual Holidays

Modern secular society no longer honors saints' days or holidays. It does have public rites and rituals, but these have become occasions for paying tribute to the new gods of modern times. Halloween, once the sacred Druid New Year, is now a holiday commemorating the morbid and satanic. The Fourth of July, established to celebrate liberty and human rights, honors its opposite, war. Thanksgiving, a time of gratitude and prayer, has become devoted to the worship of food. Valentine's Day, established to commemorate the loving sacrifice of a saint, commemorates sexual love instead. And our most important celebration, Christmas, worships our most important of gods—money—all in our new cathedrals of faith: the malls, the shopping centers, the department stores.

But while society offers little in the way of sacred celebrations, there is no reason why you can't honor them yourself. If you follow a particular religion find a calendar that indicates important weekly events in your faith. Mark them off and celebrate them at home. Don't be afraid to go all the way on this one either. Give presents, go out for dinner, decorate the house, do whatever inspires you and your child. Little ones will remember these times and will have positive spiritual associations with them all their lives. If you do not belong to a particular religious denomination, simply declare a certain day to be Kindness Day or Generosity Afternoon. Urge the child to practice this particular virtue all day long, then at dinnertime celebrate with a family party, cake and cookies, whatever. Invent your own variations.

Turn Ordinary Events Into Object Lessons That Point Out Spiritual Principles

If a toy breaks, explain to the child that nothing lasts forever. If a plant has wilted, water it, bring it back to health, then tell the child that no matter how dire a situation there is always hope. Then recite an appropriate phrase from holy writing such as: "Be of good courage, and He shall strengthen your heart, all ye that hope in the Lord" (Psalms 31:24).

If you find a dead animal in the woods or on the road explain that some religions believe we die many times, that our souls go from body to body, first into plants, then into animals, finally into human beings. This process is called reincarnation. Some persons even believe that they can remember their past lives. Can you?

If a moth flies into your room put it out the window instead of killing it. Explain to the child that everything has a right to live.

If you are walking through a dark place, holding a child's hand, explain that the child's faith will be like this handhold when he or she grows up, that it will lead her or him through dark times when it is most needed.

If you light a candle in a dark room, tell the child that his or her actions are like the candle's flame; just a little kindness can brighten the darkest places.

If fireflies appear during a summer night, go outside with the child and wander among them. Tell the child that every human being has their own light, like the firefly; it's called the soul.

If a pet or yard animal dies, explain that death occurs to all living things, that the time had come for this creature to leave the world. Some parents hold a small ceremony to mark a pet's passing which they flavor with prayers and/or religious rituals. If, moreover, you plan to purchase a new pet, be sure to emphasize that the new animal cannot replace the old one, that it is an entirely new being with a completely different personality and fate. Stress the fact that all living things are unique unto themselves.

MORE SPIRITUAL LEARNING GAMES

Peggy Jenkins has written several intriguing books on the subject of child rearing, one of which, *A Child Of God*, presents a series of inventive, interactive games parents can play with their children at home that require nothing more than round-the-house items to get started.

Without being preachy or sentimental, these exercises

teach essentials of faith and spiritual common sense. Here are some typical examples culled from Jenkins' worthy effort:

• Give children a rubber band. Have them stretch it and snap it several times. Explain that thoughts are like rubber bands. Think a good thought and more good thoughts snap back at us from other people. Think a bad thought and these return from others too, just like the rubber band. Demonstrate with the rubber bands and let the children experiment.

• Shake some salt into a bowl of water. Explain that just as we cannot retrieve the individual grains of salt from the water, so, once we've spoken nasty words they cannot be taken back. Therefore: it is necessary to think carefully before you speak. (Jenkins adds that these mistakes *can* be corrected, and that past errors can be righted, if we pray to a higher power for forgiveness and understanding.)

• Take a scissors and paper. Have children cut out several patterns. Then point out that the imagination is like a scissors, capable of shaping practically any object from the universal thought substance. Demonstrate by suggesting an item, a new house, say, or an animal, even an idea. Cut out a shape that matches this thought and have the child do the same. Explain that the child's imagination is a very powerful tool, that it can be used to think of constructive things or destructive things, and that it should always be used with care. Give examples of how people's imagination have created great things in this world, and terrible things.

• Children have difficulty imagining the notion that we came into this world from some invisible place and that we return to it after death. An interesting way of demonstrating this belief in concrete terms is to place ice cubes in a bowl of water. Explain that the cubes are human beings, and that the water is the invisible creative power of the universe. Through a certain divine process we come out of the transparent "invisible" water, just like the ice. Later on, at some distant date, we will melt back into the waters. "We come forth from the invisible to the visible," Jenkins writes. "As when the ice melts and becomes water once again, at the time of so-called death, we simply lay aside our bodies and our spirits return to Spirit, or the so-called invisible."[2]

You get the point. As a rule, it's wise not to make too big a deal out of these metaphors and to keep them simple, without employing dozens of props. Avoid too much preplanning as well. The best lessons are the spontaneous ones that seem to grow out of the moment. For teaching objects, use whatever happens to be around. If you are in the basement, tell your story using shop tools or pieces of laundry. If you are digging in the garden, a shovel and hoe will do.

More specifically: Suppose you're at the dinner table and your little one is telling you that he or she is having hostile feelings toward a friend. Pour some salt and pepper on the tablecloth, mix together, and half-jokingly remark that this is the way your child probably feels about this friend, all mixed up, like the salt and pepper. The salt is sort of like your good feelings, the pepper like your angry ones. It's that way for all of us sometimes. We feel a lot of conflicting things about the same person at different times.

Thus, in a graphic and entertaining way you have planted a prevalent and subtle social concept in the young mind: mixed emotions.

SMALL PITCHERS HAVE BIG EARS: TEACHING THE CHILD WHILE TALKING TO OTHERS

Parents are often warned that when children are within earshot it is better not to criticize them in front of others as if they were third-person pieces of furniture. We have all heard the mother who proclaims in a bullhorn voice that Johnny is a miserable eater—while Johnny sits there with, as it were, egg on his face. Or the father who carries on at length about how uncontrollably little Jennifer behaved at the drugstore this morning—Jennifer is sitting at a table nearby coloring while this monologue continues—and how he is getting close to his wit's end with this brat! And so on.

What leads some parents to say such revealing and potentially disturbing things in front of their children? There are many reasons, though surely two of the main ones are that (1) they do not think children have the psychological maturity to comprehend what is being said about them and (2) they believe that when children are absorbed in play they are oblivious of what is going on in the room.

Appearances deceive. As for understanding things said about them, children's comprehension skills are extremely advanced by the time they are five or six years old, and certainly they now recognize the meaning of "pain in the neck" or "driving me out of my mind."

The problem, in fact, is that children understand these descriptions too well, at least on a superficial level. Having a tendency to take the exclamations they hear literally, what are children to make of these phrases but that they really are, just as their parents say, pesty, mean, nasty, wild, just plain no good? Soon children who frequently hear how badly they behave start believing this message and start acting out the part, as demanded.

Though it is not always apparent, and though children do not usually comment on or react to what they have just overheard, young ones do listen in on their parents' conversations, usually with both ears aflap.

The messages that are passed back and forth during these overheard sessions, positive ones as well as negative, are then fed through the child's immature thought processes, often coming out mangled into grotesque misinterpretations.

THE POSITIVE SIDE

A child's tendency to eavesdrop is, like so many elements of childhood, a double-edged sword and at the appropriate moment can also be used for positive teaching ends. The critical thing to note here is that a child's tendency to overhear takes place in a passive state. That is, since the child is not being addressed directly, his or her defense systems remain on low, just as our adult defense systems are passive when we listen to the radio or to the conversations of others. At these moments a good deal of material which cannot be fed directly into the child's waking intelligence can be slipped in, as it were, through the back door.

In his fascinating and profound book *Meetings with Remarkable Men,* the Greco-Armenian mystic George Gurdjieff provides just such a method which he calls *kastousilia.* Here is how it works. In the presence of a child, one person asks another a spiritually symbolic question, apparently unrehearsed and spontaneous. The other person, without haste, answers seriously and logically, almost as if discussing the price of potatoes.

As a boy in Armenia, Gurdjieff relates, he would often sit in his father's carpentry shop watching his father at work. One day a priest who had taken a special interest in young Gurdjieff's education and who was just then tutoring him in religious subjects, came striding into the shop and abruptly asked Gurdjieff's father: "Where is God at this moment?"

Without hesitation Gurdjieff's father replied: "Right this moment God is in the region of Sari Kamish."

"What is God doing there?" the priest wanted to know.

The father answered that just then God was making ladders from the unusually tall pine trees that grow in the Sari Kamish forests. On top of these ladders He was placing happiness so that individual people and even entire nations could climb up these ladders and climb down again.

SYMBOLIC CONVERSATIONS
AT THE DINNER TABLE

Such strange conversations, which at the time seemed meaningless to Gurdjieff, later revealed themselves as full of rich spiritual meaning and as having influenced him on a deeply subconscious level. Parents today can employ a similar method with their own children, carrying on allegorical dialogues with one another within earshot of small ones and by so doing instilling cosmological and metaphysical concepts that children might otherwise not be willing to hear. Depending on religious persuasion or spiritual belief, parents could couch such ideas as reincarnation, retribution, illusion, grace, and so on in metaphoric terms, as did Gurdjieff's father. For example:

> *A mother says to a father, with the child nearby: "I heard a crow talking in the apple tree today. What do you think it told me?"*
>
> *The father replies: "I think he said that he had just returned from a distant country where he saw three great cities in flames. A young child was standing in the middle of each city. But the flames couldn't hurt any of the children because they were all so pure and good."*

And so forth. You can create your own dialogues based on your spiritual vision and on the temperament of your child. Elaborate rehearsals are not necessary, although parents can agree ahead of time on the topics to be discussed.

Why the use of arcane terms to express ideas that might just as easily be said in plain English? Again, because the parabolic language of symbol and metaphor seems to bypass many childhood ego defenses and to speak directly to the young unconscious. At the same time, there is nothing to stop parents from also carrying on direct and nonsymbolic spiritual conversations when the child is nearby. These can take place at the dinner table, in the living room, in the car, wherever.

Children may not appear to be very interested in what is being said at these times, especially when the subject matter has intellectual overtones. Nonetheless *something* of the exchange will penetrate, especially if a warm and sincere emotional atmosphere attends it. And in the case of spiritual messages, a little is a lot. A Zen story tells about a young boy who lived in a monastery, where he served a certain great abbot. One day the child came to the abbot carrying a handful of pieces from what had recently been a prized tea bowl.

"How did it break?" asked the monk in an irritated voice.

"I dropped it," answered the boy.

The abbot was about to lecture and punish when the child added: "I overheard you say the other day that everything in creation has its time for being born and its time for living and its time for dying. I heard you say this, and then I knew after I'd dropped it—it was the time for this cup to die today. I just happened to be the one who helped it leave the world."

The monk smiled and let the incident pass.

HAVING DIRECT RELIGIOUS CONVERSATIONS WITH CHILDREN

Children easily feel lectured to. The moment their parents launch into polemics about divine powers, saying one's prayers, and the like, they can feel put on the spot, talked down to, or just plain bored. It's catch-22 time: If you talk to children about "important things," they become resistant. If you don't they may never learn. What to do?

Basically, the success rate of spiritual conversations depends as much on how and when you say it as on what you say. This is the crux of matter, really, and here are a few useful tips to remember when attempting to communicate directly about spiritual facts:

Avoid the Pedestal Approach

Say what you have to say without sounding stagy or magisterial; express yourself as if the listener were a peer or a friend. Children will sense it when they are being force-fed ideas or talked down to or given canned materials. They will respond accordingly. This is important. Thomas Merton's comments on his father's method of spiritual instruction is particularly interesting in this regard: "The only really valuable religious and moral teaching I ever got as a child," Merton tells us, "came to me from my father, not systematically, but here and there and more or less spontaneously, in the course of ordinary conversations. Father never applied himself, of set purpose, to teach me religion. But if something spiritual was on his mind it came out more or less naturally. And this is the kind of religious teaching, or any other kind of teaching, that has the most effect.[3]

A similar description of spiritual parenting made effective because of its low-key, oblique approach comes from Peggy Scherer, ex-editor of *The Catholic Worker*. Asked to recall memories of her Catholic upbringing, one of Scherer's most prominent recollections is of her father's quiet faith and the way in which it influenced her own belief. "The presence of religion in my house was subtle but strong," she recalls. "I was aware from an early age that my father went to Mass every day. Very little was said about that, but I absorbed the fact that it was quite important to him. At the same time, I could clearly see that my father was a very kind and generous person. . . . He was forever helping neighbors out or helping with class trips or chauffeuring people here and there. With almost nothing said about it I remember, I got a sense that you kind of helped people out. And I knew that somehow that was connected to my father's faith."[4]

George Gurdjieff, too, has something to say concerning his father's own straightforward, no-nonsense style of presentation:

> *My father had a very simple, clear and quite definite view on the aim of human life. He told me many times in my youth that the fundamental striving of every man should be to create for himself an inner freedom towards life and to prepare for himself a happy old age. . . . But a man could attain this aim only if, from childhood up to the age of eighteen, he had acquired data for the unwavering fulfillment of the following four commandments:*
>
> *First—To love one's parents.*
>
> *Second—To remain chaste.*
>
> *Third—To be outwardly courteous to all without distinction, whether they be rich or poor, friends or enemies, power-possessors*

*or slaves, and to whatever religion they may belong, but in-
wardly to remain free and never to put much trust in anyone
or anything.*

Fourth—To love work for work's sake and not for its gain. [5]

Keep it Brief

This is a tough one, especially if the ideas you wish to get
across are inherently complex. Still, short is beautiful as far
as children are concerned. So keep sentences terse. Compress
and amalgamate when you can. Don't wax too long or intox-
icatedly over spiritual subjects—young children usually can't
follow such flights of fancy. In the Koran there is a passage
concerning the Creation that says quite simply: "God says
'Be'—and it is." In six words comes the perfect answer to any
child's question about how the world was made. God just said
"Be" and it was.

See Things from Your Child's Point of View

The Prophet Muhammad once remarked that we should
"Talk to each person according to their own understanding."
This does not mean that we should talk down to youngsters,
but simply that ideas are best absorbed when served up on the
child's own level.

Remember how you yourself once responded to lectures
from grownups? Those who expounded endlessly on didactic
themes quickly became bores. Those who were able to capsul-
ize an idea in a genial phrase or two and to speak in something
approximating the artless lingo of the six-year-old or the
eight-year-old were listened to with an eager ear.

I once observed a master Sunday school teacher as she
fielded religious queries from her group of bright, curious
seven- and eight-year-olds. Her answers were so concise and
to the point, and at the same time aroused such interest
among the children, that I wrote them down. They are quoted
here more or less as they were spoken:

QUESTION: What happens to us when we're dead?

TEACHER'S ANSWER: After we die, as far as my understanding goes—which isn't very great, I should tell you, 'cause death is such a mystery—our body stays here on earth and goes back into the ground. And another part of us, called the soul, goes on to a good place where God is. Other than that it's unknown.

QUESTION: What's it like in heaven?

TEACHER'S ANSWER: Think of the happiest moment you can remember. Heaven is a hundred times happier than that—and it just keeps getting happier all the time.

QUESTION: Why did Jesus say we should always love our neighbors?

TEACHER'S ANSWER: If someone is nice to you don't you enjoy it? Doesn't it feel good? And don't you like that person for acting toward you in such a friendly way? We all do. Because that person is treating you *the way you want to be treated yourself.* Just think about it. If we all treated each other the way we want to be treated we'd all be nice to each other. Everyone would be happy. Sounds pretty good, eh? Maybe we should try it this next week with our friends when we're in school.

QUESTION: How come my sister got so sick? God doesn't like her, I guess.

TEACHER'S ANSWER: God loves all of us, especially children. Sometimes He lets painful things happen to us now that help us later on. Maybe if your sister hadn't stayed home in bed she would have been hit by a car that day and been hurt even worse. Or maybe by being sick she learned what it feels like to be sick, so when she grows up she'll become a doctor to help other people. Or maybe when she was sick she had more time to stay home and be with you, so that the two of you could become better friends. You see, things aren't always

what they seem when you're talking about God's plan.
Even though something hurts now it may end up helping you later. God always knows best.

**Use Stories, Metaphors, Myths, Humor, and Picturesque
Imagery to Make Abstract Concepts More Concrete**
Don't be afraid to use spirited comparisons, analogies,
graphic images, and even historical examples when offering
spiritual ideas to a child. Usually these figures of speech
should relate to things children understand and that have
relevance to their daily life. But not always. One father, for
example, called on his knowledge of arcane archeological lore
to get a point across. His story, though alien to anything the
child had ever heard, was vivid and lent itself to easy visualization. The father told how long, long ago in a country called
Egypt, young boys were trained in special temples by holy
men. If during their training one of the boys told a lie he was
given a special punishment: he was told to sit in a large
wooden chair covered with paintings of lions and was made
to stay there for several hours, repeating the words of the lies
he had told. Later that day his teachers would come in, rub
out the pictures of lions, and repaint them. When asked why
the lions had been erased, the teachers explained that the
lions had eaten all of the boy's lies now, so he was absolved.
But in the process they had become weak and tired by all the
untruths, and now new lions were needed to replace them.
     This story is effective in several ways. It implants in the
child's mind a vivid image of the results of lying. It implies
that there are ways to punish other than violence. It helps
develop the young imagination. And it makes children aware
that there are many strange and wonderful things in this
world of which they are not yet aware.
     Another example: If you are explaining to a child the rather
sophisticated concept that different people witness the same
event in different ways—and that, hence, one should refrain
from judging things until all the evidence is in—you can let
several children who saw some occurrence (an argument, say,

or an accident) report on the event separately while you and the child note the differences. This opportunity will be a fine one to show that, while there is no intention to misrepresent, every person sees things according to individual temperament, prejudices, and mood of the moment. Moral: Before we judge anyone or anything we should question our own hearts.

Parables convey hidden spiritual messages too, even the better-known parables such as, say, "The Tortoise and the Hare." On first hearing this story seems a simple cautionary tale for the hasty. But below the surface lurks another darker and more profound meaning. The tortoise, besides standing for perseverance, is also a traditional symbol of old age and death; and the hare, with his naïveté, his mad, Roger Rabbit-like energy, and his inability to comprehend the tenacious power of his adversary, is youth.

From the start of the race the tortoise plods forward relentlessly, inevitably, untroubled by the fact that the hare has moved so far ahead. His is the confidence of experience and inevitability. He knows that the foolish hare, his initial powers spent, will soon become distracted, only to be overtaken in the end by the tortoise's somber persistence. In this way a child is subliminally warned that he too, she too, will someday be overtaken by time and old age, but that age has its compensations—it offers wisdom and experience and a mature understanding of how the human race is really run.

Yet another way of expressing various truths and summing up situations in a meaningful way, especially for older children, is through the use of appropriate aphorisms and proverbs. Carefully picked wise sayings can sum up in a single sentence how a child is feeling. No need to say more. For example:

A nine-year-old comes home from a friend's house and complains that his friend bullied him and bragged the whole time they were together. The parent replies simply: "Well, you know, every dog barks in its own yard." Point made.

A ten-year-old is bragging away and making a lot of noise about nothing. Someone nearby remarks "Empty barrels make the loudest sounds."

A sudden change takes place in Chip's life. His mother cautions him that "The wheel of life keeps turning and we keep turning with it."

William has just attended his first funeral. On the way home one of his parents remarks quietly: "At birth we come, at death we go, bearing nothing."

AND FINALLY, MOST IMPORTANT OF ALL . . .

Imitation. For the first six or seven years of life, and to a lesser extent even up to puberty, you are your child's god. Everything you say will be repeated. Everything you do will produce an impact on the child's personality, for better or for worse.

This means that if you display a reverent attitude toward life your child will do the same. If you honestly believe in a higher good, in right behavior, in ultimate justice and reward—and if you follow your principles in these matters—your belief will help the child become a believer as well.

When all is said and done, after all the sacred stories have been told, the holy games played, the deep teaching tales recounted, your primary resource for inculcating a devotional attitude into a child is your own level of being. As surely as the cart follows the horse, children will see what you do; and they will do the same.

PART · 2

DISCIPLINE
WITH A
SPIRITUAL
TWIST

7.

Authoritarian Versus Authoritative

DISCIPLINE

Discipline: The term conjures up images of spankings and tears, of browbeaten masses and drill sergeants bellowing commands. Even when associated with children the word is drapped in the vestments of pain; and so, parents come to think of discipline and punishment as peas in a pod. Too bad, because setting wholesome limits and breaking hearts need not—should not—be synonymous. "Rather than to correct and heal," writes José Maria Rivorola, "men prefer to judge and punish. It is much easier."

For the spiritually minded parent the idea of discipline must remain positive and constructive. Seen in the proper light this implies training, knowledge, learning, guidance: guidance away from what hurts a child and toward what helps. The root of the word itself is the Latin verb for learning, *discere,* suggesting that children are literally their parents' *disciplines*. Discipline, in other words, does not connote punishment so much as it does *character building*. In a nutshell, it means:

- Helping the child learn the rules of acceptable social interaction
- Instilling the instinct toward kindness, consideration, setting limits, self-control, and telling right from wrong
- Preparing the child for a sane and sensitive adulthood

At the same time, while the goals of character building are usually clear in parents' minds, the best and most righteous methods for implementing them are not always apparent. In fact, few things are more difficult then figuring out how to deal with naughty behavior in a manner that is at once effective and godly. "It seems that if you're too lenient you raise a spoiled creep," the mother of a nine-year-old boy told me once. "If you're too tough you break the kid's will. If you're too loving the kid becomes an overdependent mama's boy. If you let him go his own way unsupervised he becomes alienated. You just gotta be the Buddha to do it right!"

Not exactly. You don't have to be the Buddha to raise a child properly, though by following one of the Buddha's major precepts you can get the ball rolling. "Always seek the middle way," the Illuminated One advised. In matters of parental supervision this rule has golden applications.

What is the middle way? In a nutshell, it is maintaining a balance between a tolerant, supportive, generous, and libertarian attitude on one hand and a watchful, rigorous, strict, and conservative restraint on the other. Rupture this equilibrium, many parents have discovered, let leniency and permissiveness dominate over discipline and structure (or vice versa), and a majority of the behavioral problems that drive parents so far up the nursery walls are launched.

This balance between the hard way and the soft way has been recognized by theologians through the years. Reinhold Niebuhr, for example: "There is a hard and terrible facet to justice which stands in contradiction to love. It is not, for that reason, evil. Justice is good and punishment is necessary. Yet justice alone does not move men to repentance."

Among child psychologists this notion also prevails, though with a somewhat different emphasis. Diana Baumrind, an educator at the University of California at Berkeley, is one of a surprisingly small number of professionals who have studied the relationship between parental discipline and children's behavioral patterns. In her writings on the subject she makes the distinction between parents who are *authoritarian* and parents who are *permissive.* She then contrasts both of these categories with what she terms the *authoritative* parent. This is her analysis:

1. *The authoritarian parent.* He or she tries to control and even dominate the child's behavior using a strict, preconceived, and inflexible set of rules and standards.
2. *The permissive parent.* He or she responds to a child's misbehavior with nonpunishing, accepting, and affirmative manner.
3. *Authoritative parents.* He or she attempts to balance permissiveness with authority, according to the particular situation.

"The authoritative parents were most responsive to their children's demands for attention, but they did not yield to unreasonable demands," Dr. Stella Chess writes, discussing Baumrind's observations. "They also expected mature, independent behavior from the child, appropriate to his developmental level. Such parents tended to have the most socially competent children . . . authoritarian parents tended to have children who were less happy, as well as moody, apprehensive, passively hostile, and vulnerable to stress; the permissive parents tended to have children who were impulsive-aggressive."[1]

Balance between disciplinary modes, many believe, is thus a fundamental spiritual precept in the raising of a child, and in this regard we have the ultimate model on which to base our belief. God Himself, we are taught in many religions, dispenses His actions on two universal and seemingly opposite principles: mercy and justice. Mercy is His kindness, justice His insistence that we obey His just laws—or suffer the inevitable consequences.

Kabbalism, for example, speaks of "three pillars of the

Sefiroth." The central pillar represents material human existence. It is flanked by the pillar of Mercy on one side, the pillar
of Judgment on the other. All human behavior, Kabbalists
believe, is dependent on the tension and interaction among
all three pillars.

In Christianity the same idea is expressed, if on a more
covert level, by the concept of the Father and the Son of the
Holy Trinity. In Hinduism the existence of Siva, the destroying god, and Vishnu, the preserver, is similar. So is the concept of Yin and Yang in Taoism. "God," says the Sufi Sahl
Al-Tustari, "is only known by the union of contraries."

Since humankind should strive to mirror the divine, as we
are taught in many spiritual disciplines, it is likewise a mother
and father's responsibility to raise their child in a household
where mercy and justice are appropriately balanced. If such
a symmetry is maintained, then a balanced human being results. As Confucius wrote: "The Perfect Man is he who em-
bodies the compassion of the yin and the strength of the yang;
the knowledge of the yin and the forthrightness of the yang;
the depth of the yin and the height of the yang; the easiness
of the yin and the hardness of the yang."

What does all this mean in terms of practical parenting?
How do we translate such lofty theology into child rearing?
Start with mercy. Divine mercy can be brought to earth, as it
were, in the form of:

· Loving support
· Reasonable permissiveness
· Patience and forbearance with naughty behavior
· A fun-loving attitude, and a sense of humor
· Forgiveness, plus a warm, harboring love
· Tolerance and benefit of the doubt

Divine justice, on the other hand, is translated into parental
justice in the forms of:

· Structure and rules
· Prevention and control of a child's selfish, malicious,
and self-destructive impulses

•Fair punishments administered for wayward conduct
•Lessons concerning the moral nature of the world
•Help in teaching children to recognize and avoid harmful influences
•Lessons in the curriculum of respect, honor, humility, moderation, and self-restraint

This paradigm of God's mercy and God's wrath as alternating forces of a single divine totality can be further extended. Observe:

YANG JUDGMENT WRATH Qualities of Parental Justice	YIN COMPASSION FORGIVENESS Qualities of Parental Mercy
Strictness	Leniency
Punishment	Reward
Rules	Hanging loose
Temperance	Indulgence
Learning	Playing
School	Home
Lessons	Games
No	Yes
The serious side of life	The fun side of of life

Discipline, then, is a kind of ongoing juggling act involving both father and mother in equal but different roles. The aims: to cultivate the benevolent traits and discourage the malevolent ones. In this light, there are many actions which parents can take to restrain a child's negative impulses in, as it were, a positive way.

8.

The Tao of Discipline

The first line of disciplinary defense is to *keep children so healthy that sickness cannot take root.* If you can accomplish this bit of legerdemain, if you can spot the behavior problem while it is still in the seed and correct it before it grows into a tree, punishment will not be a problem because misbehavior will not be an issue. Here, in greater depth, is how it works.

THE PRINCIPLES OF TAOIST DISCIPLINE

Among the basic notions that constitute the ancient religion of Taoism and that, mutatis mutandis, can be applied to techniques of child rearing, are:

> *The world exists as an interplay between two fundamental forces: the positive and negative, the strong and the weak, the male and the female. Taoists call them* yin *and* yang. *The balance between these two equal and complementary forces is known as the* Tao.

The Tao is both a path and a natural law. Its principles express themselves on all levels of existence. Though the Tao cannot be described in words, everyone knows what it is deep inside themselves; everyone senses it, feels it, understands it. But not everyone follows it.

By practicing virtue one cooperates with the Tao: harmony will be the natural and inevitable result. With the practice of vice unhappiness and chaos must come. The purpose of life is, thus, to follow the path of virtue.

For the Taoist, a little energy applied at the proper place and at the proper time is more forceful than a great deal of energy misspent and poorly timed.

For the Taoist, all things in the universe have their own rhythm and cycles. Our job as human beings is to note these cycles and to cooperate with them.

For Taoists there is an appropriate moment to undertake any activity. To force or rush things when the time is not ripe is to court failure. ("You can't make the grass grow by pulling it," a Taoist sage wrote.) On the other hand, to let evil continue too long without remedying it is to invite cosmic disharmony. "Timing is all," said Lao Tzu.

All things in the universe naturally strive toward union and harmony. Gentleness ultimately prevails over force. Goodness ultimately prevails over evil.

Taking these abbreviated and admittedly simplified ideas, how can you apply the concepts to the process of raising children? Witness:

1. Always approach the question of parental discipline from a positive viewpoint. As a Taoist might, admit that your child is good and that your role as parent is to demonstrate how to express this inborn quality.

2. Foresee and remedy potential trouble spots in a child's behavior before they have time to develop into major issues.

3. Manipulate conditions so that potentially harmful influences are eliminated from the child's environment. Avoid particular trouble spots by keeping the child away from them.

4. When a small amount of correction works, leave it at that. When a few censorious words do the trick, avoid further scolding. When a raised eyebrow or a disapproving glance is enough, forget the rod. Harbor your resources; let a little take you a long way. In Taoism this method is known as *wu wei,* effortless effort.

5. Let children's own energy and discernment guide them to the right goals. Let your job be simply to aim them in the right direction. The best parent is like the best emperor: "He does not utter words lightly," explains the *Tao Te Ching,* "but when his job is accomplished and his task done, the people all say, 'Why, it all happened to us so naturally.' "

6. Avoid displays of anger whenever possible. Expressions of negative emotions rarely cure anything; they simply serve as a role model for the recipient. On the other hand, be firm, discipline when you must, and stick to your guns. But do it in a caring way, not with rancor or mean-spiritedness.

7. Let older children's innate sense of justice guide them to a proper understanding of what is right and wrong. You as parent must simply set the stage and provide the raw materials.

The following helps and hints are all based on these seven fundamental principles.

Keep the Child Busy

Keep children out of harm's way by keeping them busy. "What the eye doesn't see," says a Chinese proverb, "the heart does not yearn for." Specifically:

• Look at your child's room and at your backyard. Are there enough toys and play equipment here to keep young hands moving and young brains occupied?

• Are you well stocked in clay, crayons, paper and scissors, building blocks, dolls and dollhouses, play figures, craft sets, outside play equipment like slides, swings, and climbing apparatus? The quantity of the toys *and* their quality are important if the child is to be kept wholesomely entertained.

• Is your house arranged with the child's needs in mind as well as your own? "Concern for the health of the furniture is understandable," writes child psychologist, Haim Ginnot, "but it must not supersede concern for the health of the children."

• Set up scheduled play periods in advance with friends so that the child's time is well taken up. When you go to restaurants pack a plastic shopping bag full of coloring books, crayons, scissors, paper, small figurines—whatever is portable and transportable.

• On long motor trips be sure to bring plenty of diversions along with the sandwiches. You'll be especially wise to follow this advice if there is more than one sibling occupying the back seat. Let children fly colored crepe-paper streamers out the window—this one is good for hours. Or help them tape colored pieces of cellophane on the window so they can look at a multicolored world as the car moves along. Motor bingo, counting license plates, singing, guessing distances on the speedometer, twenty questions, telling stories, guessing games, or listening to tapes will keep children eager and occupied.

• Whether home or on the road, plan all games in advance and have them ready to go at a moment's notice. The "in advance" factor is crucial. By the time the child has become bored and is looking restively about for something to get into it may already be too late. The Tao of child raising is to anticipate a problem before it arises.

Never Let a Child Become Overtired

The day baby Brynn was born the proud father's uncle took him aside and remarked that while he was not in the habit of giving advice, he did want to pass on one small piece of wisdom. "Never, *never,* NEVER let her get tired," he said with a knowing smile. Ten years later this same father recalled to his wife that his uncle's suggestion was the wisest bit of child sense he had ever received.

Children's souls are growing in childhood along with their bodies, and any disruption of sleep will interfere with this psychic unfolding just as with physical health. Establish regular bedtimes and stick to them, even if the child pleads for more time. Junior may become especially charming and wide-eyed at this fatal hour as he begs sweetly for "just five more minutes." But if any indication of fatigue is apparent turn a deaf ear. It will be better all around.

Remember, sleep deprivation is a favorite brainwashing technique. Torturers use it to drive their victims mad. So next time the children get on a roll of nasty behavior, forget about exile or exorcism and instead ask yourself if their bedtime hour is early enough. Then try lowering it by a half-hour and see what happens. Don't underestimate this one.

What the Eye Doesn't See the Heart Doesn't Yearn for

If you want to prevent a child from craving sweets, don't keep sweets in the house. If fighting is a problem among brothers and sisters, separate all siblings during the most difficult hours of the day. If you want to cure your kids from the I-need-a-new-toy-a-week disease keep them away from seductive TV ads and colorful picture catalogs. If bad words have entered your household, check your own language; if the trouble is not here, find out which of the child's friends is setting the bad example. If you don't want your children to espouse the triple credo of guns, murder, and mayhem, distance them from military toys, violent comics, and war movies.

All in all, the easiest way to keep kids from a particular

temptation is not to. let them know that it exists in the first place. Ignorance is bliss for as long as you can maintain it—their bliss and yours.

Use Diversionary Tactics

More of the Tao: Instead of attacking children head-on for acting out, simply shift their attention. Introduce something new into their consciousness. This is especially effective with infants and toddlers, as you probably know. When children of this age begin to cry, the shake of a rattle or the change of position will quickly calm the tears.

As the child gets older the same principle applies, though now on a more sophisticated level. In infancy you diverted children through their senses. Now you work through their minds and feelings.

For example, whenever Jamie's mother sees her four-year-olds about to erupt into a tear storm she plants a diverting mental image into his consciousness. When Jamie started to become defiant about keeping his hands off the newly painted walls his mother said: "Hey, remember that book of cut-out masks Grandma got you? Let's find it. I'll get the book; you get those funny green plastic scissors in the kitchen. Let's have some fun together!" Presto! By using vivid descriptive language to lift Jamie's mind up and away from the potential trouble spot, the problem is sidestepped—and without a noisy confrontation. This method will work for a surprising number of years if employed cleverly. It can sometimes be used even with teenagers.

Nipping Tantrums in the Bud

Diversionary tactics work best when the negative emotion is in its beginning stage. Once a tantrum is in full swing don't expect to stop it by making a funny face or suggesting that everyone go out for pizza. The angry energy is out of the bottle now, just like the genie, and it quickly turns against the child, against you, against the world. Christian monks speak of this anger as "the slave that eats its master."

The trick is to prevent angry energy from developing *in the beginning, when the negativity is still small enough to control.* Like the Taoist principle of uprooting the tree when it is still a sprout, catch the difficulty early or you won't catch it all. This is a universal principle that has applications to all varieties of troubleshooting. As Will Rogers once remarked, "Once trouble's woke up it ain't so easy to get him back to bed."

Different tactics are best at different ages. Some particularly good ones for stopping tantrums in the three- to six-year-old range include:

When Tantrums Start Ask the Child a Question,
Then Follow It Up with Several More Questions

Stick with this rapid interrogation. It may take several exchanges before attention is completely shifted, but by leading children into a forced dialogue you will eventually take them out of their feelings and put them into their minds. The momentum of the anger is then broken in a natural way. Sometimes the child doesn't even notice that it's happening. Here's a typical conversation where this technique is employed:

> PARENT [When her five-year-old is about to pick a fight]: Wait a minute, is that a bird singing outside?
> CHILD: I don't know.
> PARENT: No, no, come here. Listen. Hear it? That means something very important. Know what it is?
> CHILD [Listening]: What!
> PARENT: There, that high sound over there by the apartment window? Hear it? Yippee! It means spring's here. What should we do to celebrate?
> CHILD [Shrugs]
> PARENT: Come on, give me some ideas. What do you think about. . . .

Ask a Question, Then Use the Child's
Answer as a Follow-up for Direct Action:

> CHILD: I don't care, just leave me alone!
> MOTHER: Hey, did we forget to take the groceries out of the car?
> CHILD [Shrugs]
> MOTHER: Help me remember. Did we?
> CHILD: I don't know.
> MOTHER: Think back. Did we take them in when we came back from picking you up from school?
> CHILD: I can't remember.
> MOTHER: I can't either. Let's go have a look together.
> CHILD: Okay.

Ask a Question to Make Children Aware of Their Incorrect Behavior

Dr. Thomas Lickona, in his excellent book *Raising Good Children,* advises parents not to argue with a wayward child. Instead, he suggests they use the "Ask-Don't-Tell" approach in which children are forced to answer leading questions about their wrong behavior and hence identify the problem in their own words.

For example, instead of telling children all the terrible things that will happen to them if they continue to peel off pieces of wallpaper from the dining room, you ask:

> *What's going to happen if you keep fiddling with that wallpaper like I asked you not to?*

The child's logic will be forced to fill in the missing blanks. Or when the child is acting up, a parent asks:

> *What do you think I feel about the way you're behaving?*

Or:

> PARENT: What are you doing?
> CHILD: Interrupting.
> PARENT: Right. What would I like you to do about it?
> CHILD: Stop.

Lickona also suggests that parents ask questions which refresh a child's memory concerning established family rules:

> PARENT: It's past eight and you haven't brushed your teeth. What's the bedtime rule?
> CHILD: First brush teeth, *then* a story.
> PARENT: Exactly.

Here the question-answer dialogue itself is enough and gets the job done without recourse to threats.

What should parents do if the questioning method does not elicit an immediate response? Lickona suggests that parents repeat it again and, if the child fails to answer this time, make it clear that he or she is *obliged* to give an appropriate reply. For instance:

> PARENT: Did you finish the homework assignment?
> CHILD: But you promised I could go over to Larry's tonight.
> PARENT: You're right, I did, but you haven't answered my question.
> CHILD: It's not fair!
> PARENT: We'll talk about that in a minute. Part of what we talk about will have to do with the answer to my question—which is. . . .

Change the Subject Abruptly

Among three-, four-, and even five-year-olds the wildest non sequiturs will sometimes be surprisingly effective. Observe:

CHILD: No, I won't!
FATHER: Oh, ho! The lion's belly is green again! See.
CHILD [Looks peevish and does not reply]
FATHER: I bet you can't look like a lion with a green belly.
CHILD [No reply but distracted]
PARENT: Green bellies, yellow bellies, smelly bellies.
CHILD [Smiles a little]
FATHER [Demonstrating]: There, try it. See how green my belly is?
CHILD [Laughing]: Your belly's not green.

With older children—from, say, six to nine—diversions can be more direct. Send upset children into another room. Sometimes just a change of scene will do the trick. Physical diversion is also effective. Pick up a ball in the middle of a tantrum and toss it to the child. Offer to tell a story or to go outside and play. Introduce a new toy. Sing an inspirational song. Engage the child in a conversation about something he or she is interested in. Sometimes just a hug and a loving caress will do.

Keep the Balance Between Mercy and Justice Intact by Offering Alternatives to Children

In the Middle East many legends are told about a wise fool named Mullah Nasr Eddin whose zany logic and unpredictable behavior somehow seem to expose the inner truth of any situation. One such story tells how a man came to the Mullah one day when the Mullah was occupying the position as town judge. "My neighbor has broken into my house," the man moaned as he pleaded his case, "and has taken all my possessions, my dishes, my furniture, my pots and pans. He must be punished."

"You're absolutely right," said Mullah Nasr Eddin.

The accused was quickly sent for and brought before the Mullah. "It wasn't that way at all," the man protested. "It was he who broke into *my* house. He must be brought to justice, Mullah.''

"You're absolutely right," said Mullah Nasr Eddin.

A bystander who had listened to each man's side of the argument was amazed at what he heard. "Your Honor," he said to the mullah. "The first man tells his story and you assure him he is right. Then his neighbor comes, presents a contradictory tale, and you tell him *he* is right, too. Certainly both men cannot be right."

"You're absolutely right," said Mullah Nasr Eddin.

Few issues in life are cut and dried. And thus too many absolute no's delivered without option can be as disruptive as too many yeses. Instead of doling them out without recourse, offer your little one acceptable substitutes. This will help maintain the balance between permissiveness and strictness and will hint at the divine Golden Mean that runs inevitably and silently between them.

Jeanette and her sister are not allowed to eat candy, but any time they wish they can help themselves to bowls of raisins and nuts or to an ice pop made from frozen fruit juice. When Jeffy brought home a comic book his parents did not want in the house they took it away—but they offered to buy him an activity book in its place. When seven-year-old Albert asked his parents if he could help paint the kitchen, his parents did not dismiss him with the announcement that painting is "grownup work." They laid down some newspaper, found an old brush, and let Albert learn the secrets of the painter's art on an old cardboard box.

Sandra, aged eleven, had her heart set on using the extra ticket a friend offered her for a rock concert. The concert featured a singer whose performance was exceedingly raunchy and who, everyone knew, enjoyed taking part in his own mock crucifixion at the end of the act.

Sandra did not consult her parents about attending this show, knowing in her heart that they would think her too young for such entertainment. When the time drew near for the event she simply raised the matter as if it was a fait accompli: Would her parents please drive her to the stadium?

Miffed that Sandra had accepted the invitation without asking and upset by the prospect of their youngest daughter attending an affair that seemed to them to be something between a sacrilege and a saturnalia, Mom and Dad's initial impulse was to hit the roof.

Instead, after a short consultation and a few deep breaths, they sat Sandra down and carefully explained to her their reasons for saying no. They made it quite clear that their religious principles were in direct opposition to the singer's behavior and that they felt it would be harmful to her spiritual happiness if she was exposed to such an experience.

Then they offered her alternatives: a trip to the circus with a friend of her choice or an outing on a sailboat owned by Sandra's godfather.

Sandra was disappointed but not crushed. She had had something important taken away from her. But something of approximate value had been offered in its place. Later on her parents used this event as an excuse to initiate conversations on the subject of religious beliefs and the spiritual dangers that sometimes lurk in glamorous things.

Don't Say No Simply for No's Sake

Dr. Jack Canfield reports that in a study charting the number of negative and positive commands given to three-year-old children by their parents in a single day, the tally showed 432 negatives against 32 positives.[1] This statistic shows how easily saying no can become a habit. It's like the mother who orders one of her children to "Go see what your brother is doing and tell him to stop it!"

Parents fall into the no trap primarily because they *think* it's easier this way. They think: Say no and the child will stay out of trouble. Say no and I won't have to get up and down a hundred times. Say no and life will be less of a hassle. In fact, too many needless no's spin a kind of negative web around family relationships, ultimately giving children the impression that the entire world is one colossal denial, one enormous red light. After too much of this kind of thing children start saying no back to their parents. The habit is catching. In this way positiveness, as well as the impulse toward spiritual exploration, becomes frustrated, then stifled, then deadened.

There are, of course, plenty of times when parents *should* say no. But be careful: It can become a reflex action.

At the supermarket Paul wants to feel the bottom of the cereal box. "No!" shouts Mother. "You'll knock it over."

Rachael says she needs a bandage to cover a tiny nick: "Put it back!" Father shouts. "That's a waste of good gauze."

Conrad wants to draw faces on the grapefruit with a magic marker. "You'll get your hands dirty!" is the response to his creative urge.

Rosey asks if she can climb a few rungs on Dad's ladder to see what it feels like to be "up high." "No!," commands Father, "you'll fall."

Billy wants to experiment by drinking his milk a spoonful at a time. "You'll spill it that way!" uncle assures him.

Nick asks if he can take a broken radio apart. "You'll make too much of a mess," he's told.

And on it goes, potential learning experiences turned into rebuffs: the innate desire to penetrate to the nature of things thwarted by the "no" habit. Whenever possible, when all things are equal and it doesn't cause any harm, choose the affirmative path. Say yes.

Always Accentuate the Positive

"The *main* principle of teaching children desirable behavior," writes the prominent child psychologist Fitzhugh Dodson, "is a very simple one, and I have never understood why parents and school teachers aren't given this information as part of their preparation for working with young people. The idea is that whenever you see a child behave in a way that is good—behavior that is not unfriendly or otherwise disagreeable—you reward that child for good behavior. You praise his actions or give him a smile, a hug, or a friendly pat on the shoulder. You do something to indicate that you think he is a splendid little person."[2]

A simple principle, this, yet so often neglected. Praise each positive thing children do and they will want to keep doing it. Praise feels good.

Help Children Return to Their
Spiritual Center After an Upset

One of the basic principles of the martial art of aikido is this: Whenever a person becomes hostile and attacks you, that person is stepping out of his or her spiritual center and by so doing is, in their own way, disrupting the universal harmony. It thus behooves you, the aikido practitioner, to bring this person back to his or her rightful center and hence return the world to its natural state of balance. You accomplish this by allowing the person's aggressive forward motion to ultimately return him or her to their state of rest—in this case, flat on their back.

While in aikido the return to the harmonious center is acted out literally, with children it is done through emotions and touch. Next time a child becomes upset and disobedient, instead of hurling back the same angry energy take a deep breath, then become quiet inside and contact your spiritual center. This center may be in your heart or chest. For some people it is in the solar plexus, for others in the abdomen. Find your own. You will know it from a certain feeling of balance, or warmth and security.

Once you are centered, reach out and return the child to his or her center. Try the following techniques on children two to six:

• Say nothing to children as their temper rises. Instead, simply stroke their heads and rub their arms and legs. The physical contact is what's important. If you are quiet inside, this quiet can be transferred through your touch. For children about to break into a tantrum it can be diverting and highly satisfying to suddenly find themselves caressed and hugged. Few can forgo the pleasure; something in them will prefer a quiet snuggle to an angry binge.

• For children from two to four it may possible literally to put your body into sync with theirs. Try breathing in unison with them. If upset, their breathing will be quick and hard. Breathe the same way, then slowly bring your breath rate down. Amazingly, theirs will often follow. Try clapping rhythmically. This is especially effective if the child is crying. Clap quickly at first, then slow it down. Invite the child to clap along with you. When calmness comes, rub and caress the child lovingly.

• Talk quietly to children over five when they are emotionally unruly. Speak in a low, relaxed voice. Admit that they are upset, then tell them it doesn't have to be this way. Tell them that peace and happiness are inside them right now, waiting to come out. Tell them that if they choose they can drop this painful feeling of anger and return to their center, where it's really nice. You will have to write your own material here, depending on the temperament of the child. The important thing is to speak lovingly and sincerely, and to explain that peaceful options exist right now, at this very moment. All the child has to do is say yes.

• Try quieting an angry child by singing. This will be an unexpected and disarming ploy in the middle of a hostile outburst, and it tends to work even with older children. For some youngsters, popular songs will capture attention. For others use chants or spirituals or folk songs. Whatever works. Try to get the child to join you and sing along. It may take a bit of doing, but success creates a wonderful sense of harmony between parent and child. Again, children who are captured by this technique have opted to say no to the negative within them and to return to the yes. This will make them happy and will confirm that the good feels good, the bad feels bad.

• When children from six to ten are upset, sit near them and remain silent. Hold the thought of peace, of the child's calm center, of his or her innately good nature. Some parents visualize a ball of pure white light hovering above children, covering them with warm, cherishing energy. Others imagine the child playing happily in a grove of flowers on a glorious summer day. Still others imagine a beam of radiant energy emanating from their heart and entering into the child's. They imagine that this beam has a calming, spiritualizing effect. The specific picture you choose is not as important as the quality of emotion you bring. You are trying to catch children in your net of love, to bring them back to their own state of inner tranquility. Children are extremely sensitive to feelings. If they are not too wildly upset they will sense what is happening and respond accordingly. Your peace will give them peace.

Don't Create Conditions that Make a Child Misbehave

Here indeed is where parent's spiritual aspirations earn their stripes. For if the truth be known, peevish behavior can be as much the parent's fault as the child's.

One antidote is the great universal psychic solvent, *self-knowledge*: the attempt on the parents' part to see themselves, hear themselves, watch themselves as they interact on a day-to-day basis with their children. Attempts can be made:

To hear the possible double-bind messages in one's scoldings.

To witness the inconsistencies of one's demands.

To hear the hateful sound in one's voice when a criticism is being made.

To be aware of how frequently one fails to do what one has promised.

To see one's intimidating gestures and expressions as the child sees them.

To listen to the note of boredom or insincerity in one's praise.

To see how frequently and automatically one responds to a child's behavior with a negative command.

To locate one's own selfish motivations or lurking neuroses behind rules and dictums.

A dozen times a day parents can catch themselves doling out ambiguous or even destructive discipline. A major part of our job as spiritual overseers is to become aware of these inconsistencies and to modify them as best we can.

Here are a few examples of behavior patterns an alert parent can catch and correct:

> • *Nagging.* No one likes it, least of all the free-spirited child. Ask once, ask again, ask three times, then take appropriate disciplinary measures. But *don't* keep pestering indefinitely. Nagging for its own sake is as crazy-making for a child as it is ineffective for a parent.
>
> • *Being overcritical.* "For the true guru," says an Indian proverb, "a whisper of advice is enough." While a whisper is rarely enough for anyone under six years of age, the fact remains that bludgeoning young ones with constant criticism is the stuff rage is formed of in the adult years. So be light-handed, sparing, and kind when criticizing. "Advice is like snow," Coleridge remarked. "The softer it falls, the longer it dwells upon, and the deeper it sinks into the mind." Good advice.
>
> • *Being psychologically absent.* You've probably seen more than one parent who talks to his or her children in a kind of apathetic, singsong voice and who looks at them as if looking at a stone or a wall. This parent's body is present and accounted for, but his or her attention is clearly elsewhere, and children know it. In response they may try to irritate the parents simply to get some kind of real attention. Fitzhugh Dodson terms this the Law of the Soggy Potato Chip. A child naturally prefers a fresh potato chip to a soggy one, explains Dodson. But if the only potato chip the child can get is soggy, he will take it. A soggy chip is better than no chip at all. Same with children—a negative response from parents is better than none at all."[3]
>
> • *Having too many rules.* Keep them reasonable, simple, few—and make sure you enforce them. Too many do's and don'ts eventually start to act as a noose, strangling the executioner as well as the executed. Better to have a few choice domestic bylaws and to stand by these, come what may.

• *Being too harsh.* This approach inevitably breeds harshness back from the child—if not now, then later. It's the law of the mirror. Whenever you catch yourself in an unnecessarily sharp posture modulate down, then gentle out.

• *Yelling.* My own daughter had a first-grade teacher who spent a good portion of the school day yelling at her class. Every afternoon my daughter climbed off the bus laden with stories about how this teacher, a young woman in her first year of teaching, had bellowed for twenty minutes straight or had bawled out a poor six-year-old until he broke down in tears. These stories were later verified by other parents who happened to walk by the classroom when a tirade was taking place. In November the teacher–parent conferences were scheduled, and during this meeting I diplomatically raised the issue. "But, Mr. Carroll," the teacher answered in a voice that was clearly sincere. "I *never* yell at my children. I think it's harmful for them psychologically to be yelled at." Unconsciousness hurts everybody.

Steer the Child Away from the Cause of Upset

Dr. Charles Schaefer has obviously thought a great deal about children. After working for some years at the Children's Village School in Dobbs Ferry, New York, and pondering the discipline matter, he has come up with several unique and occasionally droll methods for heading off naughty behavior at the pass.[4] Some of his suggestions are almost Zen-like in their purity and surprise. Try a few:

• When you are having trouble getting a child to do something use a picture rather than words. For instance, instead of telling children to feed the dog for the ten-thousandth time show them a picture of a starving dog.

• If you are having difficulty getting children's attention make them a captive audience: get hold of a cow bell or a loud piece of apparatus and ring it each time you want peace and quiet. Children can never claim that they didn't hear it.

• During a temper storm do just the opposite of what the child anticipates. For instance, during a tantrum say, "Hey, that looks like fun," then throw a tantrum yourself. Humor will often save the day.

• When children seem reluctant to do what is expected of them, challenge them rather than scold them: "I bet you can't . . ." or "Do you think you could . . . ?" or "I'll bet you would never be able to. . . ."

• Save your most prominent requests and demands for the dinner table. Evidence shows that people are most open to appeals while eating.

• Use a technique that salespersons call "selling up." Get a child to agree to a small demand (just as a salesperson gets you to agree to "give me just one minute of your time"). Then increase these demands in small increments. This way the child does not feel overwhelmed. Suppose, for instance, you want children to do more work in the yard. Start by having them mow a quarter of your lawn this week. In three weeks increase the amount to half. A month later have them do the whole thing.

Establish Behavioral Role Models Through Stories

"There is no duty to which a Pueblo child is trained in which he has to be content with a bare command: do this," wrote Marie Shedlock. "For each, he learns a fairy-tale designed to explain how children first came to know why it was right to 'do this,' and detailing the sad results that befell those who did otherwise. Some tribes have regular story-tellers, men who have devoted a great deal of time to learning the myths and stories of their people and who possess, in addition to a good memory, a vivid imagination. The mother sends for

one of these, and having prepared a feast for him and her little
brood, who are curled up near her, await the fairy stories of
the dreamer, who after his feast and smoke entertains the
company for hours."[5]

Many folk stories like those of the Pueblo people give children strong moral messages as well as heroic role models.
Most of these tales clearly imply that our behavior determines
our fates, and they can thus be used at appropriate moments
as a subtle form of disciplinary guidance. For instance:

> When children are prone to telling tall tales, read them
> "The Boy Who Cried Wolf."
>
> When youngsters are mean to children weaker than
> themselves, "Cinderella" shows how things look from
> the victim's side, and also that bullies get their comeup-
> pance in the end.
>
> For children who are nasty to their siblings, "Hansel
> and Gretel" shows how a brother and sister's mutual
> devotion can save the day against any kind of evil.
>
> For children who make fun of those who are homely or
> handicapped, "Beauty and the Beast" shows that beauty
> lies in the heart, not in appearances.
>
> For children who are especially gullible "Foxy Loxie
> and Henny Penny" provide object lessons in not believ-
> ing everything one is told.

Ignore Naughty Behavior Whenever Possible

You will have to be selective on this one, and obviously
there are limits. But in a number of cases simply not responding to undesirable behavior will stop it on its own. You have
only to twiddle your thumbs and pretend that nothing disturbing is happening, nothing at all. "Do not confront evil like
a ram head to head," said the eighteenth-century Christian
mystic William Law. "For then, through anger and insult, you
will become evil yourself. Rather, remain silent and find whatever good is in the moment. By turning to God's light instead

of indulging the darkness you will make the darkness lessen and the light increase."

One day Robby came back from first grade with a new phrase: "poo-poo brains." Suddenly everyone at home became a poo-poo brains including Mom, Pop, and the canary. While their impulse was to correct Robby immediately and to explain what poo poo really meant, and so on, they kept their peace. Without the raised eyebrows and protestations (read: attention) this new word was calculated to arouse, Robbie's reason for using it vanished and it soon faded from his six-year-old vocabulary.

Parents can use this silent treatment to quell a number of potentially explosive incidents, especially with trendy types of misbehavior that are picked up at school (such as name-calling, tongue-sticking-out, face-making) and usually dissipate on their own if ignored.

Use Incentives Rather than Punishments

Children can be kept on the straight and narrow if motivated by reward rather than threatened by punishment. This is another of those Oriental techniques that prevent trouble before it begins. The child's desire for a promised goodie encourages compliance with parental standards; and if the child does act out, the reminder of the reward (though not, as some believe, the threat of taking it away) is an excellent corrective.

Marcia's parents, who had raised their daughter by the book with few compromises, called this method bribery and declared they would never stoop so low. Layla's parents replied that bribery is something quite different, that bribery is "a thing or service given to induce a person to act dishonestly," as the dictionary puts it. Incentives, they explained, reward *honesty,* not dishonesty. They reinforce commendable activities and set worthy goals. Layla's mother also pointed out that, as psychological studies have shown many times over, everyone from children to white mice learn more quickly when rewarded for efforts than when punished for failure.

Layla's parents were speaking from experience. Layla, five, argued vehemently whenever asked to pick up her toys. Scoldings and threats made no impression, and punishment brought an air of gloom to the house. One day, while visiting a large museum gift shop with her parents, Layla spied a reproduction of a blue porcelain hippopotamus on display behind the counter. Falling instantly in love with the whimsical animal, she begged her parents to buy it.

The figure was expensive and Mom and Dad said no. But later that evening, after talking the matter over, they decided there was something in all this that might help them deal with the discipline situation. So they announced to Layla that they had been considering her request.

Mother than produced a drawing of a hippo. It was tinted in blue watercolor and inside it a number of small circles were drawn. Each circle, her mother explained, was for a gold star. Every time Layla cleaned her room, picked up after play, helped to bring dishes in from the table, or performed any commendatory act a star would get pasted in one of the circles. When all the stars were filled, they would all go back to the museum and purchase the statue. Within a month Layla was doubly rewarded: she had a blue hippo and a constantly . . . well, a frequently clean room.

Repeat, Don't Scold

Scolding and punishment have their place in child rearing. They definitely do, and we will discuss this matter soon enough. It's just that these methods should come later, after other, more gentle, alternatives such as repetition have first been tried. Here are some variations on the theme:

Leave Notes

The note reinforces the message and burns it into the child's awareness. It also prevents kids from bellowing that universal excuse: "But you never told me!"

Use bright, contrasting colors on your signs and write in large, bold letters. Drawings or stickers make messages more visible. All notes should be brief and to the point. A few examples:

- In the bathroom: BRUSH TEETH BEFORE BED.
- In the bedroom: ROOM CLEANING EVERY TUESDAY.
- In the kitchen: CLOSE THE REFRIGERATOR DOOR.
- In the hall: CHILDREN: WIPE FEET BEFORE ENTERING.
- In the bathroom: PUT TOWELS BACK ON RACK AFTER SHOWER.
- In the basement: TURN OFF LIGHTS WHEN YOU LEAVE.

No matter whether you tack notes on the front door or over your head, eventually everyone stops seeing them—it's inevitable. The remedy is to move signs around from time to time or, better yet, to write new ones when the old ones become a habit.

Have the Child Repeat Instructions Back to You

Whenever you issue directions have your child repeat them back immediately. In this way the message is reinforced through the sound of the child's own words and voice. Observe:

MOTHER: Tommy, when I come back from the store I want all these toys picked up.
TOMMY [NO ANSWER]
MOTHER: Tom. All picked up. Hear me?
TOMMY [NODS HIS HEAD DISTRACTEDLY AND CONTINUES TO BUILD WITH HIS BLOCKS]
MOTHER: Tommy, what's going to happen by the time I get back? Do you remember?
TOMMY: The toys.
MOTHER: What about the toys?"
TOMMY: I have to pick them up.
MOTHER: That's right, pick them up by the time I get back.

Repeat Directions Immediately Whenever the Child Fails to Carry Them Out

A variation on the above. Do not let undue amounts of time elapse between the young person's neglect of given directions and your rejoinder. If you do the child, especially a child below the age of seven, may lose sight of the causal connection between the mistake and the correction. Later on it will simply seem to them that they are being unfairly picked on. Correct and repeat the instructions *immediately* after the mistake has been made. Later is too late.

Let the Child Hear the Instructions From More Than One Significant Person

Father, mother, and older siblings can participate. Each reinforces what the other has said. If the message is important enough, the help of a teacher, a family minister, or an important authority figure can also be enlisted. Rolly is seven years old and lives with his mother, grandfather, and older sister:

> GRANDFATHER [IN THE MORNING AT THE DINING TABLE]: Don't forget, Roll, bring in the paper when you're out waiting for the bus.
>
> MOTHER [THAT AFTERNOON]: Rolly, Father wants you to toss the paper on the doorstep while you're waiting for the bus. Try to remember, okay?
>
> OLDER SISTER [THAT NIGHT AT THE DINNER TABLE TO THE WHOLE FAMILY]: Hey, Rolly's going to become our paper boy from now on, did you hear?
>
> GRANDFATHER [NEXT MORNING, OUT THE WINDOW TO ROLLY AS HE'S STANDING WAITING FOR HIS BUS]: Don't forget, kiddo—the paper. Thanks.

And so on. Continual reinforcement from several significant persons tends to help children remember rules better than hearing them from a single source.

Use Word Tricks to Dramatize Do's and Don't's

Rhyming rules will be remembered better than prose commands. Most children memorize them with amazing speed:

> *To bed at seven is next to heaven.*
> *Be a good daughter, turn off the water.*
> *A tisket, a tasket, all wrappers in the basket.*
> *When it rains and sloshes, wear your galoshes.*
> *When gum on hair and clothes gets stuck—yech!*

You can make up your own. Don't worry about creating deathless prose. The sillier these rhymes, the more effective they will be.

Another useful word trick is to let children fill in the last word of your instructions for themselves. This strengthens the message by involving the child's mental participation:

> MOTHER: Finish your dinner and *then* you get—what?
> CHILD: The Fruit Roll Ups.
> MOTHER: Right. But you have to finish dinner first.

> GRANDFATHER: Okay, wash face, comb hair, and brush—what?
> CHILD: My teeth!
> GRANDFATHER: Why?
> CHILD: So they'll get clean!

You can also give commands disguised in the form of riddles:

> FATHER: Here's a good one for you. Clean hands and the green stuff you brush on your teeth at night don't go well together. What's the stuff?
> CHILD: Toothpaste?
> FATHER: Right!

Hang Charts and Lists Up On the Wall As Reminders

Draw them in bright colors and shapes and place them in highly visible places. Let the child help you make them. They will catch the eye, act as reminders, serve functional purposes such as announcing household job assignments, bedtime hours, or the number of points gained toward an incentive reward.

Beware of Giving Messages That Appear Benevolent but Actually Reflect a Parent's Own Neurotic Agendas

Gerald Walker Smith, in his insightful book *Hidden Meanings,* has made a collection of the typical double-bind messages we all give to one another every day and which we use to disguise (from ourselves as much as from others) our true feelings and intentions. A chapter of his book is dedicated to classic parental phrases that *seem* to say one thing but actually mean quite another.

When faced with such a phrase many children instinctively sense they are not being dealt with fairly, that somewhere a hidden axe is being silently ground. But because they do not have the psychological sophistication to probe beneath the surface of adult words and body language, they can't say how or why. And if, perchance, children do object when their parents bellow out such manipulative classics as "If you really loved me you'd . . ." or "I'm telling you for your own benefit," the hurt parent angrily answers back with something like "Is that how you show gratitude when I try to help!" A true no-win situation. And too bad, too, because when children stop trusting their parents psychologically they stop trusting them spiritually as well. Witness:

Parental statement: *"Ask your mother / Ask your father."*
Possible hidden meanings:

1. I'm afraid to say no. So I'll take the easy way out and delegate this distasteful task to my spouse.

2. I get secret satisfaction from putting my spouse on the spot, forcing him or her to be the bad guy.

Parental statement: *"Act like an adult."* Possible hidden meanings:

1. I can reject you by making this impossible demand (the child, after all, cannot act like an adult until he or she grows up to *be* an adult).

2. Be more like me.

3. Don't show your real emotions with tears or displays of feeling: real feelings make me uncomfortable.

Parental statement: *"Do whatever you like."* Possible hidden meanings:

1. Frankly, I don't much care *what* you do.

2. I'm acting as if I'm a tolerant, generous parent. Actually, I don't want to spend the time getting involved with your decisions and needs.

Parental statement: *"We'll see."* Possible hidden meanings:

1. No.

2. I don't want to be bothered dealing with this question right now.

3. I can't decide right now, but I don't want to appear indecisive.

4. It depends on whether I have other plans or not.

A few other typical parent-child hidden meanings include:

• "Let's not talk about this right now." (Real meaning: I don't want to deal with this issue.)

• "When I was a kid we never . . . (Real message: I'm better than you. I was then, I am now.)

• "Go ahead, if you really want to . . . (Real message: I don't approve of what you're doing. So I'll hedge my bets by letting you do what you want and at the same time make you feel guilty about it.)
• "You're acting like this, after all your father/ mother has given you [done for you]!" (Real message: Feel guilty, kid, 'cause your parents are always keeping records.)

We often recognize or at least *sense* these ploys when we hear others use them. Unfortunately, it's not easy to catch them on our own tongues. But it can be done.

For instance, instead of saying "Let's not talk about this," be honest. Say "I don't want to talk about this issue right now; it's upsetting for me." Instead of "It's up to you," say it as it is: "I'm just not able to come to a decision about it right now—you decide." Instead of "You're too young to understand," try "This is a complicated matter and frankly, it's too hard for me to figure out how to explain it to you."

Read Between the Lines

The last and perhaps most important skill to cultivate when practicing Taoist discipline is to find out what's really behind the child's petulance, then to address the issue directly: this, instead of punishing behavior that may be a symptom of a deeper disturbance.

Ask yourself: What is the child really trying to express by this wayward behavior? What important facts might I not be reading between the lines? What is the goal, the sought-after payoff behind this behavior? How can I fulfill the child's demand in a natural way, so that he or she no longer feels the need to misbehave in order to get it? What things might I myself be doing to instigate or exacerbate misbehavior? How can I make the appropriate changes?

For example, nine-year-old Jep insisted on bouncing a hard rubber ball violently against a door in the hallway upstairs. No matter how often he was told to stop, he was at it again a few hours later, and soon the door became a polka-dotted collage of unsightly ball marks.

Jep's parents considered the matter for some time, then decided, quite rightly, that there was something peculiar about the compulsivity with which Jep, ordinarily a fairly well-behaved boy, pursued his disobedience.

Finally it dawned on them. The surface Jep was targeting was more than just a handy rebound board. It was the door to his younger brother's bedroom, which meant there was a good chance the door was also a substitute for brother himself. Had Jep's parents been neglecting Jep lately? Had too much attention been going to his younger brother? Probably. At any rate, this is how Jep's parents read the situation, and they immediately set out to make amends.

The ball throwing, in other words, was the symptom, not the disease, and many childhood discipline problems are like this. They do not stem from a child's nasty nature but from a cry of the heart that is not being answered or that parents are unaware of.

Thus, before bringing out the hairbrush and the dunce cap, look carefully at disciplinary problems for hidden and not-so-hidden emotional causes.

1. Is there a particular pattern to the child's misbehavior? Does it occur at certain times of day or in certain places? At the dining table? Before bedtime? In the presence of guests? With a sibling? On the schoolbus? With one parent in particular? The how, where, and why of disobedience always offers important clues.

2. Remember these childhood biggies:

- The need for love
- The fear of abandonment

These two impulses are among the most essential driving forces in a young child's psyche, and a majority of childhood problems can be traced back to some variation on these themes. Approach all investigations of a child's troublesome behavior with the assumption that one or both factors are involved.

3. Is the child's naughty behavior symbolic? If the child refuses to go to bed at night can this be a sign of sleep insecurities? If the child likes to kill frogs and throw stones at dogs, who is he really throwing stones at?

4. Don't assume that children will verbalize their fears and needs. They won't—not usually, anyway. And don't make the mistake of thinking that direct questioning on your part will bring the bones of contention to light. Sometimes it will, sometimes it won't. The problem is that if young persons don't know what's really troubling them (as is often the case), they won't be able to communicate the problems to you. This is true even when they are confronted with such questions as "Are you scared?," "Are you jealous?," "Are you mad?" The child simply doesn't know. Self-awareness is not a young person's strongest trump card.

5. Don't count on children to provide you explicit psychological or emotional information. *Do* count on them to display their problems through behavior. Like hieroglyphs, you must read these patterns of behavior and make sense of them.

6. Is the child testing your limits? Many do. Especially if parents have not set limits to begin with. Don Fleming's helpful book *How to Stop the Battle with Your Child* suggests that parents devise "step plans" for dealing with each behavioral area. To set limits for public behavior, for example—the supermarket, say, or on the subway—he advises that parents (1) Tell the child ahead of time the rules for behaving in this particular place under these particular circumstances; (2) Mention what the punishment (or reward) will be; (3) If the child insists on acting out, plan on removing him or her from the scene; (4) Prepare the child in the same way for the next trip to a public place, providing positive support that you know he or she will do better next time.

Similar step plans, Fleming tells us, can be devised for car trips, getting along with others, hitting, stealing, lying, and so forth. Using this stepwise device, he believes, will help parents get clear on their disciplinary modus operandi *ahead of time* and, simultaneously, let children know exactly what their limits are—and will be—in any given situation.

Why Children Misbehave

Dr. Rudolf Driekurs, a well-known psychologist and author, has identified four fundamental varieties of misbehavior which, he believes, are based on a child's frantic need to be recognized, respected, and cared for:

1. *Attention.* If you can't get positive attention, or half attention, or any attention at all, force your parents to acknowledge you by getting in their way. You do this by hitting the dog, or your sister. Or allowing the sink to overflow, blocking the TV when people are watching. There is, in fact, no end of attention-getting ploys which an imaginative child can cook up to annoy parents, to say to them: "Look at me, look at me—I exist!" It's the Law of the Soggy Potato Chip again.

2. *Power.* If children are overly controlled or browbeaten, or even if they are just passing through a rebellious stage, they may set up continual challenges to parental authority. "No, I won't!" or "I don't have to!" or "Later, Mom, not now!" are typical of children who feel helpless and/or who are testing the limits of their power.

3. *Revenge.* Since certain children are convinced that they are unloved, they find their niche in the family by becoming the "bad" one. In this role they intentionally flunk exams, tell outrageous lies, wet their pants while sitting on Mom's favorite living-room couch—and so on down the list. Children who are frequently punished for small offenses often take this option. It is one of the few ways picked-on children feel they can maintain control.

4. *Display of inadequacy.* "I'm too dumb to do this home-

work," says the child, and then flunks. "I'm too stupid for anyone to like me," says the child, then proceeds to alienate every child in the class. Claims of inadequacy can be pleas on the part of a child for recognition and for parental praise or guidance. They should be listened to.

Similar lists compiled by other experts almost all agree that naughty conduct is motivated not so much by meanness of spirit as by neglect or errors of judgment on the part of the parents.

Not to entirely blame parents. Every story has two sides, and certain unsavory childhood traits seem to come as part of the genetic package. Yet the fact remains that confronting a child's misbehavior by means of violent counterattacks can be futile and destructive. Better to determine a child's underlying needs, meet them squarely, and question one's own actions and motivations in the process.

For example, as far as Driekurs' motivation list goes, let us say a wayward child needs more attention or a greater sense of personal power and adequacy. Fine. Give that child attention and power. But do so not by becoming overpermissive; do it by becoming more psychically attuned to the child.

What does this mean? Note that it is possible for parents to be with a child twenty-four hours a day and for the child still to feel neglected. Why? Because the mother or father's attention is everywhere but on their young one. Parents are thinking about paying bills, or giving a party, or a thousand and one other adult concerns. Rarely do they take time to focus on the here and now. Clearly, they are not present to the child. Youngsters sense this absence and react to it with naughty plots to be noticed. It is as if they are being fed food that looks delicious but is made of cardboard. Slowly, inexorably, they are starving from emotional malnutrition.

Mothers and fathers who have had experience in prayer and meditation will understand the idea of emptying their minds of thoughts and of being present to the moment. They will put this technique to work in child raising in the following ways:

• During the day parents can make several attempts to stop everything they are doing and focus *fully* on the child. They must stop worrying, making plans, or thinking ahead. They must concentrate fully on the child's existence—as entirely as they would concentrate on a prayer. Nothing exists now except the two of you together. Nothing. Parent and child are alone with themselves, and with their Creator.

The very nature of this attempt will bring a stillness and specialness to the moment. Children will sense it, and will respond accordingly.

• Give your children periods of *quality time.* For a certain number of minutes each day let the child become your total center of attention. Make yourself emotionally available to each and every one of their needs. One hour of quality time spent this way is better than a week passed together in a state of distraction.

• Parents should try to *hear* what children are saying when they speak. Don't dismiss their words as mere babytalk. Their words may be mere babytalk, but they are *your child's* babytalk. He or she is trying to communicate something, and it is a parent's part to listen. Children will then feel heard, appreciated, recognized. They will modify their behavior accordingly.

A friend of mine, an engineer and father of six, recently told me that his own father had the unkind habit of not looking him in the eye when he spoke and of sometimes responding to his questions with silence. He told me how his father would gaze into the distance blankly when my friend was speaking, how he would abruptly walk away while my friend was in the middle of a sentence. "To this day," my friend informed me with admirable self-knowledge, "I still stammer and get disoriented when someone I'm talking to starts to lose interest. So I try to be absolutely there for my own kids when they talk to me. I realize how important the attention exchange is in helping them develop communication skills and in teaching them fearlessness toward others."

"Concentrate on his feelings and message," advises Dr.

Don Dinkmeyer in an article on teaching responsibility to children. "Communicate with your very being that you are present and attending. Make contact with your eyes, following him closely without interrupting. Listen to *all* that is said, being alert to the feelings he is expressing. Communicate both verbally and nonverbally that you are emphatically hearing the feelings behind the words . . . trust comes when adults are real persons, not role players."[6] Again, it is almost like a meditation; put yourself in a state of passive alertness and allow the child's manifestations to fall on your receptivity.

Take your time and try to see below the surface of things. Develop x-ray eyes and x-ray ears. Make use of all clues and cues: these can be revealed in games and play, in facial expressions and body language, in chance remarks, in emotional outbursts of joy and sorrow, in the things children like or hate. Keep at it. Bring tolerance and intuition and gentle means to misbehavior before turning to rebukes and spankings. Help children become aware of wrong behavior on their own; then take the appropriate steps to help them help themselves to fix it. Remember: If you don't want a pot to boil over, it's better to reduce the flame than to keep pushing the lid down ever more tightly.

9.

The Tao
of Punishment

In the course of child raising it sometimes becomes clear that gentle persuasion is not enough, and that punishment and deprivation are required if the tide of disobedience is to be turned. No doubt about it: When tolerant methods fail, the heavy guns must be brought in. In the last chapter the stress was on mercy. Now follows justice.

But—before letting punitive means become the sole basis on which discipline is dished out, bear in mind that there is a Tao of punishment as well as a Tao of prevention. This subtle and efficient method calls for temperate handling of a child and for corrections that teach rather than hurt. Followed with care, it can reduce negative energy expenditure on the parents' part and produce a happier, less traumatized child. Everyone profits. This is the essence of spiritual parenting.

The methods that follow are, therefore, founded on the notion that punishments should be lessons, not lashings, and that so far as disciplinary penalties go, a little bit of punishment, well-timed and appropriately placed, goes a long way.

The Tao of Punishment141

("If," a Taoist proverb asks, "you can move a block with one hand, why use two?")

Above all, discipline should ennoble, not debase. It should build good personal qualities, not destroy the budding will. It should foster trust and strength, not instill worry and dismay. It should encourage faith in the spirit, not fear of others. Discipline should build character and promote spiritual growth. That's what it's for, that's what it's all about.

Start By Having Reasonable Age-Related Expectations

To tailor-make a discipline strategy, age-appropriateness should be a parent's first concern. Here's a brief guide concerning what to expect at different ages:

Age	Appropriate Discipline Techniques For Different Ages
15–20 months	Take the first steps in establishing the meaning of yes and no. Do not expect the child to obey sophisticated orders. Do not use deprivation or scoldings as punishment. The child will not understand. Never apply any kind of physical punishment at this age.
2 years	At this age diversion and distraction are perhaps the best methods for keeping children out of mischief. Keep child very busy. Strong yes and no, do and don't commands should be obeyed, though indirect methods such as distraction work best at this age. Grant more independence, especially in can-do skills such as eating and dressing. Don't force things too harshly.
3 years	Children like to please their parents at this age and conform to rules. Your applause, signs of appreciation, encouragement, and

Age	Appropriate Discipline Techniques For Different Ages
	guided direction will help. Make commands very detailed and specific. Small chores can now be introduced. Be gentle.
4 years	Again, a rebellious stage. Praise and blame are less effective than with three-year-olds. Direct commands are necessary. Start introducing ideas of right and wrong. Simple, small punishments can be used, like standing in the corner or not getting dessert. Just be sure the child knows why he or she is being punished. Children have difficulty with the cause and effect of punishment at this age and will often feel unjustly treated. The cry of "No fair!" begins now. It may seem that child is disobedient when he or she has simply forgotten the directions or has exceeded attention span.
5 years	Needs and wants plenty of supervision and yes-and-no direction. The rudiments of the child's conscience can occasionally be appealed to at this age, though not always. Will respond to praise and applause much more than to blame. Repeat orders many times, and carefully. Repetition is very important now. Don't embarrass or discipline in front of other children. This holds true from now on through the teenage years.
6 years	Often responds with an immediate "No!" and then does it anyway. Explain why you are punishing and rewarding. The child will understand and respond. You can address certain commands to the child's reason if the commands are simple enough. Give the child time to respond to commands—avoid

Age	Appropriate Discipline Techniques For Different Ages
	demanding instant conformity. Indirect methods work best. Child wants to feel to some extent master of his or her own ship.
7 years	The child's reason is coming to bud and you can apply to it when making demands: "Clean your room because it's a mess" makes no sense to a four-year-old, plenty to a seven-year-old. Seven-year-olds must nevertheless be told what to do several times; they often suffer from instant amnesia and need constant reminding. Explain what it to be done, remind them again, then again, and punish only after repeated neglect. Procrastination is indigenous to this age.
8 years	The child will be quite argumentative. State your case clearly and do not be sucked into long, unnecessary arguments. Set rules, expect child to follow them, and let punishments be an automatic consequence of misconduct. Offer plenty of incentives—they mean a lot at this age. Don't talk down to the child, who no longer wants to be viewed as a baby. Make instructions minimum and let the child have a sense that he "can handle it"; for example, don't tell the child what to wear, just say "Get dressed."
9 years	Child learns to postpone and wiggle out of responsibilities. The age of cleverness is dawning. Be careful. Watch for lies and punish accordingly. Discourage this habit today or it will become a bigger problem during the teen years. More subtle psychological interchanges are now necessary; child will also

Age	Appropriate Discipline Techniques For Different Ages
	respond more to your body language, to uplifted brows and slight smiles.
10 years	Children tend to be at their best-behaved during the tens and elevens. But don't get drawn into long, tiresome arguments. Kids should be clear about all their responsibilities and be ready to take the consequences if not done. They will still need plenty of reminders. Child will now want to please parents and to be considered a good boy or girl. The beginnings of the wish for community service begin now and should be encouraged.

Scold but Don't Embarrass

During their fours and fives children develop a social shame that centers on the need to save face. Like adults, they want to keep up with the Joneses and not be exposed to their friends as morons and dolts.

Grownups can be oblivious to this need in children and may unwittingly make youngsters feel shamed in front of friends and peers. Publicly ridiculed children may not say anything at the time. But the monkey-see, monkey-do mentality is at work, be assured, and they may soon begin to ridicule their friends in turn: The principles of fairness and compassion you preach are at this time quickly out the window. Inside, the embarrassed child is smoldering lava; at some later date this repressed anger spills over the rim in the form of backtalk and mischievous behavior and even violence. The anger built up in such sessions can poison a child's soul and work against the spiritual lessons you are attempting to instill. If you are about to reprimand a child in front of others, consider these options first:

• Scold children in private, away from the eyes and ears of the world. This assures children that although they have misbehaved, you respect them enough not to make them feel foolish in front of family and friends.

• Absolutely *never* spank or strike a child in sight of his or her peers. If you must deliver physical punishment, execute this unpleasant task in private.

• After disciplinary action is finished, don't talk or joke about it in front of others.

• If a brother or sister ribs the punished child, stop the teasing immediately. If it continues, punish the offender.

• When the punishment is over let the matter end. Don't dwell on it. The issue is resolved, and every moment is new from now on.

• Don't punish in ways that produce bodily shame, such as spanking an exposed rear end. There is an etiquette of punishment as there is in everything else. It should be honored.

Note: Following this dictum against public embarrassment, remember that a possible exception does exist. At certain times under certain circumstances public ridicule may be just what the doctor ordered to shame a child out of particularly ugly behavior. We'll take this matter up toward the end of this chapter. Like so many aspects of spiritual parenting, rules are relative things.

Be Sure Children Understand
Why They Are Being Punished

"You're being punished because I say so!" bellows Father as the strap descends. "But what'd I do?" Junior screams in a bewildered voice. "Just take your punishment like a man!" Dad screams back as he lays to the task.

Father's "explanation," much in fashion several decades ago, is no longer acceptable in anybody's book. Better to discipline with the understanding that the punishment is being administered for a specific cause but that even in punishment a certain amount of mercy exists.

This mercy takes the form of:

1. Explaining why the penalty is being applied, and what it seeks to accomplish.

2. Giving the child a limited choice (sometimes) in the kind of punishment he or she should receive; for example "Which do you think is more appropriate for the lie you told, giving up TV this week or missing the 4-H meeting? I'll give you the choice."

3. Giving a second chance when appropriate.

4. Establishing the fact that the penalty is a temporary corrective, and once it accomplishes its goal it will no longer be necessary; no grudges will be held. Note this scenario:

> FATHER: Two Ds, two Cs. Not great, Larry. I'm going to have to ground you until your study habits improve.
>
> LARRY: Oh, come on, Dad!
>
> FATHER: You have your end to keep up—and schoolwork's it. I'm going to have to clamp down until there's some improvement in your grades.
>
> LARRY: Do I have to be grounded every day?
>
> FATHER: Well, I'll give you a choice: You can take advantage of that new study hall system your teacher told me about and stay the extra half-hour each day. Or you can come home directly and do the work here. Which do you think will help get the job done better?
>
> LARRY: I guess the half-hour at school.
>
> FATHER: Good. If that doesn't work we'll cook up another plan. Listen, Son, I just want to see your grades get better; I'm not out to ruin your day. I'll help you get on the right track and after that you're on your own.

And this one:

> MOTHER: Julie, this is the third time you've left the hose running in the yard. I'm afraid I just can't let you use it until you're a little older and can learn how to take more responsibility.

JULIA [age four]: It wasn't my fault.

MOTHER: Maybe not. But the rule is that the last person to use the hose turns it off. That's their job. If the hose is left running it wastes water, which isn't good, and we have to pay for the water, too. We've talked about this many times. You can use the watering can instead of the hose if you want.

Use a Few Simple Commands

The temptation to turn an order into an oration is irresistable for many of us; yet it is an indulgence that can also be a mistake.

Why? Because when they are being scolded, children are also being put on the spot. They feel picked on, singled out by the dark forces of the universe; all they really want to do at this moment is to get away as quickly as they can.

Children, in other words, are not psychologically receptive to lectures when being disciplined, and much of what you say will fall on closed minds. Later on, when the heat is off and the earplugs come out, you can discuss the matter with the child at length. Now, however, is the time to say what you must with a few choice words. Keep them simple, directive, explicit, unequivocal:

"Time for dishwashing, kids. No more wasting time."

"Midge, don't splash. I'm not going to say it again."

"Don't speak to me in that tone. It's disrespectful and I don't like it."

"No picking up—no playing miniature golf with Jerry. That's how it's got to be."

Let All Justice Be Immediate

Children are sons and daughters of the moment. They live in a timeless world where tomorrow and yesterday have little importance, and where the present seems eternal. This means that if too much time is allowed to elapse between a naughty deed and its expiation, youngsters may forget why they are being scolded; they may read the punishment as an unwarranted assault and an arbitrary rejection. Unlike adults, they cannot make the connection between cause and effect when events are separated too widely in time.

This crucial fact must be kept in mind when planning a discipline strategy. As soon as the mischief occurs, take action. Let no time elapse—even ten minutes may be too long. The child should be told what he or she has done wrong, that this *is* a punishment, and that it is being applied for *this particular reason.*

Sometimes even a word is punishment enough if the timing is right. A seven-year-old Hassidic boy was playing along the sidewalks of a residential Los Angeles neighborhood with several of his friends. The boys were squirting each other with water guns and generally revving each other up, as children do. An elderly man happened to be walking by on his way to synagogue several blocks away. The boy, now out of control, squirted the man with the gun.

The man stopped and the boy braced himself for the torrid scolding he knew was coming. Instead, the man stared at the boy for a long moment with troubled, loving eyes, then in a tone of utter sincerity said simply "That's not right" and walked on. This statement, along with the memory of the old man's compassionate gaze, stayed so emblazoned in the boy's memory that when he told me the story thirty years later there were tears in his eyes over this brief, three-word lesson received from a stranger.

Hear the Child's Side of the Story

Kids should be allowed to participate in the disciplinary action, at least to the extent that they are not made to feel like helpless victims. They should perceive that the punishment is a genuine attempt on your part to set a bad situation straight, a teaching transaction between parent and child.

One way to institute this method is to let children speak their piece before meting out penalties. What's interesting about this approach is that in some cases a child's explanation may throw an unexpected light on what appears to be a cut-and-dried situation. For example, nine-year-old Donnie was late to school five or six mornings in a row, so late that his teacher sent a note home reporting him as truant.

Both parents exploded when they heard the news. They were about to hand out punishments when, through teary eyes, Donnie told them a story that brought tears to *their* eyes.

Three bullying eighth-graders who lived nearby were laying in wait for Lonnie every day on the route to school. One morning they ambushed him and shoved him around with particular meanness. His calf and wrist were both bruised in the scuffle and the wind was knocked out of him. Frightened by the violence of the incident yet too embarrassed to admit his helplessness to grownups—and not wishing to be a tattletale—Donnie started walking a different, longer route to school, and this is when his lateness began. What appeared to be a transgression on Donnie's part was actually a desperate and somewhat noble attempt at survival.

Before applying discipline make sure that you have a full accounting of the situation, and that there are no hidden agendas. Two-way dialogue and hearing the child's side are both important if justice is to be served.

Let the Punishment Fit the Crime

In Gilbert and Sullivan's delirious operetta *The Mikado,* the emperor of Japan sings of his intention to discipline evildoers so that "punishment fits the crime." He describes how, in the best of possible courtrooms, con men convicted of selling quack dental cures will have their teeth extracted by amateur dentists. Billiard sharps who exploit unwary rubes will be locked in a dungeon and be forced to play endless billiard matches on "a cloth that's untrue, with a twisted cue, and elliptical billiard balls!"

The intent is wit but the point is well made: Penalties work

best when they have an obvious connection to the misdeed.
So:

> · If kids track dirt on the living-room rug for the
> umteenth time, let the punishment fit the crime: make
> them clean up the mess themselves.
> · If children refuse to eat dinner, fine—let them go
> hungry for one night.
> · If children write on the wall with crayons, make
> them scrub till the markings come off.
> · And so forth.

Try to Make Punishments Creative, Interesting, and Meaningful

This may sound odd. But when you think about it, the
dynamics of a punishment, if engineered with imagination,
can become a kind of secondary spiritual lesson. Why not? I'm
not implying that disciplinary actions should be turned into
jokes or reduced to exercises in nonsense, only that you
should try to get the most mileage possible out of each parenting action.

While you will, naturally, have to think up your own variations to suit the occasion, these case histories should stimulate your creative notions:

Punishment:

Children who have talked back to their parents are made to
stand in front of the mirror and repeat five hundred times one
or two of the angry phrases they just used. "You better get
it for me!" "You better get it for me!" "You better get it for
me!" intones Gregory over and over again as he watches his
own reflection turn silly after the two-hundredth-fifth mouthful of words. "You better get it for me!" "You better get it for
me!" "You better get it for me!" This, ultimately, can become
an exercise in self-awareness as well as manners.

Punishment:

An alternate method for children who have spoken rudely is to make them remain silent for an hour—not a single peep. For every slip add another five minutes to the term. Besides forcing children to use willpower, as a kind of side benefit this exercise will make them aware of how difficult it is not to talk, a good lesson for any child. The contrast will be its own teacher. It may also help them understand that silence has its own compensations.

Punishment:

Six-year-old Sarah has gotten into eleven-year-old Jason's *Monopoly* set. She has scattered the pieces from one end of her room to the other and dropped most of the properties into the fish tank. As punishment, little sister is made to sweep big brother's room every day, for which she receives a small "salary" from her parents. After enough money has been earned, Sarah will go to the toy store and purchase another *Monopoly* set to replace the one she destroyed. Industriousness, the karmic law of cause and effect, the role of money, and the principle of fair recompense are all stressed.

Punishment:

Ryan in a fit of anger has beaten up his little brother. Perhaps little brother deserved it, perhaps not. But Ryan's parents feel that such bullying is intolerable and that Ryan must be paid back in kind. Violence, however, is not encouraged in this home. So every day when Ryan comes home from school, his father brings him into the backyard and makes him do a ten-minute routine of exercises—including a prescribed number of sit-ups, push-ups, and chin-ups: good hard physical activity. Ryan must continue this regimen for three straight weeks (with Sundays off for good behavior) before his parents will grant that he has paid off his misdeed. Ryan, in other words, is being paid back in his own coin: physical pain—but in this case physical pain that builds stamina and strength and from which he learns moral lessons.

Be Stern—But Also Forgive

Children usually do not misbehave intentionally. Naughtiness usually stems from inattention or curiosity; from exuberance or an overabundance of energy; from focusing too intently on having fun right now or on getting their way. Quite sincerely they believe they can do what they wish and pay no price.

To adjust this notion, parents must step in and recreate in tiny pedagogic replicas the cosmic principle that if we stray we are punished. Karma. Sowing, reaping. The parents as surrogate God-figure must recreate reality for children in miniature, through disciplinary lessons, until children grow old enough and wise enough to understand the principles for themselves.

If they never receive these lessons, if they are raised to believe they can do as they please and pay no piper (parental overpermissiveness), or if they are brought up to think the world is a prison of inflexible rules and intractable people that allows freedom only to those rebellious enough to seize it by force (parental overdomination), misery and self-hatred will result. This, at least, is the attitude traditional spiritual disciplines have taken through the centuries. If you drop a stone it will fall to the ground. If you tell a lie it will return to hurt you. "The effects of our deeds eventually return to us, as if by natural means," says the *Dhammapada.* "What we are today comes from our thoughts and deeds of yesterday. And our present thoughts and deeds build our life of tomorrow." This is how God's justice works, the spiritual parent believes. This is how it is. This is reality.

A parent's job is, thus, to help children remember that though they are loved they are also depended upon; though they are individuals they are also part of a family and of a larger social unit; though they are beloved by the Divine they must nonetheless *do something good to get something good.* Discipline, in its highest form, is a way of keeping the young ego in check, of discouraging a child from always crying "me, me, me!" In this sense it is a preparation for the larger religious journey ahead when the seeker sets out to transcend his or her ego entirely.

To keep discipline couched in this spirit of selflessness, allow plenty of room for error and for misfire on your own end. In other words, when it is appropriate, forgive. The child will make mistakes, yes. But you made mistakes when you were this age—and remember how often people overlooked your misdemeanors? If you see that the child's misbehavior is not intentional or malicious, opt for the merciful path and suspend punishment.

A good way of both having your cake and eating it in this situation is to tell children that they are "on probation," and that future discipline depends on future behavior. Children will usually respond to this idea with enthusiasm. It has a certain drama, which they enjoy, and enough incipient danger to make them toe the line. Usually they will *want* to be good; they will want to please you. It's just that their energy and needs make them forget. You as parent (and as God surrogate) must provide reminders.

THE ONE-MINUTE SCOLDING

Gerald Nelson and Richard Lewark present in their book *Who's the Boss?* an ingenious and amazingly supportive method of punishment they term "the one-minute scolding" that, from the standpoint of spiritual parenting, neatly includes several of our most important principles, including the balance of mercy and justice. It works like this:

1. Touching or holding the child, the parent scolds for misbehavior. The parent explains why the scolding is taking place and continues in this way until the child shows signs of feeling: tears or sad-

ness. The scolding itself never lasts more than thirty seconds.

2. Parents now stop and change pace entirely, telling the child how much they love him or her, then giving assurance that they will help the child behave properly in the future. "I'll help you . . . every time you forget and hit your sister, I'll scold you. Soon you'll remember that we don't hit." The parent is reassuring, warm, and in control.

3. After the negative scolding and the positive affirmation, the parent checks to be sure the lesson has gotten through. Parents ask such questions as "Why did I scold you, do you remember?" "Why must I scold you each time you hit your sister?"

4. The scolding ends with a hug, symbolizing forgiveness and closure. The whole event should take no longer than one minute from start to finish.[1]

When you Punish, Punish

When it becomes clear that a punishment is in order and that forgiveness is not the appropriate mode, deliver the punishment posthaste and with vigor. When you and I misbehave we are chastened by our karma. Parental punishments should do the same. Now is not the time for waffling or inconsistency. Punishments are serious stuff. They teach children the reality principle, that their behavior counts, that retribution follows misdeeds. Whatever form you choose to deliver this message in, deliver it with serious intent.

Unless circumstances warrant, moreover, don't reduce a penalty once it has been announced. If a child is grounded for two weeks, beware of commuting the sentence to three days out of "kindness." The mode now is justice, not mercy. And anyway, such changes send mixed messages to children, with the bottom line being "My parents are not really serious when they punish; consequently, I don't have to worry about what I do 'cause in the end I'll get off free."

So much for your kindness, which is being read as weakness by the child. When you do decide to punish, punish—whole hog.

Hold No Grudges

As soon as the punishment is over, let amnesty reign. Reluctance to let go of a grievance is a profitless attitude, one that poisons the heart. Once the error is paid off, wipe the slate clean. In this way the child avoids guilt over past misdemeanors, the parent is freed from carrying around the burden of continuing disapproval, and neither feeds the ugly habit of harboring a grudge.

In this regard parents can take a lesson from their children. Watch as kids spar and squabble with one another. The most terrible insults are exchanged, remarks that would turn adults into enemies for life. Yet three minutes later all is forgiven and playtime proceeds as usual. It is this way because a youngster's ego and sense of self-importance are not as developed as those of adults. They have not yet learned to keep resentment records in their heads and hearts.

I am reminded of the Zen story of two Buddhist monks, Tanzan and Ekido, who are standing by a riverbank about to wade across when they are approached by a beautiful young maiden who asks if they will help her to the other side. Without hesitation Tanzan lifts the girl onto his back and carries her across. There he puts her down and the two monks continue on their way. After walking together in silence for some time Ekido finally turns to Tanzan and asks "Why were you so familiar with that woman back there? You know it is forbidden for us to talk to a woman, let alone carry one on our back!" "Oh her," Tanzan replies. "I left her back there at the riverbank. It is you who are still carrying her around."

**After the Punishment Has Taken Place,
Discuss with the Child What You Can
Do Together to Make Things Better**

This method, adapted from the well-known P.E.T. (Parent Effectiveness Training) method developed by Dr. Thomas Gordon, calls for taking children quietly aside after the disciplinary action is completed and discussing what can be done to prevent the problem from occurring again.[2]

During these conversations be clear about why you are upset, about what changes you would like to see occur, and about your reasons for considering the behavior unacceptable. At the same time, refrain from threats and anger. Especially avoid hostile "you-messages." For instance, say to children:

> *"I'm bothered by the fact that my sofa is getting so beaten up. I don't want to hand out any more punishments for spills. What can we do about it?"*

Not:

> *"You and your friends have practically destroyed the couch. Next time you spill something on it I'll really let you have it!"*

Say:

> *"After lunch I like to take a nap. How about if from now on you kids play in your rooms until I get up?"*

Not:

> *"Every time I try to take a nap you kids wake me up! I'm sick of it! From now on stay in your rooms while I'm sleeping until I tell you to come out."*

Approach matters in the spirit of scientific inquiry: A research problem faces you, and you and the child are going to solve it together. Ask children what suggestions they have to remedy the conflict. Then talk these ideas over together, one on one, being sure to listen carefully and between the lines.

If the child's suggestions are ludicrous, as they sometimes will be (especially if you're dealing with younger children), don't criticize or dismiss them. In fact, don't say much of anything. Just listen. If the ideas are worthwhile (as they sometimes are), say so. You could even write them down in a special notebook kept for the purpose. This will be flattering to children and will inspire them to follow their own resolutions.

After all suggestions are on the table, evaluate each one and reach a consensus on whether or not it should be adopted. Ask the child directly such questions as: "Do you think this solution is going to work?" "How about giving this approach a try for a week and seeing what we come up with?" "Do you have anything to add to these ideas?"

If the solution you choose is complicated or involves many different do's and don'ts, write it down and post it in a conspicuous place. Before ending the conference go over the points of the agreement and make sure everyone understands them. After some time has passed, have another meeting and evaluate how well the solutions have worked.

This is a tried-and-true method for family problem solving that has been used by parents for more than a decade. Instead of fomenting fights and triggering recriminations, it deals with the crisis from, as it were, an administrative viewpoint. Dispassionately, lovingly, objectively, it defines problems, identifies weak points, devises solutions—and satisfies everyone's need for feeling that they count and that their voice is heard. This is where the method's primary spiritual value lies: in letting children know that a loving approach to conflict ultimately wins out over anger and hate. Goodness prevails, as it should and must.

The Dark Side: Helping Children
When They Do Things That Are Really Bad

A friend of mine, a psychologist from Cleveland, has done a great deal of counseling work with Vietnam veterans who committed atrocities during the war. At first this man, a highly religious Catholic, attempted to treat these agonized men by convincing them that their feelings of guilt were nonproductive. He assured them that while they did wrong things in the war they were acting under unreasonable pressures and no one should be held accountable for conduct performed in the heat of battle.

It soon became apparent, however, that this method was not working very well—two of his patients committed suicide within a year's time. Another approach was needed.

Remembering his own experiences of performing penance after confession and recalling how cleansed he felt when the expiation period was over, my friend decided to adapt an unorthodox therapeutic method—to suggest this same confessional–penitential approach to his clients. His therapy now began to focus on the fact that, yes, you have done a terrible thing. Absolutely. To deny the seriousness of the act would be to make a mockery of your own inner feelings. These feelings, he explained, are in fact good. They are your conscience speaking to you, calling out to resolve festering psychological wounds, and as such they must be addressed. But while you cannot make things different for the victims themselves, you can make them different for yourself—by making amends.

Doctor and patient then sat down together and worked out a program where, for a certain period of time, the patient performed specific acts of penance. One man worked with an agency that helped Indochinese emigrants. Another did volunteer work for an adoption agency that specialized in Oriental orphans. Another spent several evenings a week working with underprivileged children. All these men reported that, although the pain of their past still haunted them, they now felt that the quality of that pain had changed, that it had become transformed from a hopeless kind of psychic pressure to a strange, deeply sad, almost mystical sense of communion with the victims they had slain.

This is not to suggest, of course, that any child would ever need such powerful medicine; it is only to make the point that the notion of penance and repentance are woefully neglected in our society today, where guilt has become unfashionable and where many forms of therapy attempt to convince patients of their psychological blamelessness without, at the same time, reminding them of their moral accountability.

Similarly, much talk has filled the air over the past decades about *never* making children feel badly for their actions. Certainly, in many instances this is a principle that should be honored. Yet such thinking can be carried too far. Religiously speaking, a spade must be called a spade in a child's life, a sin must be called a sin. Sometimes, for instance, children do things that are genuinely wrong, even genuinely bad: willingly stealing something precious or being cruel to an animal, breaking into a house, striking a parent, wantonly destroying another person's property, or physically harming another child.

These acts should not go unpunished. They are qualitatively different from childhood peccadillos. They require stronger medicine, and sometimes the best choice available is the old-fashioned act of penance.

If and when you are confronted by a serious misdeed on the part of your child, introduce the idea that special efforts will now be required to right the wrong. These penitential acts can focus on anything that helps other people or that provides service for others. Examples include:

· Performing a needed and sizable manual chore around the house—moving a pile of bricks, painting a room, etc.

· Taking part in church or charitable activities.

· Performing a certain number of prayers in church or synagogue.

· Giving away valued toys or possessions to charity or to a poor child.

· Voluntarily giving up something the child loves: chocolate, certain toys, TV, phone calls to friends.

· Volunteering once a week to work with the handicapped.

· Donating money that the child has earned to a
needy organization.
· Going to a poor section of town during the winter
and giving a homeless person articles of clothing the
child himself or herself has purchased.

Make certain that children understand the reasons behind
their penitential actions—contrition and expiation—and that
they realize that penance takes place only for a certain amount
of time, until everyone is satisfied that the misdeed has been
paid off. Also, they must realize that penance involves a sacrifice of some kind plus a certain discomfort on the part of the
doer. And last, they must understand that its purpose is to
relieve a guilty conscience and to provide forgiveness and a
new leaf. Make it especially clear that after the penance is
completed the slate has been wiped totally clear.

Practice What You Preach
A last bit of advice in the discipline department: Parents are
well advised to make sure that if they discipline children for
talking rudely they don't talk rudely themselves. That if they
punish children for making a mess they pick up after themselves as well. Practicing what we preach is a powerful teaching form in itself.
As a parent I often ask myself: Does the problem at hand
stem entirely from my child? Or do I have something to do
with it, too? Is there a part of myself speaking when the child
talks back, or throws a tantrum, or neglects his studies, or lies,
or hates his brother? Is there something I can do to change
this unholy glitch in myself as well as in my child?
Each time I perform this unpleasant little self-interrogation
I am brought back to two basic axioms of spiritual parenting:
that if children are to be virtuous parents must be virtuous
also; and that if children are to grow parents must grow with
them.
In the long run, your child will learn more from *who you are*
than from what you say. Lecture, deprive, spank with a strap,

do what you will, the fact remains that you are the role model for good and for bad. Children will do what you say, sometimes. More often they will be what you are and act as you act. That, in the long run, is the real secret of secrets: The child is mirror to the parent.

PART · 3

TEMPLE OF
THE SOUL:

Teaching Children
How to Use
and Understand
Their Bodies

10.

The Body Invisible:
Getting to Know
Ourselves from the Inside

When Timmy was seven he sliced his hand on the edge of a tuna-fish can. The cut was so deep he could lift the flap of hanging skin and peer at the muscle as it quivered and throbbed inside. It took nine stitches to close the wound at the hospital emergency room and a return visit to the doctor to remove them.

Several days after this traumatic event, when things had calmed down and Timmy had some time to think it over, he confronted his father with a serious question: "Dad, how come we have bodies?"

How would you answer this one? Tim's father's first impulse was to declare that we have bodies because nature gave them to us. We're just made this way, he was about to say. Coming from a committed but conventionally religious family, this was the answer he had been given as a boy when he asked similar questions. To his grownup's thinking the explanation now seemed fine, just fine.

Or did it? Tim's dad thought about it again. This time he

remembered how empty such phrases sounded to him as a boy, and how unsatisfying they were to some inquiring part of himself deep inside. It was a nonanswer really, a slick semantic evasion, not a great deal more edifying than, say, telling a questioning child that the reason we live is because we are alive. And so, instead of delivering a rote homily, Tim's dad pondered the matter, then replied that this was a big question and deserved a big answer. Knowing that the years between five and twelve are the period in life in which a child is most open and curious—and hence most receptive to spiritual ideas—he decided that the iron was indeed hot and the time ripe. That very day father and son began a series of talks that went on for more than a year.

Fortunately, Tim's father was well equipped for the task. Besides having a thorough understanding of science and physiology (he had spent several years in medical school before leaving it to become a Gestalt therapist) he was a serious student of Eastern and Western religious traditions, had his own spiritual teacher, and was a longtime meditator.

Their discussions ripened over the months that followed. Gradually Tim's urge to understand was well satisfied and he even began to feel that he had become privy to "special" information that none of his classmates knew anything about. Better yet, many of these ideas remained fixed in his memory for years to come, and ultimately they would help encourage his own approach to the spiritual quest.

What follows, then, is a description of the exercises a spiritually intelligent father passed on to his son. Parents anxious to see their children gain an understanding of the physical organism that goes several steps beyond calisthenics and readings in biology class can use these exercises as a working model and a point of departure for developing their own meditation methods. The techniques themselves are based on Christian and Eastern prayer and meditation techniques and will serve as an excellent introduction to the practice of psychic self-awareness. Parents should work closely with their little ones on these exercises, serving as guides throughout, and the entire family should become involved. Most kids enjoy taking part in such magical adventures, especially if Mom and Dad come along too. Approach them with a sense of wonder, an openness of mind, and a feeling for fun. The goal here is not to master these techniques with iron-willed determination. More important is that children become aware of the invisible, psychic dimension of their own organisms and that they develop a feeling for the meditatively oriented techniques on which so much of religious training is based. Later, in adulthood, these ideas will remain rooted in the body's memory bank, waiting to be tapped when the moment is ripe.

INTRODUCING THE BODY

Though remarkably aware in certain ways, children are remarkably oblivious, too. They may be more keenly conscious of their bodies at this age than grownups but, strangely enough, *they do not know that they know.* They must be told. As a Persian poem states it:

> *He who knows, and knows not that he knows,*
> *is asleep.*
> *Wake him.*
>
> *He who knows and knows that he knows,*
> *is wise.*
> *Follow him.*
>
> *He who knows not, and knows not that*
> *he knows not, is a fool.*
> *Shun him.*

A good way to break the news is to start by teaching the simple ABC's of anatomy. But do it on the child's level, not the textbook way.

Using pencil, crayons, and a pad of drawing paper, Tim's father told Tim to draw a self-portrait. When the sketch was finished he remarked on how nicely Tim had penciled in his head and legs. But was something missing? Perhaps. They could find out by looking in a mirror.

In the mirror Tim discovered that he had forgotten to put fingers on his hands and that a neck was missing between his shoulder and head. Adjustments were made. Tim's father then went over the sketch again, this time calling attention to interesting facts about the human body. For instance:

> • Had Tim ever noticed that people's noses are in the center of their faces? Why is that? Had Tim ever noticed that heads are round? How come?
> • Had Tim observed that when he walks his right arm swings back when his left foot steps ahead, and that his left arm swings back when his right foot steps ahead? It's remarkable, said the father, how few people realize this simple fact. They simply never watch themselves when they walk. Try it and see.
> • A curious fact: We have five holes in our head. Could Tim name them? Two nostrils, two ear holes, and one mouth. What does each one do?
> • In his self-portrait Tim left out the belly button. His father explained what the belly button is and why it's there. (Tim had been under the amazing notion that belly buttons are made by the obstetrician in the delivery room: "It's where the doctor gives you a shot after you're born," a schoolmate had informed him.)

Tim now sketched another self-portrait, and again they checked it against his reflection. Each time his father made a correction or pointed out a part of the body that was omitted he took the opportunity to explain what physiological function the missing part plays. He explained how the eyes and ears are attached by nerves to the brain, how the brain reads the messages it receives from these nerves and transforms them into sight and sound. He explained what happens to food after it goes into our stomachs, how it is broken down into nutrients and wastes, how our hearts beat, why our blood races back and forth through our veins, where the air goes when it enters the lungs. He discussed how our breath is full of many invisible foods and how when we breathe we link ourselves to the atmosphere around us.

He pointed out that the world has blood too: the oceans, with the rivers as veins. And bones: the continents. A spine: the chains of mountains that encircle the globe. And even a kind of flesh: the soil. Having recently read about the Gaia Hypothesis put forth by a British geologist, the father mentioned that there is evidence to support the notion that the earth is actually a living organism with all the parts of its colossal ecosystem interconnected, interdependent, and self-regulating, like the organs of our own bodies.

Using poetic language, scientific references, and well-timed metaphors (and always grounding these descriptions in reality by referring back to Tim's reflection in the mirror), Tim's father gave his son a biological Cook's tour of the entire human organism.

11.

Taking a Magical Journey Inward

But all this anatomy was simply a point of departure for Tim and his father. Once the factual data were in place, it was time to make the facts real—time to give Tim the taste of how his body works, as it were, from the driver's seat.

To accomplish this Tim's father devised a series of exercises designed to teach a kind of "psychic physiology" through the process of direct sensory experience. Most of us live unmindful of what our internal organs are doing at any given moment. We take for granted that our moods come from what we think and feel. We forget that our thoughts and feelings are linked, in turn, to our secretions, to our digestion, to our heartbeat and nerve impulses—in short, to our organs.

If these organs are functioning improperly, our psychological states will follow suit. If they are working well we will feel well—happy, cheerful, optimistic, ready to live and love. It is thus important to get in touch with these inner body parts, to speak to them in a certain kind of language, and to listen to what they say in return. Here's how it works:

The Hands

Tim sits quietly in a chair and closes his eyes. Following his father's directions, he lifts his arms in front of him and wiggles his fingers. "Visualize your fingers in your mind," father tells him. "See them on the inner movie screen of your imagination."

Tim moves his fingers slowly at first, then more rapidly. "Move each finger in a circle. Back and forth. Slow down the movements. Feel them from the *inside.*"

The Arms

With eyes still closed, hold the arms straight out in front and visualize them hanging there. Feel how heavy they are. Sense their weight. Feel them without looking at them.

Now open a small "door" on the wrist of the right arm and go inside. Tell your arm you've come to visit and that you want to see how things work in here. Walk along the muscular system and study it. What do the muscles look like? See any bones? Is it pretty in here? Hot? Cold? Move your arms a little and see if you can feel yourself inside as they stretch and tighten. Do you think you'd like to be a muscle in your own arm?

The Legs and the Magic Eye

Shift attention to the legs. Seated in a chair, with shoes and socks off, lift one leg, hold it up for a minute, drop it and lift the other. During these movements pretend you possess a special magic eye. This wondrous organ can go anywhere it wishes and look at whatever it pleases. It can float across the room, penetrate matter, have X-ray vision, magnify objects like a microscope, divide itself into several different eyes and observe many objects simultaneously. As a matter of fact, it can perform just about any feat of seeing you wish.

With the magic eye (and with your real eyes closed) travel up and down your legs, examining them from the front and back, inside and out. Move the magic eye within a half-inch of your kneecap for a microscopic look. Describe what you see. Peer at your toenails from close up, then run your magic eye up and down the back of your heel. Try seeing both heels at once. Go inside the leg and use your X-ray vision to examine your bones.

The Toes

Wiggle your toes and observe the wiggling from two inches away with the floating eye. Wiggle them quickly and then slowly. Walk around the room and observe your toes while you walk. How does it look in there? How does it feel to be in your own big toe? Imagine that you take a giant nailfile and clean the toenail. What does it feel like inside the toe to be cleaned? What would your toes say if you asked them to describe life on a foot?

The Head

Still sitting with closed eyes, circle your head in one direction, then another. Try to sense its weight and to examine different areas with the magic eye. Look inside the ears, in the corners of the eyes, in the nostrils. Use microscopic eyepower to examine the hairs on the head. Examine the back of the neck with six eyes at once. Now make several funny faces and try, with closed eyes, to see each expression from across the room.

What to Expect at What Age

These exercises should take no more than three or four minutes to complete, or a little longer if the child's attention span can sustain it (usually it won't). Concentration powers depend on age. Four- and five-year-olds will last a minute or two and no more, six-year-olds a minute or three. Children over seven usually stick at the exercise for some time and tend to enjoy the novel sensations that are produced.

While at first these exercises will seem strange to young-sters, their magicalness quickly becomes apparent and youngsters will often throw themselves into this game body and soul. Some report actually being able to perceive parts of their bodies from the inside or to see their faces from across the room—these techniques are clearly an excellent means for developing latent psychic abilities or, at least, strengthened imagination. Their main purpose is to give children a direct feel for the organism that houses them and to plant seeds that will develop into true self-awareness later.

GOING FARTHER INSIDE: A TOUR OF THE ORGANS

Prepared by the talks on physiology and anatomy, Tim is now ready to learn more about what goes on in the deeper parts of himself. His education will include trips inside his organs plus a bit of hands-on "field work." By the time he finishes he will have a fair idea of what he's made of inside and—more important from a spiritual standpoint—he will begin to think of his organs as centers of energy as well as blood pushers and food strainers.

The Brain

Think a thought, Tim's father said, and feel where that thought is coming from. Is it in your stomach? Your chest? Your head?

In my head, Tim replies. "Right here"—pointing to his forehead.

A scientist would say that's because your brain is there, replies Father. It's an odd thing though, he adds. Some people feel that their thoughts come from other parts of the body. Tibetans say they originate in the heart. Hindus say the throat. The ancient Sumerians insisted that the center of thought and feeling is in the liver. Father then had Tim try to "think" from his chest—then from his stomach and from his back.

How old are you? Father asked. Tim answered that he was seven. I'm going to ask you this same question again, Father said. This time see what part of your brain the answer pops out of. The forehead? The back of the head? The ear?

Tim did, and this time it seemed that the answers came from several parts, mostly the front. They played this question game four or five times and Tim began to sense that, indeed, some type of thinking actually *was* taking place in his brain, and that the answers really did seem to emerge from *him.*

Tim's father then pointed out how, whenever someone talks to us, we transform the words we hear into pictures in our mind. Then they played another game. Father spoke a sentence that contained several simple but vivid images; Tim tried to become aware of the mental pictures he was making as Father talked. Father would say slowly: "The fat little boy tripped on a crocodile and fell into a vat of butter" or "A green cloud carried a flock of flamingos that landed feet first in the mud." Tim would then see his own mental formations as they came pouring out of his mind. Thinking, it soon became clear to him, was more than just, well—more than just thoughts. It was a process one produced inside and which you could watch, almost like TV. For many children the experience of *perceiving themselves perceive* is strange and exhilarating.

Tim's father mentioned that people have argued for many centuries over whether our brains create thoughts or whether they simply receive them from some higher place. "What do you think?" he asked. They discussed this question for a while. Father tried to stimulate Tim's spiritual curiosity further by explaining that certain great thinkers, such as the Greek philosopher Plato, believed that ideas are actually "things" and that people can pick them up, as it were, out the air, almost like radios pick up sound waves. Father said that these ideas exist in a kind of invisible higher world and that they have been there from eternity.

Tim's father now showed his son an anatomical drawing of the brain. He pointed to the outer cortex areas where mental activity takes place, and to the cerebellum and medulla, which control unconscious activities like breathing and circulation. He told Tim to close his eyes and imagine his own brain sitting in the middle of his head. Picture the left side, he said, and hold this image for several seconds. Then picture the right side. Pretend that you have a flashlight and are shining a beam of light up into your brain. Shine it on the left, hold it there for a second, then shine it on the right. Aim it at the front part, then the back. Try to visualize the different parts of the brain as they light up.

There are certain parts of your brain that are especially sensitive, Tim's father added. See if you can feel life moving up there. See if you can see *what moves your thoughts.*

Tim closed his eyes and, following his father's instructions, focused on a spot between his eyes. After Tim concentrated there for a while, Father told him to look at any object in the room, to try to "suck" the image in through that spot between his eyes. Everything in the world is energy, Father explained. Sometimes if we concentrate on a thing and try to draw it into ourselves through this point—draw in its color and form and shape—we can take in its energy and use that energy for meditation.

The Heart

When he was preparing to describe the heart, Tim's father's first inclination was to launch into a speech about why this organ is a person's real spiritual center. He was about to recount how the physical heart has an etheric counterpart that contains the seeds of spiritual transformation, and how at a certain stage of religious development the heart is changed from an ordinary vessel of emotion into a kind of spiritual "eye" with which, the saints tell us, we perceive Divine truths. The phrase that continually went through his mind, which had so excited him when he first heard it, was Meister Eckhart's famous exclamation "The eye with which I see God is the eye with which God sees me."

But such explanations somehow seemed out of place and premature for a seven-year-old. Better to keep away from theory entirely and to plant the seeds of understanding directly.

So, instead, Tim and his father went jogging. After they had run for several minutes they stopped and tried to feel their hearts beat. Feel its beat through your entire body, Father said. The heart is connected to every part of it by a system of veins, just like streams are connected to rivers and rivers to the sea.

When they returned home, they had fun taking each other's pulses. Tim put his ear to his father's chest and listened to the beat.

Don't worry too much about where in your chest the heart is actually located, Tim's father said after they had compared physical notes. What's really important is that the heart is like a big, powerful, loving light that shines in the center of ourselves. It's there that all those good feelings of tenderness, trust, and peace come out of us. When you're kind to someone the kindness comes out of your heart. When you're happy your heart feels happy. Your heart is so important, really, that religious persons have always had special kinds of prayers they use for their hearts. Sometimes they imagine they can see light there.

Tim and his father sat down beneath a tree and practiced concentrating on their hearts. "Try to feel it right now, as we're sitting here. Send it warm, loving thoughts; see if you can hear your heart answer back. Feel your heart as if it's a light in the center of yourself. Let it warm you. Picture it as a kind of big, glowing fireball that's shooting off golden rays. Close your eyes and see it flashing and burning like the sun. Each ray is a good thought and a kind feeling. You're shooting good deeds out into the world. That's what the heart can do if you let it."

The Lungs

"Use your magic eye," said Tim's father. "Go inside your chest and look around. Watch your lungs get big and small as you breathe. When they inflate they bring fresh air into the blood. When they deflate they blow out the bad air and get rid of poisons. See how the lung muscles work. Listen to the sound they're making. Pretend you can see the air as it goes in and out."

After a few minutes' visualization, Tim held his breath. "What did you feel when you couldn't breathe?" Tim's father asked. "Like I needed air, air, air!"

"That's because air is life," said Father. "Everything that lives is linked to the air. The air is our real father and mother. Even a few minutes without it and we're finished. If you want to know if something is alive or not, just give it this test. Ask yourself: Does it breathe? If yes, then it's alive; if no, then it's not.

There are also special things in the air that God has put there especially for living beings. These things are hard to explain or describe, and most of us can't see them or feel them. They're always there, though, like special blessings, special kinds of energies. If you know how to do it you can take in extra amounts of these substances when you breathe. They'll help make you feel strong and happy, and later on when you grow up they can even help you to know God."

To prove his point, Tim and his dad sat down in their favorite spot and practiced a simple breathing technique. The point of the exercise was to learn that air contains subtle substances, and that by picturing these as one breathes in and out they can be sensed and even seen with the mind's inner eye. Here's how it works:

1. Sit quietly and close your eyes. It's especially important to keep your back straight.

2. Take three of four deep breaths. Relax. Try not to think about anything in particular.

3. Inhale deeply. Imagine that you are breathing a thread of pure silver light into your lungs. Imagine that this thread is bright, sparkling, and beautiful, like a piece of Christmas-tree tinsel, and that it is entering your lungs with great joy. You are literally pulling it in with your breath when you inhale, and when it is inside it throws off a brilliant white light.

4. At the finish of your inhalation retain the air for

several seconds and imagine that your whole upper body is filled with silver light.

5. Exhale. This time imagine that you are blowing out dark, dirty air that has been stuck in your lungs for a long period of time. Empty your lungs completely. Clean them out. Some people imagine snakes and lizards going out of their breath when they exhale. Others see smoky, polluted air.

6. After the first inhalation and exhalation cycle repeat it, breathing in a stream of silver air and breathing out a jet of dirty air. Do it five times in a row. Afterward, sit quietly and enjoy whatever nice sensations you may feel.

The Stomach

At the dinner table Tim and his father had fun feeling the food move about in their mouths as they chewed. After swallowing they pictured the food going down into their stomachs. Tim used his magic eye and watched as the pulpy chicken and potatoes moved to his lower abdomen, through the upper intestines, down into the colon.

Tim's father talked about how the stomach is a person's central point of balance. Focusing your attention here, just below the navel, will help you keep on your feet if you're walking on a narrow ledge or if you are trying to stand on one leg (an old circus performer's trick). Concentrate on the stomach when you're cold and it will help you feel warm. Concentrate on it when you're nervous and it will calm you down. If you're tired, pressing on this spot for ten or twenty seconds will give you a lift.

Tim's father pushed Tim lightly on his shoulder. Tim stumbled back. Start again, his father told him, but this time concentrate on the stomach spot with all your might. He pushed Tim, and this time Tim stood his ground. They repeated the experiment and it worked each time. Keep your attention on this point when you're running, said Tim's father, or when someone is trying to knock you over. Or when you feel weak on your feet, when you're trying to keep your balance on a train or bus—it will make you feel rooted to the ground. That small spot right below your navel is the center of your entire body.

There was something else about the stomach, too. Going through a picture book of old paintings and sculptures Tim's father pointed out how in medieval and Renaissance artworks the stomach is often painted very large, round, and strong. They studied pictures of Chinese statues and saw figures of Taoist sages with huge protruding bellies that people rubbed when they needed luck and power. They saw Buddhist temple gods with hard, rounded abdomens.

A lot of people don't know it, Tim's father said, but in the East the stomach is believed to be the place where your life energy is stored. He told Tim how Japanese soldiers would build their strength by concentrating on their stomach area during meditation, and how he had seen martial artists demonstrate stomach power by remaining unhurt after a large stone was placed on their stomachs and hit with a sledgehammer. Father described how practitioners of a martial art known as aikido can, by concentrating on the spot below the navel, prevent themselves from being pushed over by several men at a time and how by sending energy up from their stomachs to their arm they can hold their arm out straight and three strong men are unable to bend it.

Tim and his father tried one of these aikido exercises. Sitting face to face, they touched palms. Now, said Tim's father, imagine that your stomach is a furnace and that it's sending out fire into your hands. I'll do the same. Let's see if we can feel our hands heat up. If we can, then we're getting in touch with our inner power. Everybody has it, but not everybody uses it. Some people use this power to send energy and to heal others. It's strong stuff.

The Sexual Organs

When the moment came to discuss the sexual organs, Tim's father took advantage of this natural opportunity to introduce the birds and the bees. He had been wondering for some years how best to approach the subject and how to give Tim a clear, and at the same time spiritual, version of how it all works. Now the time had come.

The sex organs in a man and woman, he said, choosing his words with the care of a a man making his way from rock to rock across a rushing stream, is where the power of life lives in us. It was put there by God when we were born, and we carry this life around with us all the time. In a man it's housed in millions of tiny seeds that live in his testicles. In a woman it's in the small eggs that are produced inside her sexual organs.

When a man and a woman love each other and get married, they pass this life force through their sexual organs, through their penis and vagina. This activity is one of the great rights and pleasures of marriage. It's called making love, or sexual intercourse, and when it takes place babies can be made. The way it works is like this: The man uses his penis to plant his life energy—his seed—inside the woman. (It's not all that different from the way a gardener plants a seed in a garden.) When the seed goes into the woman it searches for her egg— where *her* life force is stored. When it finds the egg they join, the seed and the egg, and a magical, miraculous thing happens: Life is created! Together the egg and seed make a new human being.

This new little human being now starts to grow in the mother's stomach and gets bigger every day. If all goes well, in nine months it will come out and be born. Welcome to the world! That's how it happens. That's how all of us came to this place.

Tim's father stressed how the genitals are nothing to be ashamed of, even though kids at school may laugh and make dirty jokes about them. At the same time, the sex organs are one's very private belongings, he stressed—a person's "secret," one might say. When you get older and marry a woman, you'll share this secret with her and she'll share hers with you. You'll see each other naked and find great enjoyment in this. The human figure is very beautiful. You will enjoy sexual intercourse and perhaps make a child of your own. But till then our bodies and our sexual organs are something personal, something precious. We must strive to keep them to ourselves.

One more thing about the sex organs: Sex energy is a powerful force, far more powerful than we can imagine. Religious persons who dedicate themselves to spiritual enlightenment often become what we call celebate. This means they do not marry and do not have intercourse. This is not because they think sex is bad or ugly. It is because they wish to preserve their seed or egg inside themselves. They believe it has certain properties and powers that will help them make spiritual progress.

During a person's youth, Father continued, many religions believe that this energy is needed by young persons for proper growth. According to followers of a religion called Taoism in China, for instance, the vital element in sex energy makes young people's minds strong, regulates their emotions, and helps their inner organs grow to proper size. This is one reason why children have traditionally been discouraged by religious ways from having sex, Father explained. Not only is the sexual act something that cannot be emotionally understood until a person is fully grown, but the energy of sex stored in the young male and female sex organs is needed at this point in the life cycle to help children's bodies and minds develop in a harmonious way. It should not be used in any other way at this particular time.

LEARNING TO CONTROL THE SENSES

If there is one thing that's unholy, Tim's father announced during one of their discussions, it's *waste*. Some people waste food. Some waste time or money. But the worst thing any of us can waste is our energy. God gave us a certain amount of it, and we have an obligation to use it in the right way. One of the ways we can keep our energy protected inside ourselves is by learning to control our senses.

At this point Tim said he didn't really know what the senses were.

Father explained that we have five so-called organs of sense: the eyes that we see with; the ears that hear with; a nose that smells; a tongue that tastes; and a body that feels touch on its skin. The senses are strange things. We use them so much that after a while we take them for granted. Things like the ticking of a clock, our own breathing, the feel of a shirt on our back, the outside temperature—after a while we simply forget they're there. At the same time, something inside our bodies notices them very clearly. Which means that something in us is always aware of the sights and sounds and smells and touches around us, even though our minds forget.

It's because we tune our senses out most of the time that obvious impressions are sometimes the most difficult to become aware of. Your eyes don't know it's getting dark outside, for instance, until someone turns on the light. You think your bedroom is quiet. Then you spend a night in the country and are amazed by the contrast. Tuning out our senses in many instances is healthy. It can protect us from too much sensory data streaming in at once. On the other hand, we can learn also how to become more aware of these sights and sounds, and even how to use them in our meditations.

Tim's father then reviewed the organs of sense one by one and explained how Tim could learn to conserve the energy associated with them.

The Eyes

We have outer eyes and we have inner eyes—our imaginations. With our outer eyes we see the world, the covering of things. This covering is often very beautiful, but it can land us in hot water. For instance, say you are trying to avoid eating candy 'cause you know it's bad for you. Then your eyes land on a chocolate bar. It's certainly a lot harder now to say no to the candy than it would have been if you'd never seen it. What's more, when our eyes look at something attractive a subtle kind of energy flows out of them and into the object.

Once it goes we can never get this energy back. We simply have to produce more of it, and that takes time and work for the body's mechanism.

Therefore it's a good thing, said Tim's father, to train ourselves to look *away* from certain objects at certain times. A very simple thing, a very difficult thing, and a very good thing. There's even an old proverb that says "What the eyes don't see the heart doesn't yearn for."

Father gave Tim an exercise: Next time you're walking down the street and something beautiful catches your eye, a snazzy car or a toy in a store window, summon up all your inner strength and *try not to look at it.* Simple as that. It's not that the beautiful thing is bad. On the contrary, it may be very good. That really doesn't matter. The point is to go against what your eyes want you to do at that moment and to do what your willpower says instead.

Try it a couple of times a day. Pretty soon you'll be good at it. Later on in life you'll find that the ability to look away can be a powerful ally. It will make you strong, far stronger than you can imagine, and will help you turn from the kinds of temptation that cause other persons great pain.

Ordinarily the senses want to tell *us* what to do, Tim's father continued. The eyes say "Look at that pretty picture." The ears say "Listen to that nice music" The tongue says "Give me some candy—now!" If you let these voices order you around without objecting, after a while they start to run the show. They become your masters. They own you.

In your life to come, Father added, you'll hear many people speak a great deal about something they call "freedom." Most of these people will tell you that freedom is the right to do anything you want whenever you want. Actually, this is not true and is even the opposite of truth. Doing whatever your desire of the moment demands can be a form of slavery. Real freedom works in a different way. It is the ability *not* to do what your senses demand, not to be the servant of every passing wish and impulse. To *not* eat the candy. To *not* get mad when someone hurts your feelings. With this kind of freedom you have the choice of saying yes or no to your

desires, according to what your mind tells you the consequences will be and according to what your conscience tells
you is right or wrong. This kind of freedom does not come
easily, despite what some people will tell you. It must be
worked for very, very hard. But it is *real* freedom.

The Ears

Same with the ears. If you have a friend who tries to talk you
into doing something you know is wrong, there's one easy way
out: Don't listen. Remove your ears from the premises. Walk
away. Bring them to a place where you can't hear what this
person is saying. That's all. Just stay away. What the *ears* don't
hear the heart doesn't yearn for, either.

Another interesting thing about the senses is that if you
practice for a while you can teach one sense to do the job of
another.

For instance, do you think it's possible to see with your
ears? Let's try.

Tim and his father listened to several Beethoven sympho-
nies. When the horns blared out Father asked Tim what pictures came into his mind. When the violins played softly,
could Tim see the notes in his mind as they streamed out like
silken cords? What did the sounds *look like* in his mind? In the
"Pastoral" Symphony, where the music describes a spring day
in the country and a thundershower, Father told Tim to let
the sounds paint pictures in his imagination. Could he visualize the trees and the grass and the meadows? Could he see the
rain falling? Do the sounds seem to have a form and shape of
their own?

Some people, Tim's father remarked, claim they have actually seen notes come out of instruments. They claim that
besides music, every human thought and feeling has a particular shape of its own in the invisible world. Tim's father made
a drawing of a half moon. This, he said, according to a some
people, is the pattern sudden joy produces. He drew a
pointed, cone-shaped missile. This is an angry thought. It's

colored red. He drew a cloud with feathery edges. That's a feeling of affection, and it's pink.

I have never seen such shapes myself, Tim's father added, but said the idea is fun to think about. He urged Tim to make some sketches on his own, to draw what joy might look like in the invisible world, or fear and contentment, boredom or the emotion one feels when seeing a shooting star. Father and son occupied themselves for some time trying to decide which shape goes with which thought and feeling.

Still speaking about hearing, they tried still another experiment. Sitting quietly in their backyard and trying not to think of anything in particular, father and son concentrated on the sounds in this immediate vicinity, blocking out all other thoughts and perceptions. Soon it was apparent that there are far more sounds in the environment than we are ordinarily aware of. Our minds shut most these sounds off, Tim's father explained, and Tim was amazed. He listened. So many sounds! He heard a far-off typewriter. He heard dishes being washed. He heard someone talking in the next yard. He heard an airplane overhead. He heard a dog bark. He heard someone shoveling something. All these noises were going on at the same time. We are surrounded by an ocean of sight and sound and life all the time, Tim's father explained. Concentrate on the sounds around you and you will begin to see—or hear—how big the world is, and how very, very much goes on near us every moment of our lives.

Smell

Most people don't pay much attention to their sense of smell. That's a pity. Smell can tell us such a good deal about the world and about what's going on with things we can't see or hear. One especially good thing about smelling is that if you practice it you'll get better at it. Want to try?

For the next several weeks, wherever Tim and his father went they practiced smelling things. Near a hedge they aimed their noses at the leaves and sniffed. At the supermarket they put their noses to the soap boxes, the lettuce, and the cheese. Over the days and weeks they practiced smelling tractors and pens, anthills and Mack trucks, books, people and lightbulbs, cats, computers, tea. Sometimes they sniffed the air with their eyes closed and tried to tell what was going on next door. Animals can sort of "see" with their noses, Father explained. They can sense the form and shape of an object from the messages they get in a scent, sort of like radar. So they experimented trying to "see" with their sense of smell. Tim closed his eyes and his father put an object under his nose. Tim smelled it and tried to visualize its contours. You have five whole senses, Tim's father told him after they pursued this curious adventure for some time. Might as well use them all to their limits.

Taste

They played a similar game with taste. One person closed his eyes, tasted a food, and tried to guess what it was. Later on, at dinner, Tim's father explained that when we eat we don't usually pay much attention to what's going on in our mouth. But you can actually make the food taste better, he said, if you concentrate on it when you chew and see it with your magic eye.

So, as an experiment, Tim tried eating an entire meal with his eyes closed, concentrating on the food as it went into his mouth—its taste, the way his tongue moved around as he chewed, how the food became progressively liquified, how it went down his throat. When he was finished he announced he'd never realized how many tastes take place at once from a simple mouthful.

Touch

Close your eyes. Run your hands over a smooth object like a piece of fabric. Use your fingers as if they had eyes. Try to "see" the fabric as you touch it.

Tim experimented with different surfaces and tactile sensations, then his father switched the rules. This time he handed

Tim different items—a cork, a pair of eyeglasses, a hat, a can of shoe polish—and asked him to identify them without looking. Tim pretended that his fingers had eyes on them. As he ran his hands over the mystery pieces he tried to *see* them from the inside, to sense the essence of each object.

Finally, Tim's father introduced an exercise he explained was going to seem particularly strange. He had Tim, eyes open, reach out to touch a chair across the room. While you reach, his father told him, imagine that a kind of phantom arm is projecting out from your regular arm and that it's moving toward the chair. Imagine that the phantom arm has a hand on it just like your regular hand and that it's touching the chair, gripping it, feelings its texture and weight. It's as if a section of you just keeps continuing when you reach—some elastic, subtle part of yourself that can travel long distances through space.

Tim and his father practiced this exercise for some time, reaching for different objects in the room and trying to handle them with their invisible organs of sense. Making mental pictures of certain places, they even tried to reach objects across the street or in the next town. Tim concentrated on touching the blackboard in his homeroom.

Tim's father then used this experiment to introduce the idea that besides our physical forms most spiritual disciplines believe that we have another kind of body—several kinds, in fact. The one we're most interested in now is what Christians call the "soul" or sometimes the "Body of Resurrection," Tim's father told him. Hindus refer to it as the *Sukshmasharira.* Others know it as the etheric body.

We all experience one world, Tim's father continued, the physical world. Science tells us there are smaller parts our senses cannot perceive, things like gases and molecules and microbes. But besides material things there are other realms that are invisible even to the instruments of science. It is to these places that people go for a certain period of time when they die, religion believes. What happens to these parts in the afterlife, Tim's father added, depends to a great deal on how well we have developed this soul during our life on earth. If it's a strong, good soul we will prosper. If not, the experience may be confusing and painful. That's what prayers and meditation and spiritual exercises and good behavior are about: helping develop our souls.

Many of the exercises so far have been designed to get the muscles in the invisible body moving a little bit, and to acquaint you with the fact that you're made up of more than blood and bones, and that besides your physical organs each of your physical senses has a kind of double in the invisible world, which you must feed and nurture. You're a being of light and energy, Father said. That's a human being's real identity.

Right now, he added, you don't have to worry too much about all this. What's important is that you just become aware that you have finer parts within yourself, that these parts can do interesting and unusual things, and that someday these parts may help you see the invisible splendors that surround us all the time.

MINDFULNESS: SENSING ONE'S WHOLE SELF

We've toured the body every which way, Tim's father announced. We've examined different parts from the outside and the inside. Each organ and sense plays a different role, just as in an orchestra the drums make one sound, the strings another, the horns another. But the greatest sound of all is made when the whole orchestra plays at once. That's what our bodies are like—many rapt musicians playing all at once. Now it's time to feel our whole orchestra playing a physical symphony.

Tim's father talked about the idea of mindfulness, about how during the day children can stop every now and then and remember that they are here, in this place, right now, that they exist, and that their bodies are doing this or that this very moment. He explained that much of the time people, especially grownups, become distracted with thoughts about the future or past; so many thoughts, really, that there's no room left to experience what's taking place. They forget where they are—and then who they are.

If a young person learns how important it is to stop several times during the day and to think about this—here I am, a child of God, in this place, at this time—and if he or she practices it regularly, the taste of the experience will remain and will inspire children to seek this blessed sensation all their lives.

To give the concept of mindfulness width and breath, Tim's father suggested that Tim try a final exercise designed to help develop a sense of the whole body existing in the present. It works like this:

1. Sit in a comfortable place away from all distractions. Take several deep breaths. Relax.

2. Close your eyes and feel your right arm. Sense it attached to your shoulder. Feel it from the inside and outside. Put all your attention on it.

3. Move your attention to the right leg. Feel its size, its bulk, its presence. How big is it? How heavy?

4. Move to the left leg. Sense it for several moments. Then go the the left arm. End up at the head.

5. Feel the whole body all at once. Sense it in its entirety. Feel it as a single connected unity of blood and bone, energy and thought.

For children, three or four rounds of this exercise (it moves like a wheel around the body from limb to limb) is enough. The exercise is powerful and should not be done too often by a young child. Once or twice a week is fine.

Tim and his father practiced this exercise together and afterward discussed it. Tim's father asked Tim to describe the sensations he'd experienced. Sometimes a sensation of lightness and clearness can occur, said Father. If you feel this, hold onto it. It's the direction we want to go in our hearts. It's as if we're leaving the earth, floating, moving up. Eventually, if you keep at it, if you practice prayer and meditation through the years and lead a good life, you'll enjoy this feeling of peace and quiet for long periods of time. It will start to give you glimpses of great things.

From this day on, Tim's father started approaching Tim around the house or in the yard. He tapped him on the shoulder and simply said the word *mindfulness*. Nothing more. Just: *mindfulness.*

On hearing this, Tim immediately remembered to sense his body, to stop the flow of his thoughts, to feel himself centered in the present. It was a good exercise. Later he started reminding his father to do the same thing. Together they worked at helping each other. Both of them profited.

12.

Training the Body for Life in the World

WORK

There is no better way for a child to get to know the physical world than through physical work. "While the body is still supple," wrote the French philosopher Montaigne, "one should, therefore, bend it to all fashions and customs." Work builds mastery and self-esteem, two critical ingredients for the proper emotional growth of a child. Agility, coordination, reach, pace, timing, strength, balance are all developed easily and quickly in young physiques. Children who master these skills tend to remain comfortable in their bodies for a lifetime. Those who go untrained display a kind of hapless awkwardness no matter how hard they attempt to compensate for it at a later date on the tennis court or golf course.

Perhaps most important, work teaches the performance of service to others: children help at home and in the community while they build their own character and physical strength. Parents would do well to recall to their child the motto of the Benedictine order: *Labore est orare,* To work is to pray. "Put

your heart, mind, intellect and soul into even your smallest
acts," said the Hindu teacher Swami Sivananda. "This is the
secret of success."

And this is the message work teaches children: Put your
best effort into everything you do. Let work become a way of
pouring your whole being onto things so that in the end work
becomes a kind of meditation, a sort of prayer. The story is
told of an old Zen master who insisted on laboring in the
fields with his students. Concerned with his health, the students one day hid the master's tools so that he could no
longer participate in the chores. Whereupon the master
stopped attending meals. After several days the students
came to his quarters and inquired why he was absent. The
master said simply: "No work, no eat." That very hour his
tools were returned.

The Taoist, Chuang-tse, tells another story, this one em-
phasizing the notion that work and meditation are potentially
one:

> Ch'ing, the chief carpenter, was carving wood into a stand for
> hanging musical instruments. When finished, the work ap-
> peared to those who saw it as though of supernatural execution.
> And the prince of Lu asked him, saying, "What mystery is there
> in your art?"
>
> "No mystery, Your Highness," replied Ch'ing, "and yet there
> is something."
>
> "When I am about to make such a stand, I guard against
> any diminution of my vital power. I first reduce my mind to
> absolute quiescence. Three days in this condition, and I become
> oblivious of any reward to be gained. Five days, and I become
> oblivious of any fame to be acquired. Seven days, and I become
> unconscious of my four limbs and my physical frame. Then, with
> no thought of the Court present to my mind, my skill becomes
> concentrated, and all disturbing elements from without are gone.
> I enter some mountain forest. I search for a suitable tree. It
> contains the form required, which is afterward elaborated. I see
> the stand in my mind's eye, and then set to work. Otherwise,
> there is nothing. I bring my own natural capacity into relation

with that of the wood. What was suspected to be of supernatural
execution in my work was due solely to this."

WHAT TYPE OF WORK IS BEST?

Whatever work accomplishes one or more of these goals is
best:

- To train and strengthen a child's body
- To discourage laziness and encourage industry
- To teach perseverance and will power
- To be of service

Work together closely on several projects, and in a few
months the results will show. With children's quickness of
learning, their muscular systems easily become finely tuned.
Coordination also improves, along with the overall ability to
move through space with confidence and grace.

More important, inner exercises, when practiced with an
adult, give children an intuitive apprehension of their own
psychic anatomy plus an unshakable realization that mind and
body are linked, that one cannot operate or survive without
the other.

Here are some of the jobs your children can work at during
the months and years which will help prepare them for a
robust and responsible adulthood.

Cleaning One's Room

Since cleaning one's room introduces the idea of physical
work *and* service to the family unit, it's a great place to begin.
Every day like clockwork some type of pick-up activity takes
place in Tim's room: the bed gets made, toys are put back,
books and games are arranged into a semblance of order, all
as regularly as the sun rises and sets. If siblings co-occupy a
room, both should share in these chores. If children do not
have a room of their own they should be made responsible for
policing the areas where they sleep and play.

The best time to teach clean-up behavior is when a child is

very young. Two years old is a good age to begin. Toddlers can be encouraged to put blocks away or to throw dirty clothes into a hamper. Children can be trained to refrain from dropping objects on the living-room floor; they can be told that what comes off the shelf goes back on.

In the beginning do these chores with the child. Make it into a game. Find a wood or cardboard box and paint a picture of a friendly animal on its side. Then "feed the animal" by tossing toys into its "mouth." Children will love the idea of feeding a gobbling creature, as they will love the fact that they can throw their things across the room with impunity. After the child becomes accustomed to the idea of picking things up, you can phase yourself out of the picture and let the child do it all alone.

Make it clear that all family members in the house contribute their share of work to keep things tidy, that helping out with work is good, that neatness is practiced so we can know where our things are, and that everything in the world has its rightful place: books go on bookshelves, freshly laundered clothes in bureau drawers, stuffed bears on closet shelves. Just as the leaves live on the branches, just as the moon lives in the sky, so the objects we use in our room have their rightful place in the universe. Put them there.

Of course, one should also see the question of room-cleaning from the child's point of view. Possessing a primitive sense of orderliness at best and having, in their eyes at least, far more important things to do, most children will not understand why they must be bothered with the pestiferous business of housework. The prospect of cleaning an entire room from stem to stern seems an impossibly huge task to the mind of a six-year-old. Physical dimensions appear a lot larger to young eyes than to old, and what seems a quick, ten-minute fix to grownups represents an infinity of labor to the child (Remember how gigantic *your* house seemed at six?)

In response to these very understandable reservations, parents can ease the burden by breaking down room-cleaning jobs into modular chores. Each day a different pick-up task is required. Cleaning is less overwhelming to the child this way, and it gives parents more control. Make up a chart of daily chores and check off each as it is done. (This technique works best for children seven years and older.)

CHECK OFF WHEN DONE

Monday: Clean closest and empty wastebaskets
                  ▬

Tuesday: Put all books back on the bookcase
                  and pick up toys from floor ▬

Wednesday: Straighten closet ▬

Thursday: Pick up toys from floor and arrange
                  clothes neatly in bureau drawers ▬

Friday: Clean desk and all work-project areas.
                  Police areas under the bed and in
                  out-of-the-way spots ▬

Saturday: Pick up toys from floor and take dirty
                  laundry to wherever it goes in the
                  house or apartment ▬

Sunday: Holiday

Housework

Don't underestimate housework as a form of physical exercise *and* as a forum for teaching skills. Any hint of a sexual division of labor in this department is to be quickly discouraged. Both boys and girls should wash dishes, iron, fold clothes, launder, and prepare food in the kitchen along with doing the heavy chores. Let them learn these tasks not merely as a statement of sexual equality but because cooking a stew or sewing on a button will be a valuable talent to possess when the boy becomes a man.

At the same time, either sex can be assigned jobs that require the development of strength and perseverance. Let boys *and* girls carry out the garbage and mow the lawn. Help them become familiar with shop tools, snow shovels, and axes. Teach them to fix objects around the house. Encourage the practice of carpentry and mechanical skills. In a changing, uncertain world both sexes will find such skills invaluable when they are grown.

Some parents believe that children under seven are incapable of performing sophisticated household chores such as dishwashing or sweeping up. Experience has shown, however, that by six most kids are perfectly able to perform dozens of complex jobs and that with practice they can get pretty good at it. Make sure all jobs are, in fact, age-appropriate, of course, but don't be afraid to push the child a bit on this as well.

Here, in fact, an opportunity exists for parents to profit emotionally while children profit physically. When seven-year-old Tim washes the dishes, yes, a few glasses get broken now and then and the soap flies. When nine-year-old Bette vacuums, no, the house is not as clean as when you do it. When ten-year-old Val irons the shirts, he neglects the collars and cuffs. But remember, children are in training. Everything takes time, and while the process is in motion it's up to you to bite your tongue and even tell white lies when necessary. Stress the positive side of the child's achievements and keep mum over the disasters. Praise all real efforts. Children are trying. Give them their due. They will get better even as you become more patient. Eventually, they will become a real asset in the domestic department.

Outside Work

Jack Dempsey said that he learned to box by carrying rocks across an open field when he was a child. War correspondent Ernie Pyle remarked that the only way to learn how to take a beach when you're a man is to learn to plow a field when you're a boy. Exaggerations probably, but the point is well made.

Spend several afternoons outdoors with pick and shovel. Digging is one of the most intense of all exercises, and potentially one of the most interesting. It builds muscles, but it also teaches important lessons like balance and a sense of one's physical center. Children who spend time digging in a garden or field learn to distribute their weight and to coordinate their arms and legs. They come to understand the principles of leverage and the distribution of one's weight through concentrated movement.

You can even dig a hole in the ground just for the fun of it. The earth is a mysterious adventure, with its dank loam and furtive creatures that turn up in each shovelful. Once Tim and his father started digging they became intrigued to see how deep they could go. Tim's father said that if they kept on shoveling they might hit the Lost Dutchman Mine. As they removed shovelful after shovelful he entertained Tim with stories of buried gold and pirate treasure. Perhaps they might find some today.

Other Kinds of Work

Though kids may be resistant to the idea that work can be a meditation as well as a chore, repeated intimacy with exertion, rhythm, and an ultimate sense of accomplishment will slowly make work's spiritual effects known. The goal is to let love of work become a goal of its own and to introduce the child to the contemplative side of physical labor. Suggestions for activities include:

> • Neighborhood jobs. At nine or ten children can hire out to mow lawns, shovel snow, clean garages, do light yard work.
> • *Keeping a garden.* Let the child experience a full cycle of growth from the spading up of soil through the hoeing and planting, the weeding and maintenance, to the final harvesting. A whole universe of benefits can result from such an experience. God, a gardening grandfather once said to me, is a hoe and a shovel.
> • *Family work as a group.* This is an important one. At Paul's house Saturday morning is family worktime.

Paul, his younger sister, his mother, and his stepfather all do yard work together in their half-acre backyard. Paul is ten years old now, but he has been working in his yard since he was five. Not only has he become strong from the raking, shoveling, planting, cutting, and carrying but he has become familiar with the cycles of the seasons and the phases of the moon as well. In general, he feels more part of the earth and of the entire world of nature around him, even from this small daily effort.

HYGIENE

Like work, cleanliness is a subject that is not often covered in books on child raising. Perhaps there is not a whole lot to say on the subject beyond the obvious—wash your hands before eating, scrub behind your ears, brush your teeth, end of story.

True enough. But from a spiritual perspective cleanliness has a more important place in the educational agenda than just soap and water. Why? Because, religious teachings have always maintained, there is a correspondence between peoples' outer surfaces and their inner states. "Wash ye, make ye clean," Isaiah 1:16 commands, and then proceeds to make a connection between external cleanliness and purity of heart: "Put away the evil of your doings from before mine eyes; cease to do evil." Somehow, in some mystical way that we do not entirely understand, a clean body and a clean heart go together. "Who shall ascend into the hill of the Lord?" asks King David in the twenty-fourth Psalm. "He that hath clean hands," the answer comes back, "and a pure heart." Surely it is no accident that in Islam the devil is known as "the unclean one." Which may be one reason that, in both Islam and Hinduism, worshipers are obliged to perform a ritual washing before approaching prayer.

Personal cleanness is also connected to ideas of ecological purity and to veneration of nature. Certainly it is not far-fetched to assume that parents who don't hang kids up psychologically with a lot of cleanness do's and don'ts (as one parent recently explained it to me) are doing the earth a disservice, as well as their own children. For surely it is these same persons, deprived as youngsters of the cleanness ideal, who will one day fling their cream soda cans into the red-woods and dump their toxins on the beach.

A quite remarkable book entitled *Sanatana Dharma: An Elementary Text Book of Hindu Religion and Ethics,* written for children in India at the turn of the century, presents a panoramic vision of how young Hindus should be raised. Making little distinction between ordinary and religious life, its text includes long talks on such things as exercise, politics, ethics, and relations with parents, all seen from a religious perspective.

What's particularly interesting about this book is that an entire chapter is dedicated to the Hindu concept of *shaucham,* bodily purity. The featured point is that while lack of cleanness breeds disease, worse, it interferes with the subtle energies that are necessary for a child's spiritual progress. "The purity of our higher energy body depends on the magnetic currents in it," the *Sanatana Dharma* explains. "It is quickly affected by the magnetic properties of surrounding objects, and we have therefore to be careful to be scrupulously clean. Some plant-products and plants, while harmless to the physical body, are very injurious to the energy body. This body is also most seriously affected by alcoholic emanations and by the energy bodies of others."

According to the *Sanatana Dharma,* disease is a sign that some law of nature has been disregarded and, it tells us, "The wise ones—knowing that the laws of nature are the laws of God—treat obedience to [them] as a religious duty." Hence, believe the writers of this manual, "our visible bodies are composed of particles derived from the food we eat, the fluids we drink, the air we breathe, and on a more subtle level, from the constant rain of particles too tiny for us to see that fall on us from people and things around us. Everything around us, and still more, everything we touch and hold, gives us some of its particles and we give it some of ours. This means that real cleanness comes not only from careful grooming but from an awareness of where we are, what we touch, and how we behave. We must be clean, not only for our own sakes, but for the sake of others around us."

TEACHING CLEANLINESS

Best, as always, is the middle way. Teach cleanliness, of course, and teach it well and early. But teach it as a joy and privilege, not as a terrifying defense against an evil army of avenging bacilli that lurks behind every door and wall. Cleanliness, many of us have found, is best taught when it is presented as a sacred duty *and* as a human enjoyment, one that is pleasing to the higher powers and, like all virtues, makes us feel good in the bargain. Make it clear that baths are fun, that showers are refreshing, that a change of clothes can lift the spirits. I have drawn a good deal of inspiration from these lines on the subject taken from the Talmud: "Carefulness leads to cleanliness, cleanliness to purity, purity to humility, humility to saintliness, saintliness to fear of sin, fear of sin to holiness, and holiness to immortality."

TEACHING CHILDREN TO USE THEIR HANDS

Note that hobbies and crafts teach youngsters patience and stick-to-itiveness as side benefits. When building a birdhouse or repairing the cover of a book, children should be exhorted to *finish the job*. It doesn't matter how good it looks. The important thing is that it gets done, from start to finish. Discourage children from picking up a project, diddling with it, getting halfway through, then moving on to another diversion. If this habit is allowed now, later on it will promote dilettantism and lack of will. If necessary, give rewards for perserverance. Again, stress the importance of work as its own reward.

The following manual activities can all be easily learned by children and will all contribute to their betterment as adults:

Carpentry

Encourage and oversee easy carpentry projects such as a window box, a birdhouse, wooden figures, simple puppets, an easel, a drawing board, a wooden airplane, a toy box. One father told his children how in India there is a holiday each year in which carpenters bow to their tools and give them thanks. Also, how in older societies carpenters consider that each tool has a soul of its own and that if you befriend this soul it will help you in your work. The father encouraged his children to make friends with their own tools and to commune with them silently before beginning any job.

Sewing, Knitting, Weaving, Crocheting

If you have such skills you can start teaching your children when they are at least seven years old. Start with basic projects. Most hobby shops or sewing stores and even some variety stores sell starter kits for kids. After a while encourage your children to design their own patterns based on sacred symbols. If a youngster's interest is great you can take him or her to museums where prayer rugs or ritual costumes are on display.

Model-making

Model trains are still a favorite. So are model planes, which come in a wide variety of kits. Painting figurines is especially popular among older children today and is a wonderful way to learn craftsmanship and precision. Some parents help their children design entire dioramas, complete with figures, trees, mountains, buildings, and water—scenes from knighthood and chivalry, say, or great epics, even incidents from religious history.

Carving and Whittling

Children who are old enough to handle a jackknife will have hours of fun carving blocks of wood into simple animal figures or making spoons, mixing implements, walking sticks. Carving woods can be purchased from any sculpture supply store. Trips to the museum to study American Indian totem poles, Buddhist or Hindu statues, Islamic arabesques carved in wood, and the like, will add a spiritual flavor to this undertaking.

Pottery

Potting, either freestanding or on a wheel, offers excellent training in manual dexterity. You don't need a kiln to fire your child's plates, cups, figures. Many art supply stores now sell a variety of clay that can be baked in the kitchen oven. Nor should the traditional symbolism of the wheel (creation), the hands (the hands of the Creator), and the clay (flesh) go unexplained to children as they work.

Drawing

Lavish supplies of paper, crayons, pencils, and water colors should be kept on hand. Children will especially enjoy making drawings or paintings on large sheets of paper. Show them how to sketch simple forms like stick figures, mountains, trees, and water.

Calligraphy

Older children may be interested in learning the fascinating art of calligraphic handwriting. Classes are given in many schools, and books on the subject are plentiful. *A Calligraphy Manual for the Beginner* by Charles Pearce (published by the Pentalic Corporation and available at many art supply stores) is an excellent introduction for beginners.

ENDURANCE, FITNESS, AND STRENGTH

Children who work on a farm or who do heavy labor come by their work sense naturally and need little encouragement. But for the majority of today's children, confined to apartments or to suburban backyards, the only real lessons bodies receive in strength-building is from neighborhood play and from sports at school.

Sports are good in many ways, of course, though the potential dangers of contact games makes them less than ideal for developing true physical health. The competitive frenzy that surrounds them, moreover, assures that *someone's* heart is going to be broken. In many sports the egos of young winners become dangerously inflated, while the losers wallow in the shattered self-esteem the competitive system inevitably brings. In fact, sports in general seems almost intentionally engineered to promote swagger, conceit, and sneer on the part of winning participants—which is perhaps why in school most good athletes also have a reputation for being "stuck up." How then can vigor, self-confidence, and muscle power be achieved without straining the body or stunting the emotions? There are several ways.

Ordinary play

Just as baby animals develop strength and agility by cavorting with their brothers and sisters, so children's bodies become strong when they scramble around with their peers. Whenever possible, encourage children to be physically active, to run, tumble, roll, and wrestle. If you have a backyard, provide plenty of recreational equipment such as swings, climbing bars, and slides. A knotted rope hung from a tree for climbing, or an old tire for swinging are inexpensive ways to build strong limbs. Jump ropes and hopscotch courts are still favorites. So are home-made jungle gyms, safely installed ladders, shovels for digging, trees for climbing, punching bags for pounding, bicycles for pedaling, cables for swinging. Whatever *you* enjoyed most as a child your child will probably enjoy, too.

City dwellers have a more difficult task finding outdoor recreation spots, though most urban areas offer parks and playground facilities. Visit these as often as possible, and see to it that your children get a strenuous workout.

Notice how kids never seem able to sit still, how their hands and feet and heads are like perpetual-motion machines. This activity does not stem from nervousness (as it does with most adults) but from the inner force of growth energy, which wells up like a spring through the child's limbs and which is seeking constant expression in the form of exercise. Parents who keep their kids cooped up with toys and television all day long are in a sense hindering the course of nature as it yearns to express itself through the young persons limbs.

Exercise

Every child over five will benefit from some kind of formal exercise routine. Tim and his father were in the habit, even before their talks began, of taking ten minutes in the morning to do bends and stretches together. Facing one another, they practice touching toes, windmills, jumping jacks, knee bends, shoulder and neck revolutions, sit-ups, and push-ups. They end their short routine with three or four minutes of running in place and sometimes a little jogging.

For those inclined to more spiritually oriented exercises that stimulate the etheric energies of the body as well as stretch the muscles and joints, yoga and tai chi classes are becoming increasingly popular for children and come highly recommended. In the past two or three years several books have been published on this subject. In *My Magic Garden* by Ilse Klipper, for instance, the author shows how yogic postures can be adapted for use by the very young. Starting with standing and stretching positions, she proceeds to the more difficult lying and bending asanas. A few typical yogic postures inspired by Klipper's examples include these:

> • *The upward stretch.* Stand straight and tall. Have the child stetch the right arm up to the ceiling as far as it will comfortably go and hold it there for several moments. Give a good hard stretch, then bring the arm down and repeat with the left. Do ten stretches to the right side, ten to the left. Return hands to the sides and relax. Take several deep breaths.

• *The sun salute.* Stretch both arms straight up over your head, then bring them straight down in front of you, keeping the knees straight. Slowly try to touch your toes. Let your arms hang loose in this position for a count of ten. Don't strain more than you have to, but do try to touch your toes if you can. Now stand up again. Repeat several times, then relax.

• *The cat.* Kneel on your hands and knees. Pull in your stomach and breathe out. Arch your back up and let your head hang forward. Hold for a count of five, then breathe in, raise your head and straighten your back. Repeat this movement five times, then relax. Yogis call this posture the cat.

• *The cobra.* Lie on your stomach with your arms at your sides. Raise your head and torso and as you do move your hands in front of you so that they brace you as you push. Pushing with your hands, continue to raise your chest up from the floor as far as it will comfortably go. Count slowly to ten, then lower your body down and place your hands back at your sides. Relax. Repeat several times.

• *The rat.* Sit tailor-style or, if it's comfortable, in the half-lotus position. Keep the back straight. Slowly bend your head forward until your chin rests on your chest. Then roll your head to the left as far as it will go, hold it there comfortably for a count of five, and roll it to the right. Again, hold for a few beats. Then bring your head back to the forward position with chin on chest. Repeat three times. Take two deep breaths. Relax.

• *The head-knee pose.* Sit with your legs outstretched straight in front of you and your back straight. The back of your knees should touch the ground. Bring your arms straight up over your head, then slowly bring them down and *try* to touch your toes. Don't strain. Hold for a few seconds, then return to the starting position. Take several deep breaths. Repeat two or three times. Relax.

• *The mountain.* Sit in the tailor- or half-lotus position. Raise your hands above your head and bring your palms together in the prayer position. Inhale deeply, push your spine and chest upward as far as they can go, hold for several beats, exhale, and return to the normal sitting position. Repeat five times.

• *The back clasp.* Stand straight with your eyes ahead. Place your arms behind your back and clasp your hands. Without bending your knees and keeping your hands clasped, slowly bend over, pushing your chest out. As you bend your hands will naturally go up behind you. Try to lower your head so that you can look between your legs, keeping your arms stiff and straight as you do. Hold this posture for as long as you can, then slowly return to the standing position. Take a deep breath and repeat once.

Be sure to explain to young practitioners that the point of yogic exercises is not to see how far you can push yourself and not to prove that you can do them better than the other guy. The purpose is to stretch your muscles and joints so thoroughly that all your finer energies can circulate around them freely. Then you'll feel great and healthy and relaxed and happy.

If children begin a regimen of basic (and safe) yogic stretches and continue, they will remain limber in the areas that are stretched for the rest of their lives. If not, they will join the throngs of unsupple Westerners who cannot sit comfortably on the floor for three minutes at a time and who cannot touch their toes.

Martial Arts

If your child seems drawn to the fighting arts—or, conversely, if your child is small and timid and needs a confidence-builder—martial arts can sometimes help. But be cautious. The first prerequisite when searching for a good martial arts studio is not, as some suppose, the particular fighting system taught. It is the quality of the teacher.

Check out centers in your area that cater to children (many of them now do) and observe classes. Good teachers will have a winning way with children, but they will also stress the Oriental virtues of patience, stoicism, politeness, and nonviolence. A true martial art exists both as a self-defense and as a system of spiritual enlightenment. If you observe classes in which the teacher shouts "Kill!" (some do) or where a feeling of anger permeates the room (as it sometimes does), or where competition seems more important than cooperation (as it frequently is), shun them and keep searching. If it's meant to be, the right situation will come along.

Music and Dancing

While there are innumerable types of formal dance systems, the movements of youngsters under five years of age can still be said to come directly from the soul, and as such should not be tampered with. Turn the music on and just let them do their thing. At this age free form is fine. Just let them twirl.

As children reach six and seven, dancing can become more structured. Group thematic dancing is much enjoyed (playing galloping horses to the music or acting the part of a falling leaf in *Swan Lake*). Many young ones are happy with a minimum of supervision on the dance floor, and at this age a parent's job is to simply teach basic movements like turning, jumping, pirouetting, bending, and dipping. Some ideas for engaging children of this age in fun, creative, and appropriately strenuous dance activity include:

• Change records rapidly from a march to a waltz, to jazz, to symphony, to folk music and have children dance each changing mood.
• Play fast carnival-type music and have children pretend they are circus performers. Let them act out dif-

ferent routines: clown, high-wire performer, juggler, lion tamer, and so on.
  • Play music of different moods—slow, fast, happy, scary, brave, delirious—and have children make up a dance story for each.
  • Let children dance different animal personalities: a swan, a tiger, a chicken, a goldfish, a giraffe, a squirrel.
  • Let children pretend they are flower seeds being planted. Have them dance through the entire cycle of growth: sprouting, budding, flowering, wilting, returning to the earth.
  • Have children dance the parts of natural elements: fire, water, earth, and air. Have them dance the weather: rain, thunder, lightning, snow, sunshine.
  • Have children pretend they are visiting heaven. Have them move about in the clouds, talk to the angels, explore, as appropriate music plays (Bach? Monteverdi? The sitar?). Ask them what they see.

For children eight and up, real instruction in formal dance technique becomes appropriate. With so many popular songs targeted at the very young, as if to capture their psyches before their faculties of discrimination develop, children today are on intimate terms with rock music before they reach their teens. Usually, they like it—a lot.

Still, it may not be too late to counter the messages embedded in rock-and-roll dancing by introducing heart-oriented kinds of dance instead. Folk and square dancing are group enterprises that can be enjoyed once or twice a week by the entire family. The merry, nostalgic melodies have a way of working themselves into the soul of child and grownup alike and make an excellent buffer against the destructive forces of contemporary music.

Intentional Privation

A last method, this one reserved mainly for children eight and over, is the cultivation of intentional privation—learning to willingly go without.

For instance, providing there are no medical problems, parents might encourage a child over eight or nine to fast for several hours during the day. Going without breakfast, for instance, is a far more difficult task than most children imagine, and it can be an excellent exercise in self-restraint if done in an exploratory spirit. Be sure to let the child eat if and when he or she demands; be careful not to turn a benevolent experiment into an exercise in do-or-die.

Another exercise is to involve the child in an unusual and slightly uncomfortable voluntary activity. Tell him or her, for instance, to put on two shirts. Just go against what your body wants at this moment. Nothing extreme. Just gentle privation and voluntary effort. One day, for instance, when a young boy was leaving to go for a swim his mother suggested that he stay home, help out, and play with his baby sister instead. The decision was left up to the child, with no guilt-mongering about it. When he did choose this more difficult task, however, his mother was lavish in her priase, and she assured him that he would grow up just a little bit stronger now because of this decision.

Another instance: A father and son were on a bus. They had recently been talking about willpower, and the boy asked how a person develops it. The father noticed a candy bar in the boy's pocket. He reached over, took it out, and placed it on the boy's knee. You develop it by throwing this candy bar out the window, he said. Think you can do it?

In fact, he couldn't. He had been dreaming about chocolate all day. But though he was unable to marshal enough willpower to go against his desire, he remembered this incident and even tried to make up for it afterward by denying himself sodas and crunchy snacks when everyone else was enjoying them. Just a suggestion, but enough to plant a seed.

There are two persons in you, the boy's father explained. Yourself and your body. Sometimes both want the same thing. Fine. No problem. But when your body wants the candy and your inner self says no, that's when the struggle begins.

The easy way out is always to give your body what it wants. That's what most people do. But when you follow that road the body gradually takes over. In the end your other self, your higher self, becomes the body's slave.

But there is another way: Learn to deny your body from time to time and to control it with your mind and feelings. That's the harder way and the better way. Work on it.

LEARNING TO SIT STILL

The last and perhaps most difficult thing a child can ever learn to do is sit still. Quiet sitting among children flies in the face of nature and against the powerful growing force that is expanding in their nerves and blood.

And yet if a young person, say four years old or older, is trained to sit still for short moments at a time, then for longer periods, then for even longer periods, wonderful results can be seen. Quiet sitting stills the mind and introduces tranquility, a sensation that all living beings consciously and unconsciously strive toward. Later on, children's concentration will benefit, as will their ability to maintain attention and to hold a lengthy thought. Intelligence improves and so does patience. It's worth a try.

Start by having children close their eyes and sit for several moments without making a sound. Three- and four-year-olds will not last more than a few seconds at this, but they can do it, and their success is often a source of great pride for them. A year or so later these short moments can be expanded, and you can introduce certain meditative techniques along with the simple sitting. (Chapter 26 describes them in detail.)

The really helpful thing about learning to sit still, besides calming children down and paving the way for serious prayer and meditation, is that it helps cultivate a sense of *the mind mastering the body*. This, as religious communities have long known, is the most important skill anyone interested in spiritual development can ever attain.

In the long run, while strength and stamina will prepare a child for an active life at home and in the marketplace, control of the senses and physical desires will contribute to a far greater goal, that of transcending the body entirely and reuniting with the holy spirit within. All intelligent spiritual parenting should be undertaken with this central thought in mind: that the physical body, as wondrous and mysterious a work of Divine intelligence as it may be, is a vehicle for something far greater still. "I call a man passionless," wrote St. Simeon, "whose body is like a horse to its rider. When the horse rears and demands its feed, the rider reins him in and keeps him back to the trail. When the horse looks about and spies grass and hay and other lusty horses, the rider blinders his eyes and drives him steadily along to the final destination. And that destination is our spiritual home. So it must be for the soul and the body of man. So it must be that we all must be ridden home."

PART 4

A HOME
WITH A HEART:

Spiritualizing the
Child's Environment

13.

In My Room

Home is where the child is. For the first eleven or twelve years of life it is here that young ones will naturally *want* to be. The wanderlust starts later, during the teens. Until then, in the formative decade, youngsters will look to their dwelling as a haven and harbor and even as a kind of personal portrait of the way they think and feel about the world.

Thoughtful parents know this and adapt the household to suit the need. At its best this adaptation fosters a positive inner life for the child as well as an adjusted social existence. Better, it serves both simultaneously. There are many ways to negotiate these ends, and in this chapter we will meet some of the most effective.

IN MY ROOM

One of the Beach Boys' best-known recordings tells how when kids are feeling low and picked on, when they are frustrated by their friends and hit on by their parents, there is always a place they can go to find sanctuary: their room. Popular wisdom knows that a child's room is a child's castle, even if it is small or shared with a rampaging sibling. Parents will want to take advantage of this fact by making their young one's private territory a peaceful world with hints of higher things. Note:

• Children's' rooms will resonate a kind of spiritual positiveness when airy and clean, with ample windows and pleasantly colored walls. We know from scientific experiments that color and light in a living space have direct influence on an occupant's moods, and that certain colors (bright yellows, greens, and light blues, especially) have an uplifting effect on the human spirit.

Some parents paint clouds on the ceilings of their child's room or a sky filled with stars, planets, and a bright, smiling sun. Bright color, light, surprises, fun, these are the goals.

• Furnishings made of plastic, linoleum, metal, and formica may be aesthetically pleasing to many grownups, but they are inherently cold and unforgiving. Since we moderns live so far from nature anyway, why not reverse the trend for our children? Go with furnishings that speak of the earth, of wood and leaves—natural substances that help children feel cradled by the Divine forces of the earth, not exiled to a fictional world of synthetics and high tech.

To the extent possible, try decorating your child's space with organic substances such as wood, rattan, wicker, wool, cotton, cork, earth, and rock. Each natural substance has its own vibration and its own invisible message, many spiritually oriented parents believe. What the child touches and plays and sleeps next to at night has its subtle affects. As a friend of mine once remarked: "Forget about this matter-spirit separation: matter matters."

• Order and cleanliness are important gifts to give young children at any age. Start establishing the neatness precedent early by setting aside storage bins for specific toys: a basket for dolls, a basket for crayons and coloring books, a basket for blocks. Tidiness in a room subliminally contributes to a child's sense of world order and well-being.

· Photographic murals and paintings are exciting on a wall and add dimensions of whimsy to any child's room. But be careful when using life-size commercial pictures or large paste-on animal figures. Though such images appear benevolent to the grownup eye, even the most lovable three-foot-tall chipmunk can be transformed into a slithering ghoul at midnight by a young imagination. Reactions vary from child to child, and you'll know best in this department. In general, though, if your young ones are particularly impressionable do not minimize the nighttime terrors pictorial images can evoke. Remove any paintings, pasteups, or posters that display potentially threatening imagery and save them for next year.

THE DARK SIDE

Heirlooms and family furniture are appropriate objects to focus on when discussing the facts of mortality with a child. All things are in a stage of passing away, you can tell the child, and here is a good example. Point out how different your old tables and chairs are from modern furniture. Ask the child: Who made these old pieces? Where did these artists go? Do we even remember their names? Can we still see their faces? No, we can't. They have died and left behind only their artistic creations to be remembered by. They have passed away like all things; even these tables and chairs will pass away someday, too. Everything has its time to be born, to live, to die. This is a good place to then read the child the stirring words from Ecclesiastes 3: "To everything there is a season, and a time to every purpose under the heaven. A time to be born, and a time to die. . . ."

DECORATING THE ROOM

Room decorations—what you do with these is limited only by your imagination. Jan's father is an artist and has painted fantastic landscapes on Jan's bedroom walls. One depicts a fairy castle in the clouds, the other a grassy field with unicorns grazing and a blazing sunrise behind. Jan sits for hours gazing at these pictures and her imagination roams. For her the colors and images are reminiscent of a far-off place some-where, somehow, which is all good and which she believes she lived in long, long ago.

Eight-year-old Larry's father, a photographer, took a series of steel engravings from an old book of Greek myths, blew them up into life-size photostats, tinted them with watercol-ors, and pasted them on the walls and ceiling of Larry's room. Larry now wakes up in the morning to see Apollo's chariot riding across his ceiling, bringing the newly risen sun.

Eddy's parents—like Eddy—are fond of animals, but they live in a small apartment. So they purchased a fish tank with several tropical fish and made a corner of Eddy's room into an underwater fairyland complete with tank, rocks, bridges, multicolored gravel, several types of seaweed, porcelain mer-maids, and an armada of guppies. Eddy's father sometimes tells Eddy stories about his fish, about how they go on mystic quests to the land of the great sea king, and about how they, too, in their own way try to follow God's law.

WHAT THE EYE SEES, THE HEART SEES, TOO

What room and wall decorations will be most conducive to a child's spiritual strengthening? Inspiring images might in-clude beautiful landscapes, images from mythology and reli-gious cosmology, fantastic tableaux, scenes from mysterious far-off lands, gilded temples, old photographs, artistic photo-graphs, whimsical old book jackets or magazine covers, knights in armor and fair maids, illustrations clipped from children's' books or old children's magazines, tender draw-ings from fairy stories, farmyard scenes, pictures of animals and children and nature.

Family photographs and portraits provide children a connection to their own past and to their ancestors. Florence, mother of six-year-old Ann, placed a picture of herself as a child in Ann's room along with photos of Ann's grand- and great-grandparents. Florence often finds her daughter staring at these pictures or talking to them quietly. They have proved an excellent focus point when Ann asks about her family's past, as all children eventually do, or when the subject of the family tree comes up. Florence tells her daughter how our ancestors are all, in a way, still alive and inside us right now in spirit, and how we should remember them and thank them when we say our prayers.

What a child sees every morning and goes to bed looking at at night counts. I recently heard a strange tale from a neighbor, the mother of a ten-year-old boy named Vincent. While in her early twenties, it seems, this woman traveled through remote areas of Romania. During her journey she visited a small cathedral that housed a crucifix famous among the local inhabitants for its alleged healing qualities. She was so moved by the sight that she purchased several postcards of it from a local vendor. One day some years later she came upon these pictures in her desk drawer, framed them, and hung them on Vincent's wall. She explained to Vincent that in Romania people pray to this image for help when they are sick and that certain worshipers have reportedly been healed by it of very serious conditions like blindness and cancer.

Several weeks later Vincent told his mother about a dream. Almost embarrassed, he said that he had been praying to the picture of Christ (Vincent's family are not Catholic). He then announced that the Christ figure in the postcard had come down to him in this dream and told him that He, Christ, was the Savior; that He, Christ, was watching over Vincent; and that when Vincent grew up he should strive to become a man of God. "Pray," the image had said to him in a very clear voice, "and don't forget me."

Was this dream real? Vincent wanted to know. His mother said that as far as she understood it sacred images sometime have a mysterious power of their own and that sometimes, yes, if we're lucky this power can come "out" of an image and speak to us. Yes, she had heard of such things happening in dreams, though she herself had never experienced them and certainly did not understand them. How lucky Vincent was, she said, to have such a magical picture in his room. Vincent agreed.

A QUIET TIME IN A SPECIAL PLACE

All children have the right to privacy and silence. More specifically, they have the right to a time during the day when they can sit alone or in the quiet company of a parent, and simply *be*.

In six-year-old David's house his parents have instituted what they call "the quiet time." The quiet time takes place for five to ten minutes before bed. This meditative pause is held in David's "quiet place," which—in this instance and by David's choosing—is located near a window in his room where he has placed several plants and a much-loved portrait of his parents' spiritual teacher.

The quiet time is an excellent way to introduce young minds to turning inward and to the discipline of sitting still. Parents can establish a similar routine with their own children:

1. Institute the first session of the quiet time when the child is very young. Four years old is about right, though some parents start earlier.

2. At first the quiet time should run no more than thirty seconds to a minute. Even a four-year-old can sit still this long.

3. Keep at it. Four times a week is not too often to have a quiet time. The idea is to incorporate sittings into the routine, so that the child comes to expect them and eventually to look forward to them. This way the meditative habit becomes incorporated into the child's life in a natural way.

4. A form of quiet time can be practiced with toddlers, but in an abbreviated way. Approach them during a quiet moment

of play, distract them, and fasten their attention onto you or onto a interesting object. Hold their gaze for five seconds, maybe ten, then stop. Do the same thing several times a day—herein is the beginning of concentration. Hazrat Inayat Khan elaborates on this method: "When an infant reaches the age of two or three years, it is most beneficial if it is taught a moment of silence. But one might say, 'How can a silence be taught?' A silence can be taught by attracting an infant's attention very keenly, and this can be done by rhythm. When you make a certain noise by clapping your hands or by making a rhythm, and when you attract the attention of an infant fully, then if you wish it to be inactive, you can hold it in an inactive condition for a moment; and that can do a great deal of good. It could become a kind of religious or esoteric education from infancy. If an infant can keep his eyes from blinking, and his breath and the movement of his hands and legs suspended for one moment, it accomplishes even at that age a meditation."[1]

14.

Choosing Toys

In this era of Barbie clones and colosseum-sized toy stores it becomes increasingly difficult to know what playthings are right for children. Yet wholesome guidelines *can* be established, especially if parents are in accord with the belief that what children use as playthings determines, to a certain extent, what they will become. This chapter contains suggestions for evaluating toys from a qualitative and sometimes a spiritual perspective.

APPEARANCES DO MATTER

If playthings are frightening, ugly, gaudy, vapid, or useless they will leave a similar imprint on the child's soul. Beauty is said to be only skin deep, but the sages know differently. "God is beautiful and He loves beauty," the Prophet Muhammad is recorded to have said. "Let our artists be those who are gifted to discern the true nature of the beautiful and graceful," wrote Plato in *The Republic*. "Then will our youth dwell in a land of health, amid fair sights and sounds, and receive the good in everything: and beauty, the result of fair works, shall flow into the eye and ear, like a health-giving breeze from a purer region, and insensibly draw the soul from earliest years into likeness and sympathy with the beauty of reason."

Ask yourself:

> • Are the toy's colors harmonious? Are its proportions pleasing? Is it sturdy and well made? Does it seem to have been designed by someone who really cares about children or is it simply another assembly-line geegaw?
>
> • Does the toy have overtones of beauty or wisdom inherent in it—in its materials, in its form and surfaces, in the use it can be put to by the child? Does it teach a lesson in balance, intelligence, affection, discrimination, values? Or does it just sit there and look cute?
>
> • If the toy is a figure or doll, is its expression benevolent and trusting or does it have a masklike automaton's face? Masklike, automaton dolls whisper to children that their own faces should look the same way. Perhaps it is no accident that the Barbie-doll look has become a standard of feminine beauty today among the several generations of females who grew up playing with such figures.

Hannah, mother of three, recalls the critical effect a beloved doll had on her emotions while she was very young. "When I was a child growing up in Missouri," she relates, "there was plenty of prejudice all around me against black people. It was everywhere. At this time the radio program "Amos and Andy" was very popular and a toy company had come out with a black doll called Amosina, named after Amos. I begged my mother to buy it for me, and after I hounded her for months she finally gave in.

"When I got the doll home I quickly came to love it more than any of my others. I had it for years. Even though its head got cracked in several spots and it lost an arm and most of its hair, I always slept with Amosina at night and whispered my secrets to her. I also managed to grow up in my prejudice-ridden neighborhood without developing any of the negative feelings towards black people which most of my schoolmates had. One of the main reasons for this, I still believe, is because I loved and cared for that little black doll so much."

A MUSLIM VIEW ON TOYS

Although emphasis on the qualitative element in toy selection is often neglected by parents and educators, its importance has been well noted by different spiritually oriented groups—including, among others, The Muslim Student's Association of the United States and Canada, an organization made up of Muslims who have emigrated to the United States from Eastern countries. The purpose of this organization is to help fellow Muslims maintain their religious integrity while living in a society that holds values considerably different from their own. In the association's worthy booklet "Parents' Manual: A Guide for Muslim Parents Living in North America," the writers give special emphasis to the spiritual significance of toys. Though written from a Muslim point of view, the advice offered will be of interest for all spiritually minded parents and is quoted here at length:

> *What sort of toys should we Muslim parents buy for our children? We should in general be guided by the child's needs and interests, remembering that one good, sturdy toy is better than a dozen cheap, flimsy ones which fall apart after being used for a short time. . . . And we need not confine ourselves to commercial toys. The mother who has the time, interest and skill can make interesting and lovely playthings for her children, particularly ones which will help to foster their budding sense of being Muslim and will train them in Islamic ways of thinking and responding even through their play. For such homemade playthings, imagination and creativity are the main requisites. Here*

are a few general suggestions for commercial toys which are of interest and value:

• Skill building, educational toys for the young mind rather than toys which do not teach but merely provide entertainment.

• Building, designing and construction toys of durable quality which can be used for many purposes.

• Dolls and stuffed animals which do not vulgarize the human face and form (i.e., baby dolls should look like babies, not like coy and flirtatious teen-agers). There are very appealing ones available which cost the same or only slightly more than ugly and vulgar ones.

• Toys or equipment for making interesting and beautiful objects, which foster genuine creativity and originality. These are much preferable to toys offering a synthetic "creativity" such as "color-by number" sets or handicraft kits with pre-fabricated designs, etc.

• Coloring books and paper dolls which do not reflect [unreligious] values.

• Scientific sets or instruments which the maturing youngsters can use to increase their knowledge of the natural world.

• Models of various sorts which help the child build skills at doing precise, detailed work and familiarize them with the functioning of cars, planes, ships, rockets.

• Bicycles, swings and slides, roller skates and other useful equipment for outdoor play. Collections of rocks, fossils, shells and stamps, postcards and other items of interest. Puzzles and games which build skills rather than ones which merely pass time.

• Books and more books, both fiction and non-fiction of good quality.

• What toys should we avoid? . . .
Specifically, try to avoid the following:

• Toys which teach un-Islamic values and attitudes,

such as dolls and paper dolls which feature immodest fashions and the main function of which is to be preoccupied with dress or sex. This includes teen-age dolls of both sexes which are very repugnant to the idea of modesty and decency. Also make-up kits, hair-styling sets, wigs, etc. . . .

• Garish, vulgar and bizarre toys which play up a sense of ugliness and cheapness of human beings, or diabolical and sinister toys and masks which degrade humanity.

• War-type toys in the hands of a small child only result in expressions of unchannelized violence.

• Games having cut-throat competition or doing-in others as their goals, games which teach irreligious values or behavior, and meaningless games which simply pass time without teaching anything useful.

• Most comic books. All flimsy, poorly made toys which can be dangerous, especially for the young child.[1]

TOYS SHOULD SERVE A PURPOSE

Playthings that stimulate the mind and emotions, that inspire the child to build, to carry, to serve, to become strong, to experiment, to nurture, to create, to discriminate, to feel, to make effort, to figure out—these are best. Blocks, crayons, coloring books, dolls, books. Paints, Lego sets, stuffed animals, puzzles, craft kits. Cooking stoves, punching bags, dollhouses, toolboxes, musical instruments. Balls, bats, magic sets, costumes, puppets, blackboards, tricycles, tents.

While toys should play a teaching role for children, beware the "educational toy" fetish. This ploy in some instances can be nothing more than a slick merchandising trick that toy cartels have cooked up over the years to impose on parents a sense of guilt-ridden necessity: "Will my child be able to keep up if I don't buy this computer program? Or this voice-activated automaton doll? Or this mechanical speller?"

In fact, all good objects of play educate children as a matter of course. Learning is provided in an organic way, but only if we think of education as a process in which children learn about themselves and about their immediate environment, not just about state capitals. Using this definition, most of the playthings mentioned above fit into the educational niche. No need to look further afield.

Wonderful, too, are toys that teach children service and caring. A tank of goldfish or a terrarium that must be tended is ideal for training children over five years to take care of living creatures. Many young people will ask to have potted plants by their windows; this request should be quickly honored, even though you will probably end up with many of the watering duties yourself. Something will still rub off.

These objects are useful because they show the value of work and activity and beauty. They say to the child: It's good to build, and to think, and to consider, and to take care of things, and to appreciate fineness in God's great world. Life is for learning and striving; life has meaning *in* the striving.

Some children love to collect objects in nature like wild flowers, mosses, leaves, dead insects, snakeskins, pinecones, acorns, driftwood, dried plants, shells, or bark and to set them out for others to see. These and similar items can be placed in a section of the room kept especially for display, with signs to proudly identify each.

Parents can speak to youngsters, who are drawn to nature and to collecting natural specimens, about the fact that in many religions, especially among the American Indians, the natural world is looked on as a kind of living cathedral furnished everywhere with symbols of the Great Spirit. See how the tree's branches open to the sky, a parent tells a child, as if straining to reach heaven? See the day and night following one another, signs of the seasons, light and dark, and the ever-turning wheel of birth and death. Hear the bird's song. In the evening it is a prayer, at sunrise a matin. Watch how the clouds melt one into another, like the always-changing activities of our own transient lives. And the mountains, em-

blems of eternity; on them trees and waters and wild life move
ceaselessly about as if to symbolize the ever-changing phe-
nomenal world superimposed upon the infinite; as if to give
reality to the Buddhist saying "Samsarma is nirvana, nirvana
is samsarma."

TOYS SHOULD SPEAK TO THE HEART

Assess a toy for its emotional quality as well as its entertainment value. What kind of feelings will it evoke in a child? Does
it speak of kindness, constructiveness, service? Is its message
positive? Is it destructive or violent? Sleazy or sexually seductive? Wasteful? Is it loveless? Will it corrupt?

At their best, toys are spiritual counselors, their very form
functioning as a mirror for sacred truths. Allen Wooten,
writer, beloved grade-school teacher, and a man who always
attempted to put an extra "something" into his lessons, used
to point out to the parents of his students that the most
mundane toys contain hidden spiritual lessons. "Ordinary
building blocks," he would say, "are models of the building
blocks of the universe. Let a child put together a puzzle and
the child sees how in God's world it takes all the parts to make
a whole. Let the child build and the child will see unity forming before his eyes." Taking care of a doll, Wooten would say,
dressing it, putting it to sleep, loving it, shows children something of the way the universe cares for its own creatures.
Planting a seed and watching it grow, ripen, wither, and die
speaks to the child of the cycle of life and death.

When choosing toys try this. Stand in front of the object for
a moment or two, then close your eyes and try to sense it from
the inside. Let it speak to you. Hear its message. The toy in
question was conceived by human thought, designed by
human intelligence, and built by human contrivance. During
its construction something of its creator was put into it,
something of the designer's thoughts and emotions. This is
the message you're listening for now. Hear to it with your
feelings. Then judge.

SIMPLE AND LESS ARE BETTER
THAN COMPLEX AND MORE

Encourage children to invent their own toys. Encourage them to make playthings out of everyday objects. A wooden bowl will do quite well for a child under three. Or a hose nozzle, an empty soapbox, an old chessboard, some sand or string.

"There's no question but that most toy purchases are a matter of parental weakness," wrote Polly Berrien Berends in a chapter on toys in her popular *Whole Child/Whole Parent*. "If we pay attention we can find many ways to amuse and educate our children (of any age) with things that are already in the house. Furthermore, our children like to use our 'real' things because they are trying to grow up into real people and accomplish real ends. . . . One of the loveliest Christmas gifts I ever heard of was a scrap of cloth with four buttons sewn on. A two-and-a-half-year-old child had sewn them on, taught secretly by her eleven-year-old sister. There are so many little things our children would learn with joy if we did not view them as dull work, too hard for the child, or too time-consuming for us. He is often happiest (and least bothersome) by our side doing some modified version of whatever we are doing."[2]

In parts of Thailand and Burma children are not given toys until they are eight or nine years old. Instead, they are provided with the raw materials, stones, shells, paper, bundles of straw, gourds filled with chick-peas, pieces of wood. They are then encouraged to make their own playthings. Soon twigs end up being used to build dollhouses. Rattan sacks are stuffed with grass to make dolls. Dried beans and peas turn into marbles. Branches become javelins to pierce the undergrowth. Contrast this seeming "poverty" of the Southeast Asian child, who must rely on imagination and ingenuity, with the cluttered and surfeited bedrooms of American children running out of storage room for all the toys their parents have bought them. The result of this surfeit is, of course, boredom—a very unspiritual state.

To a toddler a banana, a diamond, and a plastic shovel are

all equally fascinating. When two-and-a-half-year-old Wendy
is in the kitchen she plays with water. This makes her happy.
When she is in the backyard her father shows her how to dig
in the soil. This makes her happy, too. Wooden cups, rocks,
dried flowers, spoons, flowerpots and potting soil are all toys
to Wendy. The world is her toy. Parents, in fact, are often
bemused to see that the toys they have spent so much money
purchasing are often the first to be forgotten while an empty
thread spool or an old hat totally absorbs a child's attention.
A little poem by C. S. Jennison says it all:

> I bought my daughter the kind of doll
> A parent is proud to bring.
> She opened her toy with cries of joy
> . . . And played all day with the string.
>
> She said she wanted to build a house.
> So I got her a set of blocks.
> The present, I guess, was a great success
> . . . She built a house with the box!

It is only later, from four to six, that a child's ability to be
entertained by simple things dies and is replaced by the seeking after new entertainments and ever new items of play.
Careful parents can stem the tide for a while by:

   · Shopping for toys carefully. Think and consider
before you pick one off the shelf. Ask yourself if the
child really needs it or even really wants it.
   · Keeping children sheltered from advertisements,
stores, toy catalogs, toy commercials, and massive toy
displays.
   · Encouraging play with other children whose parents view the toy situation as you do and whose house
is not laden with wall-to-wall store-bought monstrosi-
ties.
   · Staying away from the supermarket toy stores.
Shop instead at the smaller, better stores that special-

ize in wooden toys, quality imported items, nonviolent toys, and the like. (Childcraft, 20 Kilmer Road, Edison, New Jersey 08818, for instance, offers a wide selection of first-rate playthings. Write directly for their catalog.)

LEAVE ROOM FOR YOUR CHILD'S IMAGINATION

Rudolph Steiner and his followers maintain that to earn its keep a particular toy must always leave something to the child's imagination. Dolls make the best toys, Steiner claimed, when their faces are not entirely delineated. Dots for eyes and a curving line for a mouth are all that is required. Children's mental creative powers will fill in the missing features, creating eyes and ears and mouths in their mind's eye. In this way the perceptive faculties are strengthened and expanded.

The same goes for, say, toy vehicles. A slick, plastic item that includes every bumper line and door handle is exciting to children, but like television or a comic book it leaves little to the imagination. Better is a plain wooden car that contains only a hint of windows and wheels. From this point on a child's perceptive faculties will take over and make this object into a chariot, a truck, a space vehicle—or just a car. The creative faculties are exercised, and that's good. Later on this same power of imagination and visualization will be used for prayer and meditation.

KEEP ALL TOYS AGE-APPROPRIATE

Which toys are best for which ages? Here are some guidelines:

Infants

Play objects that develop grip such as rattles, stuffed animals, and squeeze toys are most appropriate for infants, as are teething toys, preferably those made out of fiber or wood. As soon as the child begins to crawl and investigate the world, let the four elements become the featured entertainments.

Playthings made from natural objects like water, wood, clay, and straw will develop tactile senses and provide a gentle introduction to the chemistry of the universe. In the bathtub pieces of wood make top-notch boats and sponges are excellent fish.

Toddlers

Toddlers will enjoy around-the-house and kitchen items. Keep materials natural and gentle: wooden spoons for mixing water, fresh fruits and vegetables for squeezing and stroking, flour for sifting, wet cornstarch for kneading (it makes a wonderful substitute for Play Dough), sandboxes with an ample supply of digging tools and clean sand. Toddlers enjoy large cardboard boxes and wheeled wooden animals.

C. N. Getman claims in *How to Develop Your Child's Intelligence* that the toy that holds a preschooler's attention more than any other is the ordinary coffee percolator. It can be used in the sandbox as a kind of nested block game, in the bathtub, at the lake, even in kindergarden class. "It provides eye-hand experience," Getman writes, "in shapes, sizes, textures, temperature, inside or outside, curved or flat, top or bottom, light or heavy (when empty or full), and is very durable."[3] Dolls, beanbag chairs, foam-rubber bouncing items, balloons, ribbons, rubber bands, blocks of wood, simple puzzles, and tents will all get played with at this age. Be careful of sharp edges and of objects that can be swallowed.

Three- and Four-Year-Olds

Most of the above toys are appropriate for threes and fours as well, but now horizons are expanded. For youngsters, who are past the pop-everything-in-the-mouth stage, chalk and crayons can be introduced, along with basic art materials: clay, fingerpaints, colored paper, Play Dough, child's scissors, and drawing paper. Children at this age enjoy having their own work area for creative enterprises. A desk or small space with nearby shelves to hold essential equipment will be welcome. Outdoors, large-muscle-development equipment such as swings, slides, and climbing ropes are good. Wooden blocks, tricycles, wagons, rocking horses, large pull toys, musical instruments, puzzles, record players, and tape recorders with story tapes are all appropriate for this age.

Four- to Six-Year-Olds

More of the same, but increasingly sophisticated. Puzzles are more complicated now, blocks more challenging (Legos, Tinkertoys, Lincoln Logs). Dolls, tea sets, play kitchenware, magnetic boards with letters. Doctor and nurse kits, too. Pegboard toys are good, as are miniature figures of all kinds: farm animals, circus performers, athletes, horses and riders. Dollhouses are a bit too advanced for this age and are usually not appreciated until later.

For children four through six, refrigerators and stoves cut by parents out of cardboard boxes will delight and entertain; allow children to paint on pictures of knobs, handles, and accessories. Cutting and pasting are fun, as are digging activities, gardening, pounding and pull toys, and simple tools like hammers and screwdrivers. Board games of skill like dominos and checkers can be started. Mattresses can be set up as forts, card tables hold blankets to make bedroom tents. Scrapbooks can be kept and dedicated to specific subjects like animals, flowers, or even religious subjects.

Seven to Eleven

Progressively more advanced. Science projects can start in earnest around the seventh year and science toys such as magnets, microscopes, telescopes, and binoculars will fall on fertile ground during the eighth or ninth years, depending on the child's inclination. At this time the sense of wonder really begins to awaken, and science is often the best way to nourish it. Do try and keep the stress away from high tech for its own sake, however, and concentrate instead on science as a door to the wonders of Divine Creation.

Complex games like checkers, chess, or backgammon can be pursued now. The toolbox should expand too, and the quality of the tools themselves can be upgraded, allowing children to make shop items such as shelves, tables, boxes, lamps, basic dollhouses. Advanced art projects are now possible: mobiles, puppets, doll construction, dollhouse furniture. Crafts like knitting, sculpting, clay-figure modeling, bookbinding, leather tooling, mosaic work, linoleum prints, and needlepoint can be started when the child turns six or seven.

From here on the toys children play with will, to a large extent, start preparing them for their adult life and should be selected and purchased accordingly.

15.

Making the Home into Sacred Ground

A family attempting to raise children in a devotional way will want to make its entire dwelling into a kind of sanctuary. Not literally, of course, but psychically a sanctuary: a humble, reverent, gracious place, the type of setting where outsiders will feel the presence of something clean and austere and righteous, something essentially good.

This ancient idea, that a family home is sacred ground and that its arrangement in some mysterious way reflects the cosmos around it, seems a difficult vision to our modern mentalities. Yet in numerous civilizations the idea is still taken quite literally. Many Southwestern American Indian families, for example, continue to enter and leave their hogans from a top entrance known as the sun door. The windows of their dwelling are aimed at the four cardinal directions; these symbolize the four elements and the four sacred tribal colors. The fire that permanently smolders on the floor is symbolic of the sacred flame that burns in the hearts of all human beings. When the father prays in front of it he is renewing both his own home and the entire community. When the mother tends the flame she does so with the assumption that she is maintaining the home fires given to her tribe eons ago by the Supreme God.

"Each part of the tipi has a meaning," explains Henry Old Coyote, recalling the hidden symbolism of the Crow Indian dwelling:

> As you face east, the left smoke flap represents the spirit of the owl who watches over the tipi at night; the right flap represents the spirit of the coyote who watches over the tipi by day. The owl and coyote are sentries; the bear and mountain lion are protectors. In addition, the base pole that faces northeast represents the spirit that controls the day coming over from the east; the one that faces southeast, the eternal summer; the one facing southwest, the point where people leave the world and follow the Old Man over the horizon; and the one to the northwest represents the eternal winter, where the weather comes and freshens the earth. They also represent the four seasons of the year. [1]

In many other traditional civilizations we find similar beliefs that the home is a minimodel of the world, and that, as the ancient hermetical code puts it, "That which is above in heaven is also like that which is below on earth." There is, in other words, plenty of precedent for making your family dwelling into more than just a place to eat and sleep.

Music

Besides its amusement value, music delivers subtle spiritual messages that cannot be conveyed in words. The doleful tunes heard in, say, Peruvian flute music communicate centuries of pain yet they also imply a kind of nobility, a zest for life, and patience. Black spirituals tell of life's injustices and of belief in a better world to come. Syncopated jazz rhythms hint at the strangeness and changeability of the universe and of the illusion that underlies our assumed sense of a fixed world.

What kind of music best conveys the messages you would

like your children to hear? If the truth be told, youngsters usually find Bach, Beethoven, Brahms, and company too complex. (There are exceptions, though I have rarely come across them.) Many children do, however, derive a kind of euphoria, brief perhaps, from light classical music, from waltzes, polkas, marches, and late-nineteenth-century romantic works.

A sample of light classical compositions that evoke this spurt of feelings and to which children will often lend willing ears include:

> *The Nutcracker Suite* and *The 1812 Overture* by Tchaikovsky
> *The Sorcerer's Apprentice* by Dukas
> *Marche Militaire* by Shubert
> *Carnival of the Animals* by Saint-Saëns
> *Night on Bald Mountain* by Moussorgsky
> *Peter and the Wolf* by Prokofiev
> *Roman Carnival Overture* by Berlioz
> *Billy the Kid* by Copland
> *The Grand Canyon Suite* by Grofé
> *The William Tell Overture* by Rossini
> *Hungarian Rhapsodies* by Liszt
> *Scheherazade* by Rimsky-Korsakov
> *The Firebird* by Stravinsky
> *Water Music* by Handel
> *Rhapsody in Blue* by Gershwin
> *The Peer Gynt suites* and *Piano Concerto in A Minor* by Grieg
> *The "New World" Symphony* by Dvořák
> *Gaîté Parisienne* by Offenbach

Any overture by Rossini is popular with kids. Also banjo music, light, happy tunes on the flute, skiffle groups, some forms of jazz (though usually only with older kids), and, from operetta, much of Gilbert and Sullivan, especially *The Mikado* and *The Pirates of Penzance.*

Other favorites that speak to the young heart include folk music, ragtime (try Scott Joplin first), ethnic folk dances (especially from the Balkans), bluegrass, "singalongs" (remem-

ber Mitch Miller?—kids still love his stuff when they hear it),
steel drums, bagpipe bands, German hiking tunes, Irish melodies—try them all and see.

Music of a more specifically spiritual nature such as
Gregorian chants, Buddhist temple gongs, Indian ragas, Indonesian gamelan, and the like may seem too strange and
cacophonous for youngsters. Still, it doesn't hurt to try. Religious and New Age music I have seen my own and other
children respond to include:

> *Buddhist Drums, Bells and Gongs* (a good recording by
> Lyrichord)
> Sufi music (try *Turkish Sufi Music* or *Moroccan Sufi Music,*
> both by Lyrichord)
> *Drums of West Africa* (Lyrichord)

Some followers of the Hindu teacher Muktananda encourage their children to listen to tapes or records of the Master's
chants. *Om Namah Sivaya* is popular.

Jazz musician Paul Horn has recorded a number of slow,
mystical horn solos in shrines throughout the world, including the Pyramids, Gothic cathedrals, and the Taj Mahal. His
music sometimes has just enough melodic line to capture's a
child's attention. The same is true of the fascinating and
otherworldly music of Paul Winter (try his *Common Ground* and
Icarus).

For Tibetan temple music, try *Tibetan Ritual Music* (Lyrichord).

For something airy and at the same time soulful there is the
music of *Zamfir, King of the Pan Flute,* (Mercury).

A good sampling of sacred Chinese music can be heard on
Ancient Melodies played by Cheng Si Sum (Lyrichord).

New Age music is a new musical genre that comes in many
styles and in many grades of quality. It is showing up now at
health food stores and New Age book shops as well as at the
record counter. The music of Stephen Halpern *(Crystal Suite*
and *Dawn)* is relaxing for some children and can help restless
sleepers get comfortable at night. Acoustic Alchemy's music
(*Natural Elements* and *Red Dust and Spanish lace* [MCAC]) is

worth a shot. So are the captivating sounds of David Naegele, especially *Dreamscapes— Higher Consciousness Music.* A group called Nature Recordings has made several soothing cuts of natural sounds (like rushing mountain streams) that make relaxing listening. Max Highstein and Jill André's recording of *The Healing Waterfall—A Guided Musical Journey* was a favorite of my own daughters. The Conscious Living Foundation (P.O. Box 9, Drain, OR 97435) sells a number of music and speech tapes designed to help children sleep better and overcome tension. Write them directly for a catalog.

Though the above list represents only a sampling, you may be pleasantly surprised at how well children respond to unusual music, especially after they have heard the same piece played several times. They will get even more out of this music if parents clap along or stand up now and then in the middle of a happy tune and do a little dance with the child (most music worth listening to can be danced to as well).

If your family is of a certain ethnicity, folk songs from the Old Country will put young ones in spiritual touch with their past. Joshua's grandfather lives in Israel and visits the United States every year. When he comes he brings Joshua records of popular Israeli folk and religious singers. Joshua now has a sizable collection, and listening to them he has learned several Hebrew songs by heart. Mujdabah, a Persian teenager whose family emigrated to this country from Iran shortly after the Iranian Revolution, was only four when he arrived. One way his parents have kept his memories of Iranian life alive is by playing records and tapes of Persian music in their home.

Even if a child's roots are not in Iran or Israel, exposure to ethnic music can be a subtle way of introducing children to the radiance of older cultures. That's why every week eight-year-old Ralph and his mother walk to the library, where they borrow taped music from foreign lands. They listen to these recordings at home and then talk over their impressions. Ralph has found that the music of certain countries speaks to his heart; the music of others leaves him cold. Ralph's mother explained that when we hear music from a particular country, or taste its food, or see its art, we sometimes get the strange feeling we have been there already.

This is all part of the mystery of life, his mother explained. Some religions believe that human beings are born over and over again in different times and places, and that some of us can remember these past lives. Ralph and his mother then launched into a discussion of death, afterlife, and reincarnation.

Books in the Home

Keep good books around. Just have them in the home. They have their own vibrations and their own benevolent influences. The child may look at them or not. No matter, the books will make their silent mark, especially the sacred ones. Have books on your shelf about roadbuilding and jewels, books on snow and ice, books on soldiers and dolls and printing, and on computers, Egypt, whittling, and ESP, books about antique furniture and pigmies and how the West was won and how to cook a wolf, big books, homely books, dictionaries, grammars, encyclopedias with lots of neat pictures (*The World Book* is especially good for inquiring kids), books on tools and tropical fish, fairy tales, volumes on rodents and the lives of great men and women, books on baseball and fire and heaven and hell, and life in the nineteenth-century Adirondacks. Keep old books, leather-bound oddities, fine bindings and antique monsters redolent of the past, and books about exotic locales that stir interest in ideas that eventually set a person looking for the Truth: science, art, music, philosophy, and nature. Books, books, books. Just have them.

The same with magazines. Copies of *National Geographic* have piqued children's interest in the exotic and mysterious for a century. *National Geographic*'s picture/nature magazine *World* does the same thing on a level specifically for children. Nature magazines like *Natural History* also are filled with images of God's wonderful earth. Science magazines are popular among teens and can speak to the parts of the young mind that feel awe and wonder. Explore on your own. Check out the newsstands for the latest periodicals, both for adults and children. Subscribe to magazines that seem to jog the right parts of your child's mind and imagination. The idea is to simply have good reading matter available around the house. Children learn best by osmosis.

Pets

Animals are people too, as the saying goes, and can add a happy emotional flavor to a home. Learning to take responsibility for a pet is good practice in giving nurturance and is certainly one good way of introducing youngsters to the ideal of service. And, no doubt about it, love for an animal can open a child's heart.

But there is something else, too, that should be considered by parents who are trying to bring their child up with a sense of spiritual perspective. Many people engaged in spiritual pursuits do not always wholeheartedly agree that having animals in the house is in a child's best interests. Animals are inevitably dirty and destructive. They often cause allergies and sometimes even disease. Having animal excrement deposited in your dining room is not, even the most avid animal lover will admit, a wholesome message to give to kids, and there is certainly something demeaning to the human spirit about having to clean it up. Children can, moreover, become so attached to a pet that other family members become of secondary importance in the child's eyes.

This is not to discourage the keeping of pets, only to put it into its proper place on the scheme of things. From a spiritual standpoint, parents might consider letting children know that, in truth, animals are *not* persons, too. They are *animals*. Period. They belong to a different order of creation and, as all spiritual disciplines agree, their possibilities for higher consciousness are limited when compared to those of humankind. As such, they should not be accorded as high a place in our affections as we reserve for others of our kind.

Parents should be careful of sentimentalizing animals too much in front of little ones. They should avoid hugging and kissing animals or showing them as much attention as they show their children. Such role models are puzzling to young ones who see their parents walk briskly past the poor on the street but who then lavish sums of money on special foods or knitted sweaters for their pet dog or cat.

A dog or cat or rabbit is a friendly representative of the animal kingdom in your own home. It can add a special feeling to a residence and should be treated with care and respect. But not the same care and respect you accord your fellow human beings.

Appreciation of Nature

Most children still possess, as the poet Marianne Moore described it, "the ability to be drunk with a sudden realization of the value in things often never noticed." Parents, too, would do well to sharpen their senses in this department, and an especially good way of going about it is to become more involved in exploring the beauties of the organic kingdoms that surround us.

One family I know makes it a point of going out on summer nights, sitting quietly together, and listening to the chirp of the crickets. During the session the parents sometimes quote poems, such as a Japanese haiku: "Nothing in the song of the cricket tells how soon it must die." Or "The cricket sings, the water spider dances across his pond in ecstasy." Sometimes they bring a portable stove along and the makings for tea. Resting quietly, they sip their tea and listen intently to nature's summertime symphony. The experience becomes for them a kind of meditation, and the satisfaction and sense of togetherness is brought back to the household by everyone.

Some families make excursions into nature carrying books to identify wild flowers. Others bring along herbal guides, which they use to recognize medicinal herbs growing in the fields and forests. They pick the herbs, dry them, label them, and use them as medicines for simple maladies. Such excursions make an excellent introduction for children to the principles of natural medicine. The important thing about nature walks is that children be exposed to beauty, that they learn about the forest, and that parents make a point of stressing that this bounty comes from the compassion of the Supreme Being.

Conversation

Still another feature that can make the home environment glow is good conversation. This topic has been discussed in Chapter 2; here I'll simply remind you again that when you talk your children will listen, listen, listen, even if they seem a thousand miles off in outer space. This means that a household with spiritually oriented conversation is a household that is feeding the people who live there.

Conversation does not necessarily have to be about religious matters as such to excite the better parts of a child. It can concern anything awe-inspiring, things that jog the sense of enigma and adventure, the desire to explore and experience and learn and do and push the frontiers of understanding. Even conversations about art, invention, nature, animals, travel, the latest wonder of science, visitors from another planet, all is grist for the child's wonder mill. Here are a few other points to keep in mind:

• Mealtime is an excellent part of the day for family conversations. Now is the moment to chat about what happened at work or school, to remark on events in the news, to describe significant encounters and feelings that you—or the child— have experienced while going about your business. Parents should not be afraid to be vulnerable to children at this time and should not hesitate to expose themselves emotionally when appropriate. The atmosphere of breaking bread together is a sacred one. Now is the time, if ever, to speak from the heart.

• Make sure children are included in family exchanges. Listen to what they have to say. Look them in the eyes when they speak. Ask them questions. Show that their ideas are valued and that you care about what they think and feel. Let them join in family discussions.

· Think of subjects that have inherent spiritual interest to a child and introduce these topics during family get-togethers. Even a conversation about the weather can be turned toward the idea of spiritual quest: What makes it rain? Why do the seasons keep changing the way they do? Is it true that Indian rain dances can really bring rain?

Talk is cheap, but speech can be sacred. Like everything else in this world, it depends on what is being said and by whom, and why—and who is listening.

16.

Death Education at Home

A spiritual household should be a happy, positive place. But it should also be a truthful place. In its own way the notion of death is as frightening to children as it is to adults, and youngsters will often go to the same lengths as adults to deny it. Yet all children must encounter this stark reality at some point along the spiritual line, and it is a parent's job to make sure that the meeting is brought off well and wisely, and in the secure privacy of home counsel. Death, after all, is as spiritual a subject as life in its own way and must be granted full honors as a religious concern. Over the past fifty years a great deal of research has been done on the topic of childhood views of death; and, while there are no unimpeachable certainties, the outlines are gradually becoming understood. Perhaps the most significant study done on the subject, and one that continues to affect death-education theory today, was carried out in 1948 by a Hungarian psychologist, Maria Nagy. Working with nearly 400 children aged four to ten in postwar Budapest, Nagy armed her young subjects with paints, paper, and pen and encouraged them to draw pictures of death and to make up stories about their creations.

One of the results of these tests, and perhaps the most important contribution made by Nagy, was to demonstrate that children are by no means blissfully unaware of death, as is often supposed, and that death is very much a part of their day-to-day consciousness. The way in which it is integrated into the awareness at different ages is where the differences lie.

Very young children, claims Nagy, between the years of three and five, perceive death as a transition or a journey, although what kind of journey they are not sure. The dead are in some sense "less alive" than living people, but they are not entirely vanished, either. Nagy records the following conversation:

ADULT: How do you know whether someone is asleep or dead?

CHILD: I know if they go to bed at night and don't open their eyes. If somebody goes to bed and doesn't get up, he's dead or ill.

ADULT: Will he ever wake up?

CHILD: Never. A dead person only knows if somebody goes out to a grave or something. He feels that somebody is there, or is talking.

ADULT: Are you certain? You're not mistaken?

CHILD: I don't think so. At funerals you're not allowed to sing, just talk, because otherwise the dead person couldn't sleep peacefully. A dead person feels it if you put something on the grave.

ADULT: What is it he feels then?

CHILD: He feels that the flowers are put on his grave. The water touches the sand. Slowly, slowly, he hears everything.

In the mind of a small child the dead return without contradiction, perishing and resurrecting in the manner of plastic soldiers or gremlins in an arcade game. Death is a fact. But it is also impermanent, really a kind of sleep, and indeed the two are viewed by very young children as being almost identical.

From ages five to nine a youngster's view of death matures considerably. Now death is understood to be final for other people, but *not* for oneself. The child alone among all human beings on earth will escape.

It is not unusual to overhear seven- or eight-year-olds bragging about their plans to live for a hundred years, which from a child's perspective is forever, or declaring that by the time they have grown up science will have "conquered" old age. The child starts to recognize beginnings and irreversible ends, but it is a conditional recognition, one that the child believes does not pertain to his or her own destiny.

Another fascinating aspect of the older child's view, according to Nagy, is that death is thought of as a kind of quasi-mystical *being*, not so much an experience as an animistic presence. Ghost stories become especially popular, as do horror movies and all the media titillations that portray death in personified terms. Death may be envisioned as a space invader or a ghoul, a kidnapper, a crook, any sinister shadow figure that hints at annihilation. This figure is neither infallible nor omniscient and only stupid children let themselves get snared. As in fairy stories and myths, death can be bargained with by a clever wayfarer, or outwitted, bribed, run away from, and at times even killed. Death itself is mortal.

Finally, there is the last stage, from the ninth year up to that uncertain cutoff age around twelve or thirteen when the older child becomes the early adolescent. At this stage an accommodation is reached with the inevitable. Death now is perceived as universal (everyone dies, including myself), irreversible (time moves ever onward and only in one direction), and internal (death is not done to me from the outside by some personified force but happens within through a biological process).

TALKING WITH CHILDREN ABOUT DEATH

Given these guidelines, where and how to begin discussing the question of death with children from a spiritual perspective?

Ironically, most modern children are already quite well acquainted with the subject on television and the movies, from newspapers and billboards, even from the more death-oriented of the rock singing groups, and especially via the ever-looming threat of collective annihilation through nuclear, military, or ecological apocalypse. Next to sex there is probably no subject to which children—and, for that matter, everyone—is exposed more frequently in our society than death.

But exposed in the most peculiar ways. Unlike children of, say, a hundred years ago who frequently experienced the early demise of a sibling or who witnessed a grandparent dying at home, almost no modern child has ever seen a dead body, and few have known anyone who has passed away.

This overexposure to the imagery of death and underexposure to its palpable reality—coupled with a kind of glorification of the gruesome side of dying, as acted out during Halloween and in the popularity of the horror film—produces in the child's eye a picture of death that is both morbid and fantastic. To this already contorted image add the modern phobia against discussing dying with children or even admitting its existence, and the matter becomes totally deformed. The modern child has not only to struggle with the difficult concept of death itself but with the overlay of contradictions and evasions fostered by the modern horror of growing old. In the end one of the most profound double-bind messages of our time emerges:

1. Death is a hideous presence that threatens one always and everywhere. Fear it.
2. Death does not exist. Don't talk about it; don't think about it. Don't even bring it up.

A spiritually oriented parent's first job is, therefore, to cut through this tissue of confusion with the sword of straight talk and right thinking. Here are some guidelines to provide you with a base of operations in this most delicate of matters:

1. From a spiritual point of view, the first and in certain ways most important point, when talking to kids about death is not to set oneself up as the omniscient last word on the subject. No matter what your spiritual bent, a child should be made to understand that death is a great mystery—the greatest of all mysteries, really—and that you as parent have no ultimate answers. If the child asks you questions that cannot be solved, admit that the answer is not known. The child will respect this reply and may come to sense some of the great mystery, too.

As a young boy I used to ask my own father a great many questions. His one response that stayed with me more than any other and that, despite the fact that he was an agnostic, turned me toward an interest in spiritual matters, was when I'd quiz him on some imponderable of existence like where does infinity end? Or what will happen to me when I die? When these questions came his way my father would smile mysteriously, pause for a moment, and then deliver that most eerie and titillating of replies: "Nobody knows."

2. Avoid overly technical explanations. Children are constitutionally incapable of listening to prolonged theorizations. Best to give them clear explanations with simple examples. For instance, try putting an explanation of death into story form: Grandpa got sick. So he went to the hospital, where we all visited him. He became so sick that it got too hard for him to stay alive. So he died. His soul left his body and went somewhere else.

3. Don't dwell on lurid details. Vivid descriptions of how the body decomposes in the grave and is eaten by worms are popular among some religious groups and may fascinate children, but there is plenty of evidence to show that it can also produce neurotic fixations. Avoid such gratuitously ghastly imagery and keep things in perspective by assuring children that dead bodies do not feel

what is happening to them, that it is as natural for a body to decay as it is for a leaf or a blade of grass to go back to the ground, and that what comes from nature always returns to nature.

4. Address specific emotional concerns. One child asks about death because he or she is afraid. Another asks out of intellectual wonder, or morbid fascination, or religious curiosity. Sometimes a child's wish will be motivated by all of these considerations or by several at once; yet there may be a single concern that looms largest among the others. Find out which one it is and satisfy it as best you can.

5. Children do not always say what they mean or mean what they say. Such evasion is not motivated by trickery, exactly. It is just that young ones do not have the articulateness or awareness to verbalize what's troubling them. Thus many of their most heartfelt attempts at communication are expressed in a kind of code, in jokes or asides, in complaints or non sequiturs. When a child asks why "the Russian soldiers are always shooting at America," the real question may be "Am I going to be killed in a war?" When a child tells his mother he's hiding in a closet so that "God won't find me," he may be reacting to having been told that we die because God calls us back to heaven.

A case in point concerns a hospital technician who deals with death on a daily basis. Returning home from work one afternoon, this man was informed that his five-year-old son was waiting to speak with him in the living room. He found the boy seated in a large easy chair wearing an uncharacteristically serious expression; it turned out that earlier that afternoon he had quasi-intentionally killed a baby mole by dropping a heavy rock on it. Try as he might, the boy said, he could not revive the creature. Would his father help bring it back to life? The boy then produced the crushed animal from his pocket, placed it on his father's desk, and looked up expectantly.

The father launched into a long discourse about the

physiological process of death and why it was impossible to revive any creature once the life had left it. The more he talked, the more restless the boy became, until he finally jumped up, ran to the window, and started talking about other things.

The father thought the matter was settled until suddenly the boy broke into tears. "Will God come and drop rocks on me?" he blurted out between sobs.

The fact was that the boy had absolutely no desire to know about death in textbook terms. He did not care about biology. His real question was whether *he* would die, and whether God would punish *him* for killing the mole, and whether he would receive the same treatment he had meted out. His real question, in short, hidden behind childish inarticulateness, was a plea for assurance and faith: "Am I safe? Does God still love me? Is my life still OK?" It related not to theory or philosophy but to distinct fears, needs, and feelings.

6. Do not entertain preconceived notions of how a child should react to discussions of death. Like preparing the birds-and-bees speech, parents sometimes worry too much about saying the proper spiritual things. If after speaking frankly about grandfather's impending death, children seem unaffected, this does not necessarily mean they are unmoved—only that they show their feelings differently from adults.

7. When providing religious explanations about death to children, parents must choose their words with extreme care. "Grandfather thought it was time to leave this earth and return to his place with God" is a lot less threatening than "God came and took Grandpa away." Young ones, remember, hear everything that is said to them *literally,* without giving the benefit of the doubt to poetic license. Don't assume that youngsters will understand celestial symbolism or fill in the figurative blanks the way adults do. They won't.

Keep all discussion concrete. Most children under six have trouble with abstract ideas and with philosophy.

Stick to the facts. Speak to children about death on their
own level. Avoid talking down to them. They sense when
you are doing this and turn off. The following conversation is an example of how such a discussion might be kept
simple and at the same time supportive and informative.
It is geared to the level of a four- or five-year-old. Up-
grades can be made accordingly:

> DAUGHTER: Is the bird dead, Daddy?
> FATHER: Yes. It died.
> DAUGHTER: Died? Where did it go?
> FATHER: It probably died because it was very old. I
> don't know where it went 'cause we can't know those
> things for sure. But if you want to know what I *believe*
> happened, I *believe* that its soul went back to where it
> came from, to its Creator. To God.
> DAUGHTER: Can't you make it better?
> FATHER: No. No one can do that.
> DAUGHTER: Am I going to get dead?
> FATHER: Someday you will, but probably not for such
> a long time that you don't have to worry about it. And
> when you do you will probably be ready for it. That's
> one reason grownups go to church, to help them get
> ready to die someday. From what I read in the [name
> of a holy book], it's not such a bad thing either to die,
> especially if you've lived a good life.
> DAUGHTER: Why does the bird look so funny?
> FATHER: When something dies it gets very quiet and
> still and peaceful. Since it's dead it's starting to go back
> into nature, into the trees and grass, so it can become
> part of the earth again. That's what it's doing now, and
> that's why it looks so strange. It doesn't feel any pain
> or unhappiness at all, though.
> DAUGHTER: Will you die? And Mommy?
> FATHER: Probably that won't be for a very long time,
> until you're grown up. Then you'll be able to take care
> of yourself. Mommy and I will do everything we can to
> be sure you'll be fine.

DAUGHTER: Why do things get dead?

FATHER: It's just set up that way. Everything is born, lives for a while, than passes on. Some people spend their lives trying to understand this idea. They want to speak to God directly and learn about the mystery of death from Him. So they pray and meditate and try to hear His voice. They're called religious persons. They try very hard to understand why we're born and why we die. Perhaps you will become one of these persons one day.

DAUGHTER: Daddy, I can't stop thinking about that dead bird.

FATHER: I know. It's upsetting. Maybe you're feeling afraid that what happened to the bird will happen to you. But it won't. Death doesn't usually happen to children. It's something that comes much later on, when you're ready for it. And remember, your mother and I and your grandparents and all your friends love you very much. We'll always be right here with you and we will all help protect you as best we can.

17.

The Television Question

You already know most of the grim news about your home television: that the average American child watches some forty to fifty hours of TV a week. That in the United States more time is passed during childhood in front of the tube than is spent in the classroom. That under controlled test conditions the behavior of preschoolers exposed to violent programs has become antisocial after just two or three hours' viewing time. That by age thirteen an American youngster will have watched more than a hundred thousand video scenes that depict violence, death, and disaster.

Study after study has demonstrated that television has a profoundly disturbing affect on young minds, and that even "harmless" entertainments such as cartoons are major anxiety-provokers. Next time you see a group of four-year-olds watching a Tom-and-Jerry cartoon observe them carefully. As the cat hunts the mouse with a meat cleaver, notice how the children clinch their fists and how their breathing gets faster. As the bomb goes off and blows the bulldog's eyes out of their sockets, see the child react with something between a laugh and a scream.

A three-year-old girl named Lonnie still questions her father about the scene she saw almost a year ago in a Bugs Bunny cartoon. In this film, made during the 1940s, a gang of malicious mice capture Bugs, tie him to a grill with hundreds of small wires, and shove him into a lighted oven to the tune of Chopin's "Funeral March." "Why did they want to hurt Bugs Bunny?" Lonnie keeps asking. "Were they going to cook him, Dad? Does it hurt to get cooked and eaten when you're still alive?"

This animated divertimento, in Lonnie's four-year-old eyes, was clearly perceived as actually taking place, just as most film stories are thought by preschoolers to be unquestionably real. To lovingly inform them that "It's just a story" or to dismiss their anxiety with a glib "Don't worry, it's only make-believe" is to miss the point. Which is that for young children the line between fact and make-believe is tenuous at best, even if the action is presented through a medium as obviously fantastic as a cartoon. Children under five live, as it were, in a continual state of suspended disbelief. Their unconscious is closer to being conscious than ours. What they see and hear is therefore what they believe, no matter how phony or improbable it may appear to grown-up eyes. And if simple cartoons are disturbing to young imaginations, consider the damage done to those who are given carte blanche to view any program they please: splatter films; murder-a-minute police dramas; soap operas full of materialist values, kink, and tawdry disasters.

Predictably, the networks (along with their hired guns from the college psychology departments and motivational research companies) continue to protest that a link between what children see on television and the way they behave at home has never been authoritatively confirmed, never "scientifically" established. One is reminded of the tobacco companies who cite "scientific" evidence, derived from studies they themselves finance, showing that the dangers of cigarette smoking are still "unproved."

Such disclaimers by the networks aside, a majority of child therapists will inform you quite directly that violent programming on TV contributes to the development of violent youth—end of story. Moreover, the same media pundits who promise us that nothing children see or hear on TV influences their behavior seem to entertain no such doubts concerning the coercive power of ads and commercials. Neither, for that matter, do the sponsors who pay for it all.

TV and Children's Values
While it may, in fact, be true that any well-adjusted child will not be transformed into a murderer by watching a few cop dramas, this is missing the point again. It's not so much that TV makes good children do bad things (although there is evidence that it does make bad children do bad things). It's that TV inculcates wrong values into children at a time when right values are so desperately needed.

In his *Raising Good Children* Thomas Lickona refers to several of the primary negative influences exerted on kids by TV when he speaks of television as a "moral teacher." One of the few authors in recent times to address the ethical side of child rearing, Lickona points out that besides the obvious fact that criminal behavior on TV sets a miserable example for young watchers, there are other subversive messages that do almost as much moral damage, among them:

> · If you can't get what you want through ordinary means, try getting it by violence.
> · Violence is commonplace. No big deal. Everybody does it. Nothing to get worked up about.
> · Females are incompetent and inferior to men.
> · Drinking is fun, neat, and socially applaudable.
> · Material things will make you happy.
> · Grownups are idiots. Children are the people in our society who *really* know what's going on, and they're the ones who should be running things. (During the 1960s young people used to say "Don't trust

anyone over thirty. Today the line could read "Don't trust anyone over seventeen.")

To Lickona's list of common television messages several more important items can be added:

> · Sex before marriage is something to be expected and encouraged. Multiple sexual involvements are cool. The whole purpose of being grown-up is to pursue members of the opposite sex. The real and only happiness in life comes from finding a person with whom you can have good sex and romantic adventures.
> · Revenge is sweet. If people are unkind to you, give them back double.
> · Money solves all problems.
> · The authorities are your enemies. Society is run by an establishment of faceless, money-grubbing, A-bomb-dropping plutocrats who hate kids and are out to ruin the world.
> · Adopting an appearance that is hideous, macabre, and/or robotlike will make you into a different, unique, and interesting person.
> · Anything that interferes with your physical enjoyment is to be shunned. Work is a burden; it is to be avoided at all costs. The sole purpose of existence is to have fun.
> · Grow up as fast as you can. Adulthood is where the power lies.

In *Raising Good Children* Lickona refers to the insightful work of Dr. Neil Postman, professor of communications at New York University, and to Postman's interesting thesis that the knowledge barrier between children and grownups, once so bulwarklike, has been severely eroded during the past several decades specifically by TV.

One of the features that formerly separated adults from children, Postman believes, is that adults knew things about the seamy side of life that children did not. Children were innocent, it was assumed; most adults wished to keep it that way. "Time enough for adult concerns later on" was the prevailing attitude among parents and educators alike. "Keep them clean as long as you can" was the byword.

Today, attitudes have taken an abrupt turn in favor of "honesty." Read "total, uncensored disclosure about anything and everything." Which means that at eight years old most children know a good deal about the kinds of shadowy human behavior that once upon a time—*literally*—would have made a convict blush. Things such as incest. Or transvestitism, sexual perversion, ritual black magic, torture, bestiality, suicide, gang rape—you can fill in the rest of the list by glancing at the week's TV programming guide.

Lickona describes how, in one of his courses at NYU during the 1970s, several teachers informed him that almost without exception their students' favorite TV program was "The Dukes of Hazard." A "hilarious spoof" popular a decade ago, "Dukes" was about two handsome ex-cons in a small Southern village who fill their days cracking up cars and other men's jaws, bootlegging applejack, seducing women, and making a moron out of the local sheriff. One might assume that in any sensible family such a program would be off limits to five- and six-year-olds. But to the contrary: During the 1970's "The Dukes of Hazard" was one of the most popular *children's* TV show in the world. Like so many programs of its kind, a majority of American parents considered it clean-cut, good ol' family entertainment.

Why Children and TV?

Why is it then, one might ask, that so many well-meaning mothers and fathers allow their children to view programs that quite obviously encourage antisocial and even criminal behavior? What has happened to the minds and hearts and good judgment of parents across the land who so willingly expose youngsters to the types of words and pictures that less than fifty years ago would have sent their creators to jail?

In some cases, clearly, it is a matter of personal values:

Parents simply do not consider carousing and mayhem inappropriate messages for a child. No further discussion. There are many parents like this; more, perhaps, than we realize.

In other instances, parents honestly do not agree that TV exerts the kind of subversive psychological impact educators would have us believe. They convince themselves that such warnings are highbrow alarmism, that the nightly serials really *are* the frivolous, harmless amusements the media power brokers bill them as, and that viewing these programs causes no more harm to a child's psyche than does, say, a fairy tale.

All in all, however, a majority of parents who allow their offspring to watch seamy TV shows are rationalizing away the unpleasant truth of its harmfulness, even though they may expound on how these programs are good for a child's "sense of reality" or how they prepare children to meet life in "the real world." For, whatever criticisms one may wish to hurl at the great silver eye that sits so triumphantly in the middle of our homes today—and transmits messages that a culture with even a modicum of spiritual sensibility would instantly recognize as being overtly satanic—it nonetheless has one virtue that is unarguable: it is the most efficient babysitter that humankind has ever produced. And this, when all is said and done, is nine times out of ten the real reason so many parents allow so many children to watch so many television sets for so many long and unrelieved hours of the day.

A PLAN OF ACTION

But enough of criticism. As mentioned, you probably know all of these facts already. What you are more interested in is discovering what you as parent can do to reduce the negative impact TV has on your children.

Stop them from watching it entirely?

Well, that's one approach. If you find it a satisfactory solution by all means start the wheels turning today. There's no doubt about it, the most direct answer to the television dilemma is to remove the TV from the house entirely and to guide children toward other, more creative forms of entertainment.

Of course, you may wish to watch a little intelligent TV yourself once in a while. You do have some rights in this department, after all. You will likewise have to deal with the fact that most of your child's friends will have a television, which means that if you want to preserve your youngster's media virginity you will have to keep him or her at home most of the time as well. Also, be aware that at a certain age, when their classmates begin discussing the latest television programs at school on a regular basis, and when friends start having sleep-over parties that feature a night of television watching, your children will feel left out. Let's face it, American culture today *is* television, at least on the popular level, and to bar it from the child's life completely may not be the best approach.

Is there then a happy medium between total TV withdrawal and the forty-hour-a-week syndrome?

Probably not. Probably not a *happy* medium. The prevailing fact is that even a little television viewing can have a hurtful impact. Thomas Lickona mentions that children who were allowed to watch "The Dukes of Hazard" just once remained imprinted with its aggressive story line for months afterward, playing auto smash-up with toy cars and calling one another Luke and Bo, the names of the program's heroes.

At the same time, however, there is a strategy which, if not a happy one, will guide parents to make a sensible compromise between complete TV deprivation and total immersion. Here's how it works:

1. Do not expose children under four years old to *any* television. Even the most innocuous cartoons and kindly talking heads can be confusing to very young minds. Better to let books and trees and kittens and crayons be the featured experiences before nursery school begins.

2. Once children reach four, establish a conservative viewing policy based on: (a) the quality of the program, (b) the length of time the child is allowed to watch, and (c) the child's

emotional state at the moment the program comes on. Stick to this policy like glue. If, for instance, you decide that a little viewing is okay, be precise about what you mean by a little. A half-hour is a half-hour. No longer. No exceptions.

If children are petulant or upset, moreover, TV may not always the best way to deal with their emotional state. Though an hour's watching can have a sedative effect, it may also leave the conflict unresolved. Perhaps it would be better if the child was kept away from the tube entirely at this time and consoled by the parents directly. You must be the one to decide on this issue, of course, but bear in mind that when children are in turmoil they are emotionally impressionable as well. Choose what they watch at these times with particular care.

3. Some further guidelines to consider when establishing watching limits:

· Limit TV watching to a few carefully selected programs.

· And/or: Allow TV viewing only on the weekends.

· Place the television in an uncomfortable part of the house. Make it difficult for children to reach. Place it behind closed doors or arrange it so that the set must be taken down and set up each time it is watched *by the child.* Very often the rule of "out of sight, out of mind" will put a self-limiting muzzle on the monster.

· Allow children to watch only public and cable TV programs: "Sesame Street," "Mr. Rogers," nature documentaries, old 1950s serials such as "Lassie," "Flipper," or "Mister Ed." and the like. This approach has been followed by millions of parents since public broadcasting and cable have become popular and has proved an excellent compromise between watching and not watching. If nothing else, the absence of commercials on public television ups its stock several hundred points.

· Don't leave children under six in a room alone with the television set for more than a few minutes at a time. Keep checking in, making sure that they're not switching the dials to harmful programs. Let them know you are here and available, should they become frightened. Sometimes you might also consider watching a program or two along with the child, salvaging at least some family feeling out of the affair by cuddling as you watch, popping popcorn together, discussing the program afterward. A certain affection will flow when parent and child are together enjoying a mutual experience, even if it is as mundane as a television show.

· Monitor your own TV-watching habits. What children see, they do. If you watch TV several hours a day your offspring will imitate you. One good trick is to keep viewing times confined to the evening, preferably after all young ones are in bed. If children never see you watching TV they will assume you never do. This is a "white lie" worth perpetuating.

4. Programs to keep your children 100,000 miles away from at all times include the following:

· Police, war, spy, detective, and horror shows of any kind.
· News programs. Contrary to popular opinion, it is not particularly "educational" for a child to see the bodies of children burned to a crisp in the latest fire or to learn how many captives were gunned to death by terrorists during the weekend.
· Science fiction shows. With few exceptions, these are gruesome, formulaic, atheistic, and full of "technology will solve all of humankind's problems someday" messages. The better sci-fi dramas can sometimes stimulate a sense of wonder in older children, perhaps, but such shows are *never* appropriate for preschoolers and rarely for those under seven.
· Soaps, sitcoms, and adult dramas. Even though certain sitcoms seem innocuous, their values, with one or two exceptions, are usually pretty unspiritual.
· Adult movies and prime-time dramas. These can

be too raw, too adult, too full of incomprehensible grown-up conflicts and mishaps for the young mind.
· Quiz shows of any kind (talk about instilling materialistic values!).
· Rock-music videos. Pure chaos: just about everything you would not want your child exposed to.

Programs that may occasionally be acceptable for older children but that should be screened with the upmost discretion include:

· Cartoons. Stay away from most of these. Possible exceptions include well-made, intelligent, and morally upright versions of standard children's' stories, fairy tales, myths, and the like. At all costs avoid the violent superhero, high-tech, robotlike cartoons flooding TV these days, along with animated offerings that sponsor violence, greed, vanity, consumerism, and so forth.
· Nonthreatening, nonviolent evening hourlies. Family variety shows, though far from perfect, are sometimes okay for occasional viewing. Use your discretion.
· Grown-up educational and discussion shows. These are often harmless, though children will be bored with them most of the time anyway.
· Family-style feature films, especially those made before 1960. The adventures and comedies in this genre are solid entertainment for older children, but be wary of problem films: war movies, gangster pictures, and the like. Certain older classic films such as *It's a Wonderful Life* are actually religiously inspiring in a Hollywood kind of way.

Finally, shows you may wish your children to see include:

· Carefully screened and selected children's' shows such as, to take two classic and long-running examples, "Mr. Rogers' Neighborhood" and "Sesame Street."

· Selected cartoons. See above.

· Selected children's movies. Again, your very discretionary choice. Remember, just because a movie is made for children does not mean it is good for children.

· Classroom education shows that teach interesting and appropriate lessons. "Mr. Wizard" has been a prototype of the best of this genre for years.

· Nature shows and age-appropriate educational documentary films. There are, fortunately, more and more of these on TV, especially on the cable channels.

· Old-time children's comedies such as *Our Gang,* Charlie Chaplin films, *The Keystone Kops.*

· Keep your own home stock of approved videos. There are many decent children's entertainments now on tape. Most are affordable, and it can be fun for the child to build his or her own film library.

5. Carefully screen all television programs yourself before allowing children to view them. Yes, this means parents must plunk themselves down in front of "Captain Kangaroo," "Sam and Jodie," "The Smurfs," and "Lassie" for a morning or two and see exactly what it is that will be going into their youngster's brains. Pay close attention to the commercials as well as to the programs. After watching several of these you may opt for a public TV exclusive.

When you do find a show worthy of your child's time, give it a passing grade and include it on the viewing agenda. If you are unimpressed, strike it from the list. Don't be afraid to be harsh in these matters. When in doubt, say no. There are many children's programs on the air today that, though they are touted as being wholesome and (that magic word again) "educational," do not hold up to the scrutiny of parents concerned with moral education as well as with entertainment.

6. Be on the alert for feedback from children and act on it immediately. Every afternoon six-year-old Roland watched a show on cable TV called "Belle and Sebastian." This well-made European cartoon told the story of an appealing young

boy named Sebastian who, along with a giant dog, Belle, was separated from his mother by a strange accident of fate and who spent each subsequent episode wandering from town to town across the Pyrenees, searching for her.

At first glance this show seemed acceptable enough to Roland's parents. Sebastian was a well-mannered, kindly boy, and his dog Belle rivaled Peter Pan's Nana for patience and affection. The animation was sweetly drawn, but what pleased Roland's parents most was that the action was slow and evenly paced, unlike the frantic, laser-speed cartoons that populate most prime-time shows.

After watching "Belle and Sebastian" for several days running, however, Roland started asking anxious questions: Why did the butcher drive Belle out of his shop with a meat cleaver? How come that pretty woman Sebastian thought was his mother tried to turn him in to the police?

Roland's worried tone conveyed a concern that was beyond mere curiosity. So the next day his mother took a closer look at "Belle and Sebastian." Sure enough, the story was full of the kinds of terrors that would ruin any child's day—abandonment by a parent, betrayal at the hands of friends and local townspeople, relentless pursuit by a gang of police who believe Belle to be a mad dog, narrow escapes from murderers and heartless scoundrels. On and on the list of nightmares went, even down to the quietly ominous music that droned on continuously in the background. In all, Roland's anxious questions were well warranted. The next day his TV-watching schedule was accordingly changed.

7. Use whatever positive messages children receive on television shows as opportunities for discussing related moral questions. "Sesame Street," for instance, though short on religious consciousness, makes a good try at conveying positive emotional ideals like sharing and caring. Even more so "Mr. Rogers." Take advantage of these concepts. Why doesn't anyone like Oscar the Grouch? Even though he's mean, how come the people who live on Sesame Street try to be nice to him? That seems like a very kind way of behaving, doesn't it? And Cookie Monster—he's funny all right. But

he's greedy, too. And notice how his greed gets him in trouble. He's always getting a stomachache or having an argument with a friend. Does greed do that to us? Let's figure out how.

When and if children do happen to witness disturbing scenes on TV, this experience can be turned into a learning event as well. Take time out and talk it over. What was there about the way that TV father yelled at his son that bothered you so much? Why do you think he yelled? Maybe he had a stomachache. Maybe he was just a mean guy. Do you know any fathers who act like that? Did you feel scared when the puppy fell into the well and Lassie tried to pull her out? Sometimes things like that happen in real life, too. Accidents. We have to be careful sometimes. Let's talk about this a little. . . .

8. Establish WATWs—Wholesome Alternatives to TV Watching. One of the main reasons children are so mated to the tube is that nothing else is offered in its place. This may sound odd to parents who have stocked their child's room with toys and gadgets. But remember, many children are not self-initiating. The toys may be there all right, but the child's creative faculties do not always know how to use them. Sometimes they'll need your help.

If your child is already a TV addict it may be necessary to put a plan for WATWs into action slowly. Start small. Find a show he or she feels lukewarm about. Suggest that instead of watching such-and-such you take a nature walk together or build a gigantic block city or go down to the local playground. Make the alternative as attractive as possible, and let the child know that you will share the experience.

Next step: After you've offered yourself as bait, and after the child gets accustomed to this particular WATW, take the next leap of faith: Announce that you'd like to begin a really great project together. Explain that it will take lots of time, but that it will be lots of fun.

What kind of project? Something that turns the child on and can be continued over a long period of time. You might, for example, start building an electric-train diorama. Or a dollhouse. Is your child interested in nature? Purchase a cheap telescope and a book on astronomy and set up a small observatory near a handy window. If the child likes plants and animals, purchase a microscope and establish a small lab. For kids who like plants, start a garden in the backyard or on the windowsill. Something more ambitious for the landowner might be to set up a tiny nine-hole miniature golf course in your backyard. Sounds expensive, but it's not, really. All you'll need is some landscaping imagination and the golf equipment. If children are interested in music and if you play an instrument, teach it to them, or bring them to a local teacher and be sure they practice regularly. Other interesting WATWs that will lure kids away from the TV set include:

· Building a tree house.

· Making your own movie. With a video camera or Super-8 camera, and with your help, the child can write a script, direct, and shoot his or her own "feature film."

· Constructing a backyard playhouse.

· Founding a home family drama club. Take a simple play from a book of fairy stories, rehearse it, make costumes, sets, and give a scheduled performance for friends and grandparents.

· Planting and nurturing a small orchard.

· Setting up a tank of tropical fish.

· Starting an aviary.

· Purchasing appropriate art materials and setting up an "artist's studio" in your home or apartment. Paint and draw together, then plan an exhibition of your work in your living room. Invite family and friends. Send out announcements.

· Working on building a radio-controlled boat or plane. Plan a special launching day and invite your friends to the occasion.

· Setting up a small carpentry workshop and starting on household projects like repairing chairs, building bookends, and the like.

· Setting up a leatherworking area for projects like making belts and wallets.

· Giving the child horseback lessons at a local barn or stable. Let the child work around the house to earn money to buy his or her own saddle and riding equipment.
· Setting up a loom and weaving a rug together.
· Joining the Girl Scouts or Boy Scouts.
· Taking ballet lessons.
· Playing a musical instrument.
· Building hand puppets and giving a family performance.

Whatever grips you is the way to go. The idea is to get young people interested in more active pursuits, pastimes they can participate in on an ongoing basis. Now there will be two juicy carrots dangling in front: the WATW itself and your loving involvement.

What is really crucial for parents to understand is that children do not "need" TV to survive, no matter what the sponsors and the educators may tell us. Children did, after all, get along without it for a million years or so. They can continue that way today.

Nor is it a law of nature that if young ones watch a little TV they must watch a lot. Like all habits, TV can be controlled and perhaps even turned into a friend. But everyone in the family will have to work hard at it first before this occurs.

18.

The Home as a Haven: Protecting a Child from Harmful Influences

Keeping harmful influences away from children these days is about as easy as poking your finger into several hundred leaks in a dam at the same time. Somewhere, somehow, the water is going to get through.

The impossibility of such a task notwithstanding, there are things that can be done to keep the floodwaters at a level somewhere below the nose. Myra, a mother of two boys and an old friend of mine from our teaching days in Hawaii, has raised her children on the assumption that, in her words, "What kids *don't* know is as important as what they do."

Myra has lived for some years in eastern New Mexico as part of a fundamentalist Christian commune. Within this tightly knit group members raise their children according to a code of moral and religious principles, and members make heroic efforts to practice what they preach. Despite their rigorous standards, "the long arm of society and television," as Myra calls it, has still made its incursions into their private lives, and members recently have had to come face to face with the fact that no one, child or grownups, can entirely escape the Zeitgeist.

How then have parents in this upright, struggling little community adapted to the realities of the outside world? I spoke with Myra at length on the subject. She offered many sound suggestions both for preserving children's integrity and for protecting them from society's insults. Several of her points might serve as general principles for spiritual child raising everywhere. Here's an excerpt from our taped conversation:

> *Since I didn't want my kids getting into things the neighbor kids were doing like hunting animals, I had to sit down with my husband early on when the kids were still in diapers and decide what things we wanted to keep them out of. We made a list and we've tried to stick by it. The thing is, you have to start by identifying the diabolic forces you wish to protect your children from, so you know in advance which battles you are going to pick.*
>
> *We made our list and set our brains to figuring out what to do about each problem. Oh, there was a big inventory: What to do about television. About knives (a lot of the local kids carry them). About pressures to date in the early grades. Drugs, yes, and even more around here, booze at an early age. About movies and buying candy. About going off alone with a bunch of friends and "scofing," as the kids here call it—doing whatever mischief you want like breaking windows or stealing from people's garages. About sex, too. That's right, sex in fifth and sixth grades.*
>
> *It was hard sticking by our guns, but—listen—being clear about what is and is not allowed into a religious home is very important. About what the boys are allowed to do after school. Who they can be friends with. How late they can stay out. When they can go out. We have to set times and ground rules. Whether they can watch this program on their friends' TV (we solved the TV problem at home by not having one). The best way of all is to keep them protected from the trouble spots. What they don't know definitely won't hurt them. Definitely.*

Based on Myra's viewpoint and on further conversations with spiritually oriented parents, there are three basic steps parents can take to protect their children at home from negative influences. These are:

1. Identify and define the unwholesome forces you wish to protect your children from.
2. Devise a protective strategy against it.
3. Persist, and be consistent.

Let's go over these points in detail.

1. Identify the Unwholesome Forces You Wish to Protect Your Child from

In the Islamic tradition a system has been worked out that has guided parents for centuries. This system is designed to determine whether an act or situation is morally and spiritually acceptable. The method is simple, yet remarkably inclusive. People who hear about it wonder why they never thought of it themselves.

It works like this: A value scale of one to five is established to grade every person, place, thing, deed, and condition that comes into consideration. The five value correlatives on the scale are:

1. *Mandatory.* The condition in question *must* be done, no matter what.
2. *Highly encouraged.* You'd certainly like to see it done.
3. *Neutral.* Neither good nor bad—it doesn't matter if it is done or not.
4. *Discouraged.* This condition will be tolerated but not encouraged.
5. *Not allowed under any circumstances*—no matter what.

Every moral decision a parent must face fits somewhere on this scale. Every idea, every person, every entertainment, every fashion, every offer and undertaking a child could dream up has its appointed ranking.

For example, the question arises: Should an eleven-year-old be allowed to see an R-rated movie? Parents confer, talk it over, and decide that number five on the scale is most applicable: never. From now on R-rated movies are placed in category five: Not allowed under any circumstances.

Or, should the same eleven-year-old be allowed to attend a rock concert? Generally, this child's parents do not sanction rock music. In the case at hand, however, a classmate is having a birthday party and all the child's friends will be attending. A special exception is thus made. Category four on the scale: Discouraged but not forbidden.

Another example: Should Bobby be allowed to play with two of the neighborhood children, Jerry and Max? Jerry is a quiet boy, not very intelligent or imaginative, but not mean or neurotic, either. He ranks as a number three: Neither a plus nor a minus. Bobby's parents will not seek him out as a friend for Bobby, but neither will they discourage the relationship. Max, on the other hand, is a sensitive and kindly boy, loud and overly energetic, but with his heart in a very right place. He is a two: Recommended.

You get the point. The method may sound a bit simplistic and formulaic, and perhaps it is. But what does it matter? The critical thing is that it works. Parties, events, entertainments, invitations to a friend's house, toys, games, books, movies, practically everything pertaining to a child's life can be assessed and evaluated according to this ancient religious measuring stick. Try it and see.

2. Devise a Protective Strategy
Specific to the Problem at Hand

Once the assessment is made, a plan of action can be devised. Let's see how such plans might deal with the most potent, most prominent societal problems parents face today: pornography and sex, drugs, alcohol, films, and rock music.

Pornography and Sex

With the infiltration of hard-core porno into the very fabric of American life, and with the high visibility such materials enjoy, familiarity has come to breed not contempt but indifference on the part of many otherwise sensitive adults. Given the ubiquitous nature of salacious materials in our society and the general apathy that exists over its influence, how is it possible to protect children from porno's many jaded messages?

Perhaps the best thing you can do is realize that if protection is to be afforded it must be done *within the child's consciousness,* not without, and that while children can never be totally shielded from unwholesome messages in our very permissive world they can be given, as it were, spiritual and psychological immunity shots against them.

This means (and it should go without saying) that parents should begin by setting an impeccable example themselves. X-rated literature of *any* kind must be verboten in the household. It should be a a resounding number five on the ranking system above: Forbidden.

Parental attitudes toward sex, moreover, are best kept unambiguous. If parents present sex as a wholesome, pleasurable, but purely personal activity that takes place behind closed doors between married persons, and if they themselves are free from embarrassment and kittenish snickerings on the subject, their children will be, too. Pornography, by definition, relies on the assumption that sex is dirty and illicit. Its illicitness is part of its allure. In the spiritually minded household, parents who talk freely about sex when the subject is appropriate but who do not dwell on it or overemphasize it, have a good chance of raising relatively unhung-up kids.

When speaking to young people, appeal to their natural sense of modesty and to their common sense. Address the matter from two perspectives. One, that sex is the most beautiful, intimate, and pleasurable experience a man and a woman can share together. It is a sacred act, one that the Divinity has given to humankind for enjoyment and procreation. You might even mention how in the East there are spiritual disciplines that involve special sexual practices between husband and wife in which couples use the energies of sex to achieve ecstatic and transcendent union. Sex is a big thing, a luminous thing, a sacred thing.

But—number two—that sex is also a *private* affair and something that you, the child, cannot fully understand or enjoy until you are grown up.

Besides setting your own example and keeping youngsters shielded from suggestive materials, moreover, talk frankly to the preteen about its dangers—VD, AIDS, promiscuity, unwanted pregnancy. Try not to hem and haw on the subject, and don't pretend these things are not issues. They are. When discussing pornography in particular, stress the fact that some individuals who simply want to make lots of money publish books and pictures that show sexual acts. These books and magazines can be very fascinating, granted. But after you read them you will probably feel pretty unhappy about it. Assure children that no one wants to feel this way about themselves, and that the best thing they can do when they see pictures that show sex between people, or naked bodies, or sexual sadism, is to look away and walk away. Tell them they will feel a lot better if they do. Because they will.

Finally, parents can help children come to grips with the sex and porno problem by teaching them a simple psychic prayer/meditation to be invoked whenever they are faced with a sexual conflict of any kind. It works like this: Children who come into contact with pornography and who find themselves confused or attracted by it, can immediately recite "Oh Higher Self, please come to my aid and protection."

Explain to the child that we all have an indwelling spirit within us—a guardian angel, if you will. That if we call upon this angel and ask it to help us, to show us what to do, to steer us away from danger, to give us the wisdom to handle the situation, it will. Believe in it, and it will.

Children can come to rely on this simple phrase whenever they are troubled or threatened or confused. They should turn inward at these moments, become calm inside, and ask for help. Tell them that the inward being will hear and will answer their call.

Films

We've already discussed TV and the galaxy of problems that surround it. Most of what was said applies here as well.

With films, however, it is generally easier to keep things under control because:

1. It costs money to go to the movies and you're the bank.
2. It's more difficult for children to go to a theater than it is to turn on the TV.
3. You can know the reputation of a film ahead of time from reviews and from word of mouth. This allows you to have some knowledge concerning which films should be seen and which should not.
4. The film code, at least to a certain extent, will serve as a protection.

At the same time, monitor film-watching activities carefully. Be sure that you've screened a movie before the child watches it, or at least that you know something about it in advance. Movies with innocuous titles can sometimes turn out to be horrifying or tasteless. Don't judge on name alone.

Perhaps the biggest pitfall are films kids are exposed to on their friends' VCRs. This is a relatively new problem and a vexing one indeed. Nine-year-old Lea developed sleep disorders for several weeks after seeing hanging bodies and bloody eyes at a sleep-over party. At seven, Pat was allowed to remain in the room while the family of his best friend watched a film about terrorism in the Middle East. His games for the next several weeks revolved around locking a man in a box and torturing him with acid and lighted cigarettes.

If your neighbor's VCR is a trouble spot, speak directly to the parents in question. Explain that your child is sensitive to certain subjects and that he or she has had trouble in the past when viewing disturbing materials. On the day of the visit politely inquire which films the child will be seeing. If the list is unacceptable and if the hosts seem insensitive to the problem (or even hostile to it, as a surprisingly large number are), you must simply play the ogre, make your excuses, and not allow your child to visit again.

Drugs

The best and perhaps *only* real drug deterrent for children is to prevent them from experimenting with drugs in first place. Because once the high is experienced the battle is already half lost. How many eleven-year-olds do you know who can resist feelings of utter freedom and euphoria on the limp grounds that they've been told "It's not good for you"? Once again, the Taoist approach to child rearing is called for: Prevent children from catching the disease so that you won't have to worry about finding a cure.

How can parents accomplish this feat? There are several possible strategies:

1. *Set an example at home.* Obviously, if you don't want your child using drugs, don't have them around. This sounds like an obvious point, but it's amazing how many parents keep a bowl of marijuana on hand for guests to dip into, or who wear a cocaine razor around their necks, yet who are shocked when their own children start experimenting.

2. *Avoid drug jokes and drug innuendos.* Be careful of displaying a "hardy-de-har-har!" attitude toward "harmless" drugs like pot. Drugs have become so common a part of American life that many people, even nonusers, condone their use with a collusive wink or a helpless shrug. But children pick up on these mixed signals, and they, too, will come to adopt the same "tolerant" standards.

3. *Let your child know where you stand on the drug issue.* Make clear that you are positively, resolutely, and uncompromisingly against them. As a father or mother practicing spiritual parenting you have moral and ethical standards. Without

being pontifical, let children know what they are. Children recognize sincerity when they see it, and they will want to emulate it. This is good.

4. *Provide drug education.* Some parents think it frightens children or sullies their innocence if they are told the sordid realities of drug addiction. This might or might not have been true in a quieter age. But common sense says that if a hungry wolf creeps into the pasture now is *not* the time to let the lambs sleep. The situation is urgent, drugs are everywhere, and there is no excuse for pussyfooting. Talk about the issue with children at an early age, especially if there is a problem in your neighborhood; if you live in or near an urban community there probably will be. Talk about the different types of drugs that are around, explain how one drug works and how it affects the mind; describe in detail the kinds of damage it does. Explain that these substances are like a slow-acting poison that ruins brain and body alike. Give an account of addiction and withdrawal and the social misbehavior drugs cause.

5. *Talk about the criminal consequences of drug use.* Drug-taking is a criminal offense and users, even juvenile ones, can get into a lot of trouble if caught. Let children know this fact. You don't have to terrify them with details of jail cells and reform school, but it's good if they know the ground rules. Fear, in this case, is a valuable deterrent. Don't be afraid to use it.

6. *Let the child witness the results of drug abuse first hand.* Nothing sobers a child more quickly than the real evidence. If you are walking along the street with a young person and you see a drug user sprawled out on the sidewalk, call the child's attention to it: This is what it does. What a terrible thing. Too bad, if he hadn't used drugs he might be as happy and as healthy as you and me.

The child will quickly get the message. No lectures are required. If youngsters want to talk about what they have seen, as they often will, now is an excellent time for discussing the drug question in greater detail.

7. *Stay alert for possible signs of abuse.* Parents must remain sensitive to their children's behavior and be on the lookout

for telltale signs that drugs are (or may become) an issue. Danger signals include:

· Excessive joke-making about drugs.
· Discovering that your child is hanging out with new friends who are known to use drugs.
· Any odd physical, social, or behavioral changes: glazed or dilated pupils, nervous tics, lethargy, hyper-active behavior, evidence of a sleepy-eyed, half-lidded marijuana look, the snorting and sniffing of cocaine users, the drugged-out posture of heroin users.
· Any atypical demands on the part of your child for money. Exactly what is this money being spent on? Find out.
· Reports from teachers, friends, or other parents that your child is acting strangely. Such reports should never be ignored.

8. *Protect the child with your prayers and love.* Here's a protective prayer you can use. During quiet times of the day form a mental picture of your little one. Hold it for several moments, then imagine that a kind of psychic bubble is forming around the child. The bubble is light red and is composed of pure love. It is transparent, yet it is strong and resilent. It cannot be penetrated by negative or evil forces of any kind. It especially cannot be broken through by the demon of drugs.

Hold the image of the child encased in the bubble for several minutes each day. When you concentrate on this picture try to make the bubble powerful and your force of protective love strong. Tell yourself that you are building an impregnable wall of love around your child, and that no matter how diligently such things as anger, alienation, boredom, and rebellion try to penetrate they will be warded off.

If such feelings can be kept from creeping into the soul of a child at an early age and from lodging there like so many cancers waiting to erupt, more than half the battle is won. Children who are secure concerning their family and home life, who see the good sense of obedience and feel little need to rebel, who have been psychologically supported and physically well trained, who have a sincere desire to serve and to do the right thing, who are busily involved in a range of wholesome activities, and who have a basic grounding in spiritual principles will, with with some luck and many blessings, come out unscathed by the drug monsters of our time.

Rock Music

Keep your children shielded from the worst in heavy rock music, especially the overtly salacious and satanic kind. Do it as well as you can, for as long as you can. Don't allow youngsters to watch music videos. Monitor their listening activities at home and in the homes of friends. Yes, children like rock music. Children like everything that glitters and makes a lot of noise. But they will also like the better forms of music if you give them a chance: show tunes, jazz, ragtime, singalongs, New Age, ethnic, folk, symphonic, religious—there's plenty to choose from.

Eventually, when a youngster enters the teenage years and when rock music becomes his or her anthem, as it has for almost every young person in our country today, then perhaps it will be time to make exceptions. Then, perhaps, it will be time to bend.

But now, during childhood, during the most impressionable years of life, you have the right and the *obligation* to prevent youngsters from being marked by the destructive powers of low-grade popular entertainments. Music, bear in mind, is a phenemonally powerful persuasive force, a magical messenger that exerts far more control over our unconscious minds than we normally suppose. It is no accident that tyrants from Napoleon to Hitler have known that marches and anthems can make populations perform the types of bestial acts that words alone cannot inspire; or, conversely, that in religious myth deities like Orpheus or Apollo or Krishna bring the word of God to humanity with the power of music alone.

Carl Jung once remarked that popular entertainment is a

way of working out our private neuroses in public. This is clearly the case with contemporary music today. Guard your young ones against it, even though you may have to swim against the tide to succeed. If your friends announce that you are being an alarmist, that there is nothing wrong with a frisky beat and good showmanship, just remember the telling words of Baudelaire, no stranger to the darkness himself. "The devil's finest and most seductive trick," that brooding poet once remarked, "is to convince you he doesn't exist."

3. Persist, Be Consistent, and If You Fail Try Again

On the one hand, you will want to support the ideal of protecting your child against every harmful influence in the universe; on the other, you are well aware that you can never live up to such a ridiculously lofty goal.

Good. Bravo! This is as it should be. Life is process as well as progress, and the quest for making things better is part of the human imperative: no pain, no gain. In this difficult time, when so many pitfalls lie in wait for the father and mother of a child, be assured that your efforts will not be in vain no matter how futile they may seem at the time. Be convinced that, as all sacred texts point out, the Divine powers are not oblivious of our attempts.

Apropos this crucial fact is an ancient Christian story that tells how one night many years ago an anchorite received a vision. This venerable man saw a wide sea and on its shore a monk. The monk leaped high into the air and with bright wings soared effortlessly across the water to a heavenly land on the other side.

As the hermit wondered over this strange vision a second monk approached and he, too, spread his wings. This time the flight was far less smooth, and though the monk reached his destination he had all he could do to keep from falling into the lashing waves.

Finally, a third monk appeared. So feeble was his flight this time, however, that more than once he tumbled into the roaring waters. Only with the most heroic efforts did he keep himself moving ahead in the dark night, and only eventually, half-dead and thoroughly drenched, did he reach the far shore.

After much pondering the monk went to his superior and asked him the meaning of this dream. The superior interpreted: "The first monk was the believer who aspires to fly to heaven in our own time—now religion and good persons are everywhere, and going to heaven is a relatively easy task.

"The next monk stands for those who try to reach heaven in the years to come. Their journey will be a good deal more arduous.

"Finally, the third monk is the believer who makes spiritual efforts in the very distant future, when religion and righteousness have almost vanished from the world. During this dark millennium it will be difficult beyond imagining to reach the other shore. So rejoice that you live in our blessed time. But do not forget this: The third monk's efforts are worth far, far more than those of all the rest."

PART · 5

———

TEACHING CHILDREN VALUES AND VIRTUE

19.

Instilling Virtue Without Breaking Hearts

Pick up any number of recent books on child rearing and you will read several hefty chapters on how to build your child's self-confidence. Likewise you will find much information on instilling good self-images in children, on teaching useful communication skills, and, most of all, on helping children "feel good about themselves." All these techniques will help produce nicely adjusted youngsters, of course. And all are absolutely necessary for the raising of any healthy, happy human being.

Yet in many of these same books, filled as they are with techniques for bolstering ego strength, you will search in vain for one particular missing ingredient: teaching virtue. Where are the sections in these books on moderation, say, or on humility and patience? Or dignity, awe, temperance, forgiveness, sacrifice, industriousness, charity? There is much in the canon of parenting books on how to make a child feel loved, little on how to help a child *to love*. There are many rules for self, few for selflessness. Psychologist Kendra Smith, speaking of the modern therapeutic system in general, wrote: "Wholesome factors of consciousness like mindfulness, selflessness, detachment, shame, sympathy are valued (in Buddhism), like money in the bank, a hedge against karmic debt. Never do these factors—and rarely do the courage, humor, and idealism so movingly apparent in so many patients (in therapy)—appear in the buff-colored sheets titled 'Diagnostic Summary.' "

Common sense tells us that what makes good men and good women are good traits of character. That if we are going to foster kindly, adjusted persons we must teach them virtue at an early age; later on it will not be so easy. Spiritual teachers through the ages have concurred, stressing that the real path to happiness is not through self-assertion but through selflessness. "I don't know what your destiny will be," Albert Schweitzer wrote, summing up his credo, "but one thing I know; the only ones among you who will be really happy are those who have sought and found how to serve."

CATALOGING THE VIRTUES

Let's call these positive spiritual qualities *virtues.* The word is a bit lackluster, perhaps, and doesn't express the full, heartfelt vigor of its Latin antecedent *virtus.* But for want of a better word it will serve. A similar and related, somewhat more secular word is *value* and it, too, has its place. "Man's chief purpose," exclaims the American critic and writer Lewis Mumford, "is the creation and preservation of values; that is what gives meaning to our civilization, and the participation in this is what gives significance, ultimately, to the individual human life."

While naturally there are many values that you and I would like to see our children develop, each parent will have his or her special list.

If you have never actually made such a list, try doing so now. Write down the character traits you would like to see your children develop as time passes and place a star by those you consider the most desirable.

If such a list does not come easily to mind, there are a number of traditional models to use as guide. Plato posited four cardinal virtues: prudence, temperance, fortitude, and justice. To these Christianity added three more: faith, hope, and charity. The seventeenth-century hermeticist Philalethes believed that in order to succeed spiritually a child must be taught to be "persevering, industrious, learned, gentle, good-tempered, a close student, and neither easily discouraged nor slothful. . . . Above all, let him be honest, God-fearing, prayerful, and holy." Even in our own time such sayings as the Boy Scout oath offer wonderful ideals: A young person should be trustworthy, loyal, helpful, friendly, courteous, kind, obedient, thankful, thrifty, brave, clean, and reverent.

Such collections of virtues represent an ideal, of course, and could be fully embodied only in a messiah. Important for us to realize, however, is that virtue is taught to children not simply to make them "holy," but to protect them as well. "The thing you have to realize about keeping the religious law," I recently overheard a rabbi tell a group of young listeners, "is that the law is not just a series of prohibitions designed to deprive you of your fun. No. It is a collection of practical advice written down by learned men to *guard* you from the things that bring harm, and to encourage you toward the things that give you real profit in life. Virtue, you see, is armor as well as goodness."

INSTILLING VIRTUES WITHOUT BREAKING HEARTS

How does one go about teaching values and virtues to creatures who are already half saints, but who are wild banshee maniacs as well? For, as any parent knows, children are an inscrutable composite of insight and ignorance, of maddening rigidity and supernatural malleability, of selflessness and egomania, of the deep sleeper and the awakened sage.

Given this confounding mixture, special medicine is called for. The following chapters will concentrate on these contradictory elements with suggestions on how to best get them across to your children.

20.

Teaching Honesty

Honesty is not inborn. Unlike perseverance, say, or courage, which some youngsters display at amazingly early ages, the wish to treat other people fairly and squarely has to be taught.

To make the matter a bit difficult though, honesty wears several hats.

There is the honesty of possessions: not taking what belongs to other persons.

And the honesty of words: learning to tell the truth.

And, finally, the honesty of behavior: not cheating or victimizing others, and its flip side: being emotionally forthright, sincere, and direct.

1. STEALING: TEACHING THE HONESTY OF POSSESSIONS

Let us start with the first and in certain ways the easiest of the three, honesty of possessions. And let's start at the beginning, with toddlers.

And let's start by saying that you shouldn't be surprised if children from one to three stare at you blankly when you correct them for taking what doesn't belong to them. They probably don't get what you're miffed about. If they do, they don't much care.

At the same time, you can start laying the foundations of honesty by acquainting toddlers with the concept of private ownership. An easy place to begin is with danger spots around the house: "No! Hot stove!" "Uhuh, sharp!" "Be careful, it's slippery!" Besides protecting little hides, these warnings create an association in the child's mind between concepts of do and don't and specific physical objects.

By two and a half years you can apply the don't-touch rule to items of value around the living room, bedroom, and kitchen. Stress their functional and personal importance:

> "Don't handle the vase, sweetie, it's grandma's and she'd be sad if it fell and broke."
> "Don't paint on the tablecloth, Bobby. Mom just washed it. She'll have to wash it again if it gets dirty."
> "Those are Daddy's; leave them in the jar. He needs his pens to write with."

After a while a child comes to understand that the vase really does belong to Grandma and that distressing consequences will follow if her proprietary rights are violated. Or that tablecloths are eaten on and are not for soiling: Fingers off! And that Dad does become perturbed if his pens are messed with. In these simple prescriptions an awareness of "mine and yours" is developed.

When youngsters reach their third year, parents can then continue applying the same commands, but now with an increased emphasis on *possession:*

> "Don't touch! The typewriter belongs to your father."
> "Be careful not to sit on that coat. It Mrs. Wexler's."
> "If you are going to borrow those scissors I'd like you to return them to me as soon as you're finished. They're mine and I need them."

Five to six is still an uncertain age as far as the ethics of property go, and the child's dominant litany is "What's mine is mine, and what's yours is not yours." Some young people have an abstract idea that they should keep their hands to themselves. But, oh, that remote-control car of Larry's! Ah, those crumb cakes at the supermarket! Wow, coins in Grandma's purse!

This line of thought, not so far removed from the rationale used by adults at times, is in the child's case inspired less by larceny than from ignorance of the way life's social games are organized and played.

"There is something almost wistful and charming in what [the child] steals and the way he steals it," write the authors of the famous *The Gessell Institute's Child Behavior* guide. "At five he may prefer pennies to half dollars. They have meaning to him. At six he responds to the beauty of some trinket and takes it before your very eyes even though he denies it when accused. At seven his passion for pencils and erasers is so strong that he wants more and more and more—any within hand's reach. And by eight the loose money in the kitchen drawer is indeed a temptation . . . when the theft is discovered he is punished and admonished. He probably excuses himself that 'he didn't mean to' and he certainly promises that he will 'never do it again.' "[1]

THE HUBCAP SYNDROME

When stealing does take place parents become alarmed— sometimes too alarmed. Today pennies, tomorrow hubcaps. Rest assured that by almost everyone's estimation stealing is a phase all youngsters pass through and that occasional pilfer- ings rarely warrant pushing the panic button. For most youngsters it a testing of the waters more than an expression of incipient criminality, part of the age-old process of learning through trial and error.

At the same time, however, parents must not allow habitual stealing to go unremedied, especially if it occurs with increas- ing frequency. In such cases parents are advised to monitor this tricky activity *v-e-r-y* carefully, both because it can mushroom into a habit and because raising it as an issue can be a excellent tool for honing a child's sense of right and wrong.

APPEAL TO THE WHOLE CHILD

Appeals to a child's moral sense concerning theft should be two-pronged: through the emotions and through the mind. Often parents avail themselves of the first prong exclusively, the emotional—even when dealing with preschoolers who do not yet have much of a conscience to be appealed to.

Feelings should indeed be addressed in cases of stealing. But the remedy is incomplete unless an intellectual understanding is also given. "I never saw a person go wrong or get lost," one mother quoted to her child, "by following the right road." This is the message parents will want to get across most clearly. Here are some examples of how to bring it home:

Case One

Three friends came to swim at six-year-old Alex's backyard pool. After several hours of splashing around the children were picked up by their parents and taken home. An hour later Alex discovered that his snorkel-and-fin set was missing. One of the boys had obviously taken it. But which one?

"That's the trouble with stealing," said Alex's mother to Alex. "One of the boys will have a new set of goggles and fins tonight. He'll have all the fun. But another kid—you in this case—will be without them. When something gets stolen an innocent person suffers. That's why stealing's lousy."

Alex's mother called up the parents of the day's guests and the culprit was soon discovered. He was duly punished by his parents, and Alex's mother reported this fact forthwith. "Nick should have thought twice about taking what didn't belong to him," Mother said in a confident and confidential manner. "If someone takes what's not theirs they get punished for it. As far as I'm concerned, when stealing happens nobody wins."

Case Two

At Larry's school several unidentified mischief-makers broke into the school building at night, trashed a classroom, and stole three computers. The next day Larry's sixth-grade teacher made a point of bringing her entire class to the scene of the crime. She showed them how the thieves had smashed in the window and scattered glass on the floor. She showed how the inside of the room had been scarred, pointing out the overturned fish tank and the several dead fish lying nearby—innocent creatures had to suffer because the robbers were so mean. And, of course, now that the computers were stolen the computer class, a favorite in all grades, would have to be canceled until new machines could be purchased.

"Just because a few persons were dishonest and greedy," said Larry's teacher, "our whole class and our whole school is deprived. Stealing is mean. It hurts everybody. Even the people who do it usually feel badly later on. Nobody gains anything, and everyone loses."

Case Three

Five-year-old Leslie sneaked into her mother's room and helped herself to a pile of rolled-up quarters on the bureau. Leslie's parents quickly realized where the money had gone. At the dinner table that night Leslie's mother announced matter-of-factly that the roll of quarters had disappeared.

"What a shame," her father replied. "I needed those coins. I thought we'd take them and give them to the animal shelter so that the dogs and cats could get food. Now they'll have to go hungry."

Nothing more was said about the matter, but that night the coins magically reappeared on the bureau. The next day Leslie and her father brought the coins to the animal shelter and afterward went out together to spend the few quarters her dad had held out in order to buy ice cream.

Case Four

A new kid in Mary's class named Blanche came to play at Mary's house one afternoon and left with Mary's dollhouse refrigerator in her pocket. Mary told her mother about the theft. Mary's mother said that she guessed they would not invite Blanche over again 'cause she couldn't be trusted.

"You see," Mary's mother said. "When someone steals something we love we don't *trust* that person any more. We don't believe the things they tell us and we don't want to be their friend. I'm so proud to know that you don't steal from your friends. That's why they all trust you so much."

When watching TV programs or reading stories the idea that stealing hurts everyone can be reinforced. Each time the thief gets caught and punished, stress the fact that this person is experiencing the consequences of his or her deeds. Karma. Once this idea takes root, once the child sees that it is not profitable to deprive others of what is rightfully theirs, a good part of the honesty battle is already won.

FINALLY, APPEAL TO THE CONSCIENCE
When stealing occurs, make it clear that you feel bad about it. Don't get mad. Get sad. Let it be known that stealing goes against your beliefs. As far as you are concerned it is not spiritually or morally or humanly right to take what belongs to others. "Stealing makes me want to cry," one mother said when she discovered that her child was taking coins from her purse. "Stealing breaks my heart," said another.

21.

Teaching a Child to Tell the Truth

Every person's fate, the Buddhists believe, is determined by three actions only: What we think; What we say; What we do. In that order. Notice that what we say is given priority over what we do. Because, as the expression goes, "When the tongue speaks, the whole world moves." Words count, therefore, and this is one of the most important understandings a parent can convey to a child. The things we say influence people. They produce change. They set the wheels of suffering or pleasure into motion. They make others like us or hate us. They determine karma. They count.

Lonnie's father, a Hebrew teacher and Talmudic scholar, is fond of quoting Jewish proverbs concerning the importance of words whenever Lonnie steps out of line. When Lonnie talks back, his father warns that "One false word can start a war." When Lonnie says nasty things in the heat of anger, Father reminds him that "A human being can forget a slap; an unkind word one can never forget." While watching a political debate on TV, Lonnie's father remarks that "The

sign of a fool is that he uses a lot of words to say a little."
When Lonnie tries to talk his way out of paying back money,
his father informs him "Words don't pay debts." When Lonnie is yelled at by a teacher or is belittled by friends, his father
consoles him with "God is closest to those whose hearts are
broken." When Lonnie complains about his life his father says
"If people thanked God for all good things they wouldn't
have time to complain about the bad."

HELPING CHILDREN NOT TO LIE

A young child's fibs often seem outrageous and inexcusable
to parents. Junior denies breaking a plate after having just
dropped it on his mother's foot. Sister insists that she had no
part in tearing the coverings off baby brother's bed while she
stands there holding the blankets. Parents cannot understand
such flagrant untruths. They punish accordingly.

What parents do not always recognize at age four, five, or
six, and even up to seven, is that a youngster's sense of reality
may not be entirely developed and that what seems a morally
obvious fact to grownups exists only in embryonic outlines to
young perceptions. Children, immersed in a magical dream
world where to think a thing is to make it so, may simply be
developmentally incapable of processing sophisticated concepts of real and pretend, good and bad, with the result that
they honestly believe that their lies are true.

It is, moreover, not always an easy matter for children to tell
the difference between a lie and a figure of speech or a joke,
say, or a tease, a politeness, an exaggeration, or an estimation.

A six-year-old boy listened to a weather report that sol-
emnly stated the skies would be sunny and clear next day.
Next day came, bringing with it fun-spoiling rain, and the boy
angrily announced to his mother that the weatherperson had
lied.

"It wasn't really a lie," his mother told him.

"It was!" answered the child indignantly. "He said it would
be nice today. He was making it up!"

"He wasn't making it up. The weatherperson believed that

what he was saying was true. A lie is something you know isn't true, but you say it anyway."

"But why'd he say it would be sunny?" asked the child, still not convinced."

"From all the information he had at the time he thought the weather would be nice today. He said what he sincerely believed. But he was wrong. So what he said wasn't a lie. It was a mistake."

Many children have special difficulty with the idea of saying—or not saying—what they really think. Reasons the child: "Dad bugs me to always tell the truth. But when I say Granny's breath smells, or if I tell Uncle Ralph he has dirty teeth, or if I mention that I think dinner doesn't taste good, everyone gets mad at me. All I did was tell the truth."

The concept of white lies versus real lies is a puzzling one for children. While there are no foolproof formulas, explanations can be given that bring this and other cloudy issues into better perspective. For instance:

• Stress the fact that words that hurt people, even honest words, are often best unsaid. Appeal to children's innate feelings of sympathy. Remind them that if they see a person with one arm or who walks with a limp, this person probably feels self-conscious about this handicap already. The kind thing is to remain quiet and not make that person feel worse. Teach the rule of thumb: If you're not sure whether your words will hurt someone, stay silent. As Thumper the Rabbit said in *Bambi*: "If you can't say somethin' nice, don't say anythin' at all."

• Stress the fact that the kind of "truth" that causes others to feel badly about their physical or psychological problems is not necessarily truth at all. "You're weird!" "You smell yuchy!" "I don't like you"—such phrases, you might explain, are opinions, not facts. They are just a blurting out of our negative thoughts and impulses. It's best to keep these thoughts to ourselves, you can tell the child. Later on, if you like we can discuss them together in private. But not to the person's face. It hurts too much.

· Stress the fact that we must say polite things to people even if we don't always mean them. Why? Because sometimes it's more important to be kind than to be frank. For example, we say a cordial "Thank you" to a person who has just handed us a present even if we don't really like it. This is a graceful and grateful thing to do. It makes the other person feel good. Or we might tell a father and mother how beautiful their new baby is even if we secretly think it looks like a toad. This is a sort of lie, perhaps, but a compassionate one. We tell it because saying the opposite would hurt the new parents' feelings very badly. In other words, lies told to help other people or to make them happy are different from lies told to cheat others or to steal or to deceive. We call the former "white lies." Sometimes they're necessary.

INTRODUCE IDEAS OF HONESTY
AND DISHONESTY THROUGH STORIES

An excellent tale for children who frequently fib is "The Boy Who Cried Wolf." In this familiar fable a bored shepherd entertains himself by shouting falsely to the townspeople that a wolf is attacking his sheep. The good citizens heed the cry of "Wolf! Wolf!" and come running with picks and spears. When the real wolf invades the boy's camp, no one now believes his shouts for help and his sheep are eaten. He slinks off a sadder but a more honest shepherd.

Another story that shows the folly of lying is "The Pied Piper of Hamelin." The town council assures the pied piper that if he drives the rats from their county he will be handsomely rewarded. But the council goes back on its word and the piper is not paid. He then punishes the town for its lie by luring their children away forever. Because of the falsehoods of a few everyone in the town suffers.

A number of popular children's favorites highlight the struggle between honesty and falsehood. The candy decorations that cover the witch's house in "Hansel and Gretel" and the witch's pseudo-kindly welcome at the door are dirty tricks to gain a selfish end. So is the little tailor's boast that he has killed "seven with one blow." In the story of Aladdin, Aladdin's so-called uncle tries to deceive him about the real power of the magic lamp. In "Little Red Riding Hood" the wolf lies to Grandma and Red Riding Hood alike. In "The Emperor's New Clothes" it is the honesty of children that finally brings people to their senses.

Especially interesting is the mirror on the wall in "Snow White." It can never lie. So when the mirror tells the wicked queen that Snow White is the fairest in the land, terrible things happen to good people, and it seems that the mirror's honesty has served only to bring on Snow White's death. But it only *seems* this way. In the end, after many travails, Snow White and the prince are united and the truth the mirror tells turns out to have influenced events in a most fortunate way after all. Moral: The truth will out. Similar instances of honesty and deceit appear throughout the Bible, the stories of Joseph and his brothers and of Samson and Delilah being among the most interesting for children. They can also be found in popular children's tales such as *Pippi Longstocking, Treasure Island, Charlotte's Web, The Hobbit,* and many more. (See the book listings in Chapter 4 for particulars.)

When telling stories, give special attention to issues of lies and truth, even if some judicious retelling becomes necessary. Then discuss the story afterward. Ask questions: Why did the townspeople stop coming when the boy cried wolf? What caused the boy to tell such lies? Why were the townspeople punished so severely by the pied piper? What questions would you ask a magic mirror if you had one on your wall? What would you do if the mirror told you a truth you didn't want to hear, like it told the queen?

STRESS THE DIFFERENCES BETWEEN A FANTASY AND A LIE

As a rule, it is best not to automatically correct young children when they tell you they have seen a zebra in the bathtub or Santa Claus by the bed. Perhaps they have, who knows? At any rate, a tall tale and a lie are not the same, and the difference between them should be grasped by parents, if not by the child. A lie is an out-and-out attempt to mislead and misinform; a tall tale is whimsy moving at large, imagining, fantasizing, pretending, wish-fulfilling. Magical thinking again, but this time with illustrations. Let it be.

If at age eight or nine, however, elaborate fantasizing seems to be increasing and if children have difficulty telling the real from the pretend, this is another question entirely.

Often you can put things into perspective by helping children differentiate between the real truth and the imagined truth. Thomas Lickona in *Raising Good Children,* tells of a father who dealt with his daughter's fabrications in a particularly clever way. The father introduced the child to the idea that there are "true-true stories" and "true-false stories." A true-true story is really true. It actually happened. A "true-false story" is one you *wish* were true but isn't. Whenever the father suspected that his daughter was telling a tall tale he would ask her "Is this a true-true or a true-false story?" Applying these labels and forcing the child to make these distinctions helped her sort out the differences on her own.[1]

Lickona's method can be adapted to your particular situation. While watching TV together point out the difference between a documentary and a pretend drama. Or between a cartoon and a film with real performers. Point out whimsical drawings of animals and discuss how they come from the artist's sense of make-believe. Compare them to photographs of animals: these show the real thing. Is it a true-true animal or a true-false animal? Ask children to tell you a fantasy story and explain why it is a creation of the imagination. Then ask them to tell you a "real" story about things that have actually happened. Discuss the differences.

DISAPPROVE OF LYING
BUT DON'T GET MAD AT IT

Children at five and six often lie out of fear, and angry reactions on parents' part can serve to turn this fear into a self-fulfilling prophecy. In general, severe scoldings and punishments do *not* make successful remedies against living and may even exacerbate it, especially if youngsters are not certain of the differences between truth and falsehood in the first place. A touch of humorous body language may get the point across better then a tongue-lashing. Try using the following routines when an obvious lie is told:

- An extended "hmmmmmmm"
- A steady, unbroken stare with a slight smile
- An ironic lift of the eyebrows
- A puzzled, bemused expression
- A confused roll of the eyes and a bewildered scratch of the head
- A doubtful glance with an "are-you-kidding-me" kind of expression

Each time the child says something dubious repeat one of these techniques. After a while the visual signal will speak for itself and the child will know when he or she has bent the facts too far. Lying often tends to self-correct itself when mirrored back to the liar, especially if done in such good-humored and nonaccusatory ways.

A more direct approach for older children is to let it be known gently but firmly that you disapprove of lying on moral and spiritual grounds, and that what was just said is simply not the truth. Typical explanations might go something like:

> *"What you say sounds like it would be nice, but I'm afraid it's not true. The plate is broken and I saw you drop it. Come on now, let's pick up the pieces together. Next time tell me when it happens. Truth is more important to me than my possessions."*

For older children (nine and ten), parental reaction to lies can be delivered with more clout, though the same rules of humor and polite directness still apply. Unless the lie is a malicious one that causes other persons pain, it's better to: (1) Make the child aware that you know he or she is lying; (2) Make it plain that you do not approve; (3) Explain alternative methods he or she might use next time to avoid lying.

When Jon broke a treasured antique silver pen and assured

everyone he had nothing to do with its destruction, his parents took him aside. They told him that when he makes a mistake like breaking a pen he should come to them. He should tell them he had something important to report but that first they should agree not get mad. "Our part will be to not get mad." his parents said. "We may ask you to make up for what you've done in some way. If what you did was serious you may have to be punished for it. But the punishment will be a lot less if you tell the truth. And you'll feel a lot better about it, too."

Try to determine why the child lied—out of fear, fantasy, convenience, anger—then address the motivation directly. According to Dr. Allan Fromme, one-time chief psychologist of the Child Guidance and Well Baby Clinic at St. Luke's Hospital in New York City, children lie for four main reasons:

> To gain praise and affection
> To conceal guilt
> To avoid punishment
> As an act of general hostility

"The first step in teaching a child not to lie," says Dr. Fromme, "is to reassure him sufficiently *so that he feels that he does not have to lie.* This is another way of saying that we make a mistake of overimpressing our children with our moral authority. If they feel deeply sure of our love for them, our children would have very much less cause for lying. They are frequently prompted to lie to us because they are afraid to tell the truth. We translate this advice into action by reminding them that we are on their side."[2]

Finally, never set up a situation in which children are tempted to lie.

> POOR: *Parents ask their son "Did you leave your jacket at Billy's house again?" The accused is forced to answer yes or no. If he is frightened of the consequences, and if he already has the lying habit, chances are he will fib to save his hide.*

BETTER: *Parents say "Your jacket is missing. It's probably at Billy's house. Will you call and see?" Through a direct statement rather than an interrogative, the temptation to lie is not presented. And if perchance the parent happens to be wrong, if the jacket is not at Billy's house, the youngster will say where it is and no one gets their feelings hurt.*

POOR: *Parents say to a child "There's water all over the floor! Did you splash again after I asked you not to?" Obviously, if the child was the last person to take a bath, it was he or she who splashed. The fact is self-evident. So why make it into a an anxiety-provoking showdown with a confrontative question? Say instead:*

BETTER: *"There's water all over the floor from your bath. Please clean it up immediately."*

22.

Teaching Honest Behavior

In certain ways learning what we might call the honesty of behavior requires greater maturity than simply refraining from a lie or from a theft. When you think about it, many of us continue to work at honing this skill throughout our lives.

Small wonder, then, that between the ages of four and seven children lack the moral equipment to understand fully why human beings should deal with one another in anything approaching a fair and equitable way. They *honestly* do not see the good sense in cooperation and fair play, in what's wrong with glancing at their neighbor's cards in a game of Crazy Eights, or why they should allow another kid a turn looking through the binoculars.

In some ways it even seems that children take a delight in exploiting one another. The sense of power it brings is intoxicating stuff, and if truth be told Hammurabi's code and Dog Eat Dog are far more popular credos on the playground than the Golden Rule. Why give it up, Junior wonders, just because Father tells me it's nice not to gyp my best friend out of his allowance? Or because Mother thinks it's wrong to break my word? What's in it for me to play fair?

What is in it for them, children wonder? Not much, so far as they can figure. But something *is* in it for them—several important things—and if children discover these bonus points early in the game their life will be smoothed considerably.

HELPING CHILDREN PERCEIVE THE LOGIC OF HONEST BEHAVIOR

The forthright way is also the smart way, and youngsters who are taught this fact already have a leg up on the world.

Why is it the smart way? the child may wonder. Because, the parent replies, if you treat others fairly and squarely they will return the favor to you, sometimes with interest. Swindle them and they will swindle you back. That's just the way things work. The world is a mirror that reflects our behavior and our intentions back to us.

Yes, there are exceptions, the parents explain. Because sometimes we run into people who cheat us even if we play fair. But not usually. Usually, others treat us about as well as we treat them.

And so forth. You get the idea, which is to stress the all-decisive fact that honesty is not simply a finger-waving rule promulgated by adult do-gooders, but a practical, efficient, self-serving mechanism by which children can get what they want and at the same time make themselves and everyone else feel good about it too: an all-win proposition.

Honesty of actions has other benefits, too, and you might tell children about them. Honesty assures us that our life will run smoothly. Without it even the most simple transactions such as buying a toy (we *trust* that the money is good) or agreeing to meet a friend (we *trust* that the friend will show up as planned) would be impossible. Honesty makes people admire us and respect us. It makes them like us, perhaps even love us. Best of all, treating others in a just and kindly way makes us feel just and kindly about ourselves. It is a spiritual action, a reverent way of walking through the world and a sign of respect for God. Guaranteed. Try it and see.

Using this line of reasoning and backing it up with solid

evidence (more on this below), parents can transform a child's inclination toward selfishness into an attitude of care and integrity. It's a bit of a trick, but a benevolent and efficient one. "How do you make a man honest?" a reporter once asked Mahatma Gandhi. "By showing him that honesty pays" was the Mahatma's realistic reply.

Here are a few suggestions:

Show the Child That It Is
the Cheater Who Gets Cheated

In life experiences are the best. Use them when they occur. For instance, when a child has just been double-crossed or otherwise taken advantage of, seize the opportunity to point out why this behavior harms both the cheater and the cheated.

Take the case of eight-year-old Terry. While swapping baseball cards he and a classmate made a trade: a hundred of Terry's National League cards for seventy-five of his friend's American League cards, with two new Dave Winfield cards thrown in to clench the agreement. Fine. The boys counted the cards out in separate piles and exchanged. But at home Terry discovered that his trading partner had stuck in at least twenty wrong cards plus several worthless duplicates. This could conceivably have been an oversight had it not been for the fact that the boy had made such a big deal about how carefully he was counting the cards and about how he would put the Dave Winfield cards on top of the pack. He hadn't.

"That kid cheated me," Terry cried to his father. "I trusted him. He's a rat."

"Sounds as if he acted like one," said the father. "Do you think you'd trade cards with him again?"

"No way!"

"I can't blame you. When someone cheats us it makes us want to cheat them back. That's what I've noticed happens to cheaters—they get cheated themselves. When you see this kid again tell him you know about the fast one he pulled. Tell him you don't trust him any more and that you won't trade cards with him. Nobody wants to play with a cheater, tell him. Tell him that because of his cheating neither of you will be able to get the cards you want. Tell him you will have to suffer because he didn't play fair."

Terry's father is not really concerned about whether the other boy receives this message. He is addressing something in Terry, who has been having problems himself acting in a forthright way. Father is using Terry's sense of betrayal as a means of helping his son see that it hurts to get cheated, that no one likes a cheater, and that everyone loses when cheating occurs.

Stress the Value of Mutual Trust

Incorporate the word *trust* into your everyday conversation. Use it in many different contexts:

"Sarah, I'm *trusting* you to remember to feed the fish every morning."

"I *trusted* that you'd give back the fishing pole this morning like I asked, Billy. But you didn't. I'm disappointed."

"We agreed that you'd pick up your room by bedtime. It's still not picked up. You didn't live up to our *trust.* Please try harder next time."

"I'm going to *trust* you to bring this tape over to Jill's house, 'cause I know I can *trust* you. Please don't let me down."

Cultivate a Mutual Atmosphere of
Trust Between Yourselves and the Child

Children respond to being trusted, especially older children who by age nine or ten have developed the scaffolding of a social and moral conscience. Youngsters at this age will feel honored that parents believe in them even though they are "just kids," and this feeling will inspire them to live up to parental expectations.

Allow a sense of trust and approval to permeate your home. Let children know that you think their motives are genuine and their hearts good. If their behavior seems dubious, give the benefit of the doubt until proven guilty. "It is happier to be sometimes cheated," Samuel Johnson remarked, "than not to trust." In most healthy human situations trust breeds trust.

Expose the Child to Stories that Champion Fair Play

Before the fetish for "realism" took over in our culture most stories, novels, plays, and even films made a point of showing that fair play breeds success. This moral assumption was, of course, unquestioned during the Victorian era, when entertainments that focused on the wages of vice and virtue were the norm. To a certain extent it prevailed even up to the Second World War, and, in fact, as late as the early 1960s it was still forbidden by the film code for characters in a movie to get away with a crime.

This ethic still limps bravely on today in some forms of children's entertainments, though on a voluntary level only—filmmakers can now give a story any kind of moral twist they desire, from crime-doesn't-pay to crime-pays-with-interest.

While those responsible for weakening the moral code felt at the time that the crime-doesn't-pay moral was goody-goody and unrealistic and that the public should be exposed to life "as it really is," they missed an obvious point: that by showing people getting away with crimes, certain viewers are encouraged to try these crimes for themselves. The crime-doesn't-pay ending was, many believe, a valuable social protective device that, once breached, invited a massive reevaluation of right and wrong. There is no proving it, of course, but, it is perhaps not entirely coincidence that between 1960 and 1970, the period of time in which this code disappeared from media entertainment, that the crime rate in the United States rose almost 20 percent.

Be that as it may, the point is that if parents wish to impress the rules of honesty on their offspring they must present stories and games that encourage fair play, not foul. This means two things. Parents can:

(1) Expose children to stories, games, literature, films, and entertainments that emphasize good triumphing over evil and suggest that fair play is a legitimate method of gaining suc-

cess. The Horatio Alger stories, corny as they now appear with their interminable sermons on the value of hard work and unselfishness, undoubtedly contributed far more to children's positive character development than *Miami Vice* does today.

(2) Keep children away from books, comics, computer games, and TV programs in which antisocial behavior is extolled and in which cheating, exploitation, lying, cunning, recklessness, and hucksterism are held up as models of behavior. You won't have far to go to find such examples. Teenage films (most of which are also watched by children), movies about crime or getting rich quick, comic books, and even some juvenile novels all make a point of showing how their protagonists profit (oh, so cleverly) at the expense of others.

Use Jokes, Fantasy, and Vivid Imagery

One father enjoyed playing "Imagine if" with his two daughters. Along with ordinary "imagine if" questions such as "Imagine if all books were made of bananas and we could eat them after we read them," he slipped in ethical "imagine if" messages as well. "What if everyone on earth trusted everyone else?" he once asked, "and if no one ever took advantage of others? Just imagine: we wouldn't need police any more. 'Cause no one would commit a crime. We wouldn't have to bolt our doors. 'Cause every house would be safe. We wouldn't need burglar alarms, or vaults to hide our money, or locks for our bikes. We wouldn't have to put bars on our cellar doors. We wouldn't have to say 'I promise' because everything we said would be true." The father then asked his daughters what *they* thought the world would be like if everyone cooperated and lived in a state of trust.

One mother I know through mutual friends plays with her children in which she has them imagine what the world would be like if no trust of any sort existed:

"Imagine if I didn't trust the milk company," she suggests. "Every time I bought a carton of milk I'd have to open it up to make sure there really isn't lemonade inside."

"Imagine if I didn't trust the toothpaste makers. I'd have to smell the toothpaste each time to be sure they hadn't put in whipped cream."

"Imagine if I didn't trust the people who build the ferryboat. I'd have to swim across the bay instead."

And so forth. Ask the child to give *you* some examples. Then discuss how important it is that we all learn to treat each other fairly in this world.

Reward Children for Keeping a Trust

When children carry through on a promise or when they behave equitably in a difficult situation, make sure they are praised. In six-year-old Bobby's house Bobby's family keeps a "trust list" tacked to the kitchen wall. Bobby's parents make a point of telling him that he is *trusted* to clean his room without being told. That he is *trusted* to take out the dog in the morning and the garbage at night. Each time Bobby carries out one of these trusts he makes a check of the appropriate entry on his trust chart. When he gets fifty checks the whole family gets to go out to dinner and celebrate.

**Let the Child Discover What Rightful Pride
and Peace Can Come from Admitting a Wrong**

The Catholic church has long understood that the act of admitting a misdeed to a benevolent authority figure and then undergoing an appropriate penance is not only spiritually satisfying but psychologically therapeutic. While children especially benefit from such unburdenings, many are afraid to admit their acts of dishonesty to parents for fear of harsh reprisals. Instead of unburdening their guilt they internalize these feelings and sit on them. Later on these feelings become the stuff of anger and self-hatred.

This process can be nipped in the bud by parents who play the part of benevolent father confessors. "To prevent unnecessary guilt," writes Dr. Haim Ginott, "parents should deal with children's transgressions the way a good mechanic deals with a car that breaks down. He does not shame the owner; he points out what has to be repaired. He doesn't blame the car's sounds or rattles or squeaks; he uses them for diagnostic purposes. He asks himself, 'What is the probable source of the trouble?' "[1]

The child has a problem. He or she wishes to speak about it and be rid of the bad feeling it generates. On hearing these admissions parents maintain a steady balance between firm acknowledgment that the act was wrong (if indeed it was) and a positive acknowledgment that the child's act of confession is a courageous one and that it will in no way imperil their love.

Michael's parents make a point of sitting down with him whenever he seems anxious. They ask him what's wrong, encourage him to speak out, listen fixedly to what he says, and comment appropriately on his confessions. They then ask him what he thinks should be done to remedy the problem, and Michael frequently comes up with sensible suggestions for his own punishment. In this way the problem is self-solving. After this meeting is over an air of complete forgiveness pervades the household (this is important, too) and Michael is praised several times for having told the truth. When the affair is over he feels cleansed, strong, and proud of himself for having acted forthrightly in the face of difficulty. "You're good," Michael's mother tells him. "You've learned what strength can come from swimming against the stream."

Point Out That Being Honest Makes You Feel Good

"Virtue is its own reward." But why? Perhaps because virtue makes those who practice it feel so good. "One moment I remember as a child," wrote Franz Kafka, "was giving away to my sister a bonbon which I especially coveted at the time, then feeling a kind of joyous warmth travel through my body, as if I was on fire with a delectable inner light. I realize now, and perhaps I even realized dimly then, that this was my first moment of conscious realization that good faith towards others stirs one's own heart in the most pleasurable and unimaginable ways."

Next time children catch themselves in a lie or make an effort at honesty, after congratulating them ask them to notice how good they feel. Explain that this is our inner spirit's own way of rewarding us for a job well done. Explain that some deeper spiritual part is always rooting for us to be honest. Tell them to try not to let it down.

A PROMISE IS SACRED

Brenda's mother does not make promises to her daughter often, but when she does she *always* honors them. She believes that giving your word is a sacred act, even if it means exerting a great deal of extra effort to live up to it. Overheard in Brenda's house:

> "*I promised you we'd go to the beach today. Even though it's raining, if you still want to drive out there, we can. A promise is a promise, isn't it?*"

> "*I gave you my word that I'd stay home from work tomorrow and play with you. So I will. I made a promise and I have to stick to it now no matter what, don't I?*"

> "*I know you're upset 'cause we can't go to the puppet show. But I absolutely* promise *we can go to the film at the community center next week instead. And you know: in this house a promise is a promise!*"

Don't be shy about laying on the bravura. A promise is a REALLY BIG THING, something v-e-r-y special and v-e-r-y exalted.

This extra bit of body English will impress children. They will find comfort in the fact that an agreement can exist between people that is entirely reliable and secure.

To further emphasize the idea tell your child stories that highlight the golden concept of promise-keeping. Children are often intrigued by the fact that in "Rumpelstiltskin" when the little man comes to claim the queen's firstborn child, the queen does not take advantage of her new position and have him tossed out on his ear. She is, after all, now the queen. Instead, she sticks faithfully to her vow and is about to give the child up when Rumpelstiltskin relents and makes *his* promise: that if the queen can guess his name in three days he will release her from the oath. Other well-known fairy stories stories that include promises both kept and broken include "The Frog Prince," "King Hawksbeak," "The Pied Piper," "Aladdin and His Magic Lamp," and many more.

When children reach five or six, parents can take the next step in promise-keeping, which is to reverse the process and extract promises *from the child.* Start with secrets. Tell the youngster a secret and explain that he or she now has a duty not to reveal it. If (or more like it, when) the child spills the beans, point out that this behavior is wrong. A deal is a deal, after all. Next time you'll expect better.

Do make liberal allowances if children fail, of course, which they will, and don't be draconian about extracting compliance. On the other hand, stick to your guns. If a promise is broken, let it be known in no uncertain terms that you do not approve. Tell children that you will expect them to try harder next time—let them see that you consider this serious business. Then let them try again. You might even mention that there is something magical about a secret; that when children wish for a thing and don't tell it to their friends, the mere act of keeping it hidden can help it come true. That's why you're never supposed to tell your wish when you blow out the candles of a birthday cake. "When the heart becomes the grave of your secret," the Persian poet Rumi wrote, "that desire of yours will be gained more quickly."

Breaking ground in this way, continue to emphasize the specialness of promises. Even ordinary promises—promises to pick up the crayons, to finish the food on the plate, promises that are easy to keep and that produce visible results for both parent and child. Make it plain that a promise is different from all other agreements, that it is something sacrosanct that

you make before your God and that you must try to follow
with all your might. Children brought up hearing all this will
become thoroughly familiar with the concept and will have it
fixed in their minds, if not their hearts, that a promise is an
obligation we must honor, come what may. It is, in reality, a
kind of warm-up for a later age when persons will make sacred
promises to themselves, to their spiritual teacher, and to God.

SET AN EXAMPLE

"Children," remarked the French writer Joseph Joubert,
"have more need of models than of critics"; and, indeed, the
examples parents set come close to being the whole ball of
wax as far as the teaching of integrity is concerned. Thus, as
parents we would all be well advised to:

Practice what you preach in front of a child. Behave fairly and
avoid lying to children. When you play a game don't cheat,
even in fun. When you make an agreement stick to it, even if
the agreement is silly or annoying. If you do slip, apologize
and let it be known that you have made a mistake. Well-timed
apologies can make a deep impression on a child. They will
help children develop the concept of repentance and of
humility.

Do what you say and say what you do. If you announce that you
are going to take the child to the playground this afternoon
or to the movies this evening, stick to your word. Otherwise
children will read your change of mind as a lie and will feel
accordingly deceived. Pretty soon they will say to themselves:
If Mom or Pop can lie that way, why can't I? The prevarication
machine is now set in motion for a lifetime.

Watch those half-truths. Adults often take their daily social
and business fibs so for granted they forget that children are
listening in. "One half of the world doesn't know how much
the other half lies" goes the expression. "I just loved your
Christmas present," says Mother—but the child has heard
Mother ranting on about how useless she thinks this gift really
is. "I'd have loved to join you guys the other night at your

house for dinner,'' Father tells Charley on the phone—but the child distinctly heard Father say that he wouldn't be caught dead at Charley's house. And so on.

Watch those inconsistencies. Richard's parents make a point of telling him that it's wrong to take another person's property. But Richard is confused. He sees Dad steal magazines at the barber shop when the barber isn't looking. And sometimes Mom sneaks into the neighbor's yard at night to help herself to the apples on their trees. Sometimes when getting on the bus Richard's grandfather lies about Richard's age to save the fare. And Richard has distinctly seen his father cross at a red light after saying that it's wrong to break the law. Remember, it is unreasonable for parents to expect their children's principles to be any higher than their own.

23.

Patience

"Perhaps there is only one cardinal sin," wrote Franz Kafka: "Impatience. Because of impatience we are driven out of Paradise; because of impatience we cannot return." Almost all spiritual authorities agree: Patience is the ground on which the other virtues are seated. "Adopt the pace of nature," said Ralph Waldo Emerson. "Her secret is patience."

As far as children go, this special virtue is needed on both sides of the fence: the child must learn it, the parents must practice it. "No doubt a great amount of patience is required to take care of an infant," wrote Hazrat Inayat Khan. "But patience is never wasted; patience is a process through which a soul passes and become precious. . . . To raise an infant, to look after it, to educate it, and to give oneself to its service is as much a good work as the work of an adept [devotee]; because an adept forgets himself by meditation, a mother forgets herself by giving life to the child."

TEACH CHILDREN TO WAIT

Instant gratification is thy name, oh child, and it is a parent's job to tame this dragon early. Even when children are less than a year old they can be made to wait short periods of time before being fed or picked up. Later, toddlers will want their stuffed rabbit or their blanket or their tangerine when they want it: now! You can introduce the idea of patience at these moments by establishing a period of delay between request and response. One father, playing blocks with his two-year-old daughter, asks her which block she wants, then waits several moments before handing it to her. During the waiting time he sits very still, as if in suspended animation. Then he returns to life and hands her the block. After a while he reverses the process. He tells her to give him a block but to wait for a moment, to be *patient* for a moment before handing it over. In this very unobtrusive way the concept of waiting is introduced into the mind of one toddler.

Other opportunities for teaching the waiting process occur throughout the day. During meals the child should refrain from eating until everyone is seated at the table. All family members should be finished before the child has permission to leave the table. Small things mount up. Make youngsters wait ten minutes after a meal before getting dessert. Say to the child "Yes, I will play dominos with you. But not right away. Play quietly in your room for fifteen minutes, then I'll come."

If children want to know how long fifteen minutes is, tell them it's about as long as it takes to eat a meal. Patience and the time sense are related and during childhood, when clocks mean so very little, young people will enjoy measuring out their hours by natural intervals. Speak to them about waiting quietly for approximately the period it takes to get dressed in the morning or the amount of time it takes the bus to get to school.

Let waiting become the rule, not the exception. You will be bucking the push-button syndrome, of course, but all the more reason to persist. Tell the child that, yes, he or she can watch an hour of television, but *only* after finishing the homework assignment, or only after carefully picking up all scattered toys, or only after stacking the blankets neatly in the closet. Don't deprive unreasonably, but don't be immediately forthcoming, either. Let a time gap exist between desire and fulfillment. In this way impulse control is strengthened and an implied lesson is put forth: One must work and wait patiently in life before pleasures are granted.

USE PHYSICAL WORK TO TEACH PATIENCE

There is a mental patience, an emotional patience, and a physical patience. Teach all three, but especially physical patience. One good way of doing this is to encourage children to work with their hands, an activity that builds inner persistence as well as manual skill. Set children a goal with a hobby or project and help them attain it, step by measured step. At the same time, remember that the aim is for youngsters to develop tenacity and mental focus, not to build a better mousetrap. Emphasize the importance of the process, not the result.

If a children become impatient with their project and are about to chuck it in burst of frustration, encourage them to take a break and come back later. Suggest that they go outside, walk, run, change their impressions, have something to eat or drink, then come back and finish. Just keep at it. This message, that one can temporarily leave a taxing problem, rest, refresh, and return is a valuable lesson in patience, too.

Finally, let children witness your own patience in the face of a tough gluing job or a difficult stitch. Let them watch you overcome frustration with patient resolve. Psychological studies have shown that most children have the ability to assimilate manual skills simply by *watching* adults at work, and that adult ways of approaching a task will be copied by young observers. One child watches her mother's careful, Zen-like hand movements while she chops vegetables. Another sees his father cut wood with measured, graceful swings of an axe. A third witnesses a parent's calm, meditative state while modeling clay on a wheel. The implicit and nonverbal message is that working slowly, carefully, diligently can be a kind of meditative act in itself.

ENCOURAGE ACCEPTANCE

"With children," says the cleric and child psychologist Diane Lyric in a letter to this author, "the goal is to show them how to be happy with what they have this very minute. To show them the joy that comes from *not* wanting more, from savoring what is presently in their cup and not what is in their neighbor's cup. To show them the angelic ease that accompanies contentment. I like Albert Einstein's quote: 'Be willing to have it so. Acceptance of what has happened is the first step to overcoming the consequences of any misfortune.' Our whole life today in recent civilization is spent in anticipation of what's next. What material things or what sensory experiences will come tomorrow. A pity it is too that so little emphasis is placed in our schools or in our family groupings on teaching the child to be pleased with what God has rendered unto us this day, and to be grateful for it. Contentment, I have come to believe, is one of the last stages in the spiritual journey. It is, I think, only one or two faltering steps behind real peace."

How does one teach true spiritual acceptance to child?

Here are some ideas:

• *Don't surround your child with too many material things.* "The irony is," a mother of two children remarked, "that the more you give them the more they expect. And the less happy they are with what they already have." Go easy on presents and toys, on objects that fill every square inch of the closet but leave the heart empty. A few well-chosen items presented at special occasions will be more appreciated than an endless stream of gifts.

In this regard, single parents especially tend to indulge their children in lavish giving to offset their sadness and guilt over the divorce. But the message relayed to the child is an unfortunate one: When you're feeling badly salve your wounds by consuming. A considerably better offering is the gift of a parent's own company. Trips to the museum, working side by side in the yard, assembling a photo album together, folding laundry, a group swim, a walk in the forest, just plain talking and laughing and fooling around will make a child far more content than a store-bought toy. It will also bring home the lesson that the things that make us feel most satisfied in life are not physical objects but quality contact with persons we love and trust.

• *Give thanks.* Make sure the child gives prayers of thanks at night and that included in these prayers are expressions of gratitude to agencies human and divine. Some parents feature a "thank you" list after the lights go out. Ask children what they are grateful for today; they will reply as they will, sometimes in amusing ways. Overheard in my own nursery:

> Thank you, God, for protecting me when I fell on the blacktop this morning. A skinned knee is better than death.

> Thank you, earth, for white daisies and petals.

> Thank you, Mom, for driving me to Benny's house and picking me up later on, even though I was fresh.

> Thank you, sun, for shining when I asked you to.

> Thank you, electricity, for going on and lighting those Christmas lights that broke last Christmas.

• *Stress the concept of social gratitude.* Make sure children are encouraged to say thank you to others and to acknowledge all kindnesses. Ingratitude is an ugly trait; a child who is ungrateful is never satisfied, and a child who is never satisfied is never happy.

Urge children to write thank-you letters and to make thank-you phone calls for recent kindnesses. Ask the youngster what he or she thinks they can do to repay the kindness.

• *Avoid the "If only" syndrome.* "If only it hadn't rained we could have gone to the carnival." "If only the sale had lasted

a little longer we could have afforded that new air condi-
tioner." "If only Norma was the head of the team things
would run a lot smoother." As an Egyptian friend once said
to me after having lived and taught in this country for a year:
"You Americans—you survive on three phrases: If, I hope,
and in the future. In my country such terms are discouraged.
They are considered to be insults to God, who knows best
what we need."

· *Hold contentment up as a trait to be praised and emulated.* Ned
fell off a horse, bruised his ankle, and could not play in a
much-looked-forward-to tournament soccer game. He suffered with silent dignity, and his parents praised his courage.
"If you can do something about a problem, do it," Ned's
father had advised. "If you can't, then accept what God gives
you graciously." He then quoted Reinhold Neibuhr's famous
prayer: "O God give us serenity to accept what cannot be
changed, courage to change what should be changed, and
wisdom to distinguish the one from the other."

· Make a point of the fact that there is a hidden opportunity
in every problem and that patience during adversity brings its
inevitable rewards

"Grace under pressure," John F. Kennedy often said, was
the quality he admired most in others. A brilliant spiritual
example of this quality is cited in Richard Wilhelm's preface
to his translation of the Chinese classic, the *I Ching.* The
incident took place, Wilhelm explains, during the Second
World War amid the siege of the Chinese city of Tsingtao.
Wilhelm was in charge of the Chinese Red Cross, and in
between shellings he attempted to buoy his spirits with a
study of the Confucian classics. "Happiest of all, however,"
he writes, "was an old Chinese who was so wholly absorbed
in his sacred books that not even a grenade falling at his side
could disturb his calm. He reached out for it—it was a dud—
then drew back his hand and, remarking that it was very hot,
forthwith returned to his books."[1]

Few of us can muster such sublime detachment, of course,
though even small efforts in this direction will help. Take the
case of Hank, who spent his thirteenth summer getting in

shape for junior varsity football. After working out with incredible determination he finally made the team. The week before the first game, however, he took a header and sprained both wrists. The doctor informed him that he would not be able to play for at least a month.

Hank's first reaction was despair. His mother stayed close and insisted that what seemed like a problem can often turn into a blessing, if only we keep the proper perspective. She urged Hank to sit quietly and meditate on the problem. "Don't ask for your wrists to get better faster," she advised. "Pray for the courage to accept what's happened to you and for the ability to learn the proper lessons from it."

Four weeks later Hank's wrists had healed. By this time he had joined the photography club at school and decided not to continue at sports. He confided to his mother that he enjoyed taking pictures far more than scrimmaging, and that he now realized that if he hadn't hurt himself he would never have had so much fun in photography class. His mother agreed.

Hank's mother might have driven her point home with even more emphasis had she told Hank a particular Chinese story that Wilhelm's old Confucian scholar no doubt knew by heart. I have seen this story reproduced several times throughout the years, and whenever I read it it packs the same spiritual wallop. Perhaps no other tale of its kind expresses so vividly the importance of acceptance and the peace that is to be found by surrendering to a higher will:

> An old man lived on a farm with his son and their horse. One day the horse ran away and the old man's neighbors came to console him. "What a pity," they said. "Without the horse you will be unable to plow, and without plowing, no harvest. You have had great misfortune indeed."
>
> "Perhaps yes, perhaps no," replied the old man.
>
> The neighbors looked at each other in a puzzled way. "What a strange reply," they said under their breath, and went home.
>
> But a day later the horse returned, this time wearing a saddle studded with jewels and pieces of gold. Where it had come from

no one knew, but when it was sold it made both father and son rich men.

The old man's neighbors came again. "What great good fortune has shone upon you from the Immortals," they said all at once. "You are indeed most fortunate among men."

"Perhaps yes, perhaps no," replied the old man.

"What an ungrateful fellow" was the neighbors' only comment as they departed.

The next week the man's son attempted to mount their newly returned horse, but the animal was feeling irritable and bucked the boy off. He fell to the ground and broke both his legs.

"How dreadful," the old man's neighbors now fretted. "You have a crippled son. No one will tend your fields. How evil your luck has become."

"Perhaps yes, perhaps no," replied the old man.

Several weeks later a troop of soldiers marched up to the old man's door. A great battle was about to take place nearby, an imposing officer announced to the old man, and the imperial army had come to conscript all young men in the valley. Where was the old man's son?

The boy came forward. But when the officer saw that both his legs were in splints he turned up his nose in disgust. "This one will never make a soldier," he announced, and off he and his army marched.

"How fortunate you are," exclaimed the old man's neighbors. "All our sons have been taken to the army and some may not return. Yours alone remains to serve you in your old age. The Immortals indeed despise us and hold you in esteem."

"Perhaps yes, perhaps no," the old man replied.

This time the neighbors understood. They smiled and made no reply.

BE PATIENT YOURSELF

Remember that each child grows at his or her own pace, and that parents will surely be called upon at some time to show patience toward their youngster's deficiencies. Certain children will be poor eaters. Others will be slow to talk or to accept toilet training. Some will be stingy, or have learning disabilities, or be afraid of the water. Every child will show an Achilles heel in *some* area, and parental tolerance must flow like milk when this moment arrives. Comparing your child with others is a dangerous game at best and one that can make both parent and child feel like failures. The more parents accept the child as he or she is, the more that child will feel accepted; and as an adult, the more that child will be able to accept others.

24.

Manners and Forbearance

TWO IN ONE: MANNERS AND FORBEARANCE

Real manners are *kindness.* They make other people feel respected, they ease their burden, and in the process they chip away at our own selfishness and self-importance. Manners are a way of helping ourselves spiritually while we help others.

In many countries, especially in the Middle and Far East, manners are heavily formalized and often appear ludicrous exaggerations to the Western eye. But there is method in this madness. Human beings tend to be selfish and self-seeking, the ancients knew, and constant reminding is required to prevent them from forgetting others' rights entirely.

A mannerly response serves as a check against this tendency, even if it appears utterly rote and ritualized to an outsider's view. When one visits a Japanese household and the father introduces his family by saying "This is my frivolous, ill-bred daughter. This is my low-born, unworthy wife. This is my headstrong, foolish young son," he probably does not mean any of this in his heart. But something in this age-old form of introduction reminds him, however deep in his unconscious, that it is spiritually important to be humble. The medium is the message in this case; manners are a tried-and-tested formula that somehow reminds both adults and children that serving others is the highest form of behavior. Here are some ideas for inculcating this principle into young minds:

1. *Show gratitude toward the child.* Start by saying *please* and *thank you* to preschoolers whenever they hand you an object. But say it with all your heart. Let the child sense that you are, indeed, grateful for what has been given you. Let an emotional quality pervade the exchange. When such moments are vitalized by real feelings they take on a deep meaning for young people. Many children will naturally start saying *thank you* back as a matter of course, simply because it feels so good.

Many years ago I visited pre-Russian Afghanistan and stayed several weeks at a small hotel in Kabul. Having traveled through the East for several months with a trunk that was barely hinged together, I made a trip to the local bazaar and purchased a spanking new Chinese model, complete with brass hardware and combination lock. Back at the hotel I was planning to bring my old trunk down to the desk for disposal when I heard a knock at my door. It was the hotel porter, come to clean the room.

This porter was an elderly man dressed in the pajama pants, brown shirt, and wound turban of his countrymen. It was impossible for me, an outsider, to gauge his social and financial standing but I decided to risk the chance of offending him and offered him the trunk, hoping he would not see through this impromptu attempt to save myself a trip downstairs.

At first he seemed dumbfounded, like a man who has suddenly offered a throne. He said nothing, but simply picked up the trunk and started to walk out of the room with it. At the door he then turned, placed his hand over his heart, and made a short bow of gratitude. Then he left.

To this day I do not know what it was about this moment

that so moved me. It was nothing but a simple head nod and a quick, burning expression of the eyes, made with neither obsequiousness nor defensiveness. Yet before or since I have never received anything approaching such heartfelt thanks. The imprint of that old porter's appreciation—his pristine gesture of acknowledgment and recognition—seemed literally to enter my body. I could feel it inside me, as if something palpable had been placed into my heart. I can still sense the feeling twenty-five years later.

2. *Use everyday experiences.* Train children to wait for others at the dining table before starting to eat. Explain to them that it's polite to chew with their mouth closed; no one at the table, after all, enjoys looking at half-digested food. Encourage the child not to interrupt during family conversations. Encourage picking up around the house. Why? asks Jason. Because helping is a *kind* thing to do—and because we *need* your help. Encourage the child to be of service, to hold the chair at the table for Grandmother. Why? asks Heather Jo. Because Grammy has trouble with her legs, and this way you'll be making her more comfortable. I'm proud of you.

3. *Help children to go against the grain.* "Assume a virtue if you have it not" is perhaps a less hypocritical saying than it might appear. Children complain that they "hate" Mrs. X. So why act polite to her? Parents answer: Because it's a kind thing to do. And because it's excellent training to go against one's negative feelings and to make ourselves act politely to persons we don't care for.

What does this mean exactly? Well, to force our mouth into smiles when there are none in our hearts. To shake hands warmly when our antagonist's hand is cold and unfriendly. To help someone up from a chair when we would as soon knock him down. To look a disliked person straight in the eyes without rancor. To go against the little voice that says "I can't stand the ground this guy walks on." The person before you, parents should make clear, is a human being. He or she is as much a part of God's creation as we are, and as such we owe them respect. Children should be taught to give this respect, even if it hurts.

Is it hypocritical to act courteously toward people we dislike? Perhaps. But only if we do it to exploit other people, or to deceive them for our own profit. Otherwise it is simply a technique for going against one's negativity and for keeping the peace.

Children, moreover, who learn at an early age to control the impulse to frown or stick out their tongue or use abusive language are taking big steps toward self-control. Later these efforts can become the stuff not only of real kindness and forbearance but of internal power and will as well. "You feel sad, or worried, indignant, or jealous or suspicious," wrote A. R. Orage. "Exactly at that moment when you are experiencing one of these emotions, and are involuntarily about to betray it, resist the impulse. Don't let your muscles suit their action to your mood. Make them at least keep still. If this effort of non-expression is made at the moment when our body is most eager to shout our secrets on the house-tops the results will be found to justify themselves. . . . A man who can deny his muscles their habitual luxury of automatically acting his moods and emotions is on the road to the greatest powers."[1]

4. *Be polite to the child.* Although the idea is somewhat foreign to Westerners, in parts of the East respect and politeness toward one's children are an integral part of family life. Once upon a time in China a son would bow to his father and the father would bow back to his son. While in the cradle a child was addressed with special honorifics, since it was believed that newborns are receptive to exceedingly fine words. Children were given special places of honor at banquets, and parents took elaborate pains to speak respectfully to their offspring even when they were very young.

Today parents can transpose these methods into modern application. For instance:

Avoid disparaging children publicly, especially when friends or important adults are nearby. If children are acting up in a social situation, take them aside for criticism; never criticize them harshly in front of others. The memory of scathing reproofs given in public can leave indelible scars.

Address children in a sincere tone. Avoid the singsong, condescending cadence so many adults affect: "Well—and how are *youuuuuu* today, Bobby? Have you been a goooooood boy today, Bobby? Oh, thaaaaaaat's good."

Allow children their psychic space and physical privacy. When a child wants to be left alone, let it be. Don't pester or cajole. Allowing children room for their private worlds is one of the most mannerly things parents can do.

Lend them a hand when you can. Be on the spot to help. And if children want to perform the task themselves, honor this impulse with equal willingness. Sometimes politeness is in the things we do *not* do for a child as well as the things we do.

Insist on instilling manners that have meaning. It really doesn't matter a great deal, after all, if children take their hats off in the elevator. It *does* matter that they refrain from pushing in front of others, or shouting in another's ear, or wiping their noses on the tablecloth. Youngsters will know the difference, too.

Michael Schulman and Eva Mekler note in their fine book *Bringing Up a Moral Child* that a group of psychologists, after having observed dozens of classrooms, found that children from two-and-a half years to adolescence all clearly understand the difference between rules based on bureaucratic demands and rules based on real human values.[2]

Youngsters, they found, tend to pay far more attention to the human rules—rules against killing animals or hitting, stealing, or playing unfairly—than to the conventional rules such as what part of the lunchroom they must eat in or where class assignments should be done. Most children maintained that harming a classmate was wrong even if there were no school rules against it. "This finding," conclude Shulman and Mekler, "is particularly important because it helps explain why children don't usually resist moral rules while they often fight conventional ones with all their strength."

Parents should follow this lead and insist only on those acts of courtesy that help or protect or comfort other persons. The remainder belong to the fashion of the hour and to the brittle exhortations in Emily Post.

Use a variety of supportive phrases in daily conversation to make children feel honored and valued. Young ones are often starved for affirmation, yet parents tend to overlook this relatively easy way of making them feel good. Typical conversational examples include:

"You're absolutely right, Rick. That's a great idea."

"That's a very good point you're making. I never thought of it that way."

"Thank you for reminding me of that. I would have totally forgotten."

"How kind of you, Jesse! You've really saved the day for me."

"You're a good sport, kid. Not everyone would have waited that long in the rain."

"You really have a skill at that. I'm impressed."

When children make mistakes, it is polite on the parent's part to help them save face:

CHILD: I dropped my notebook in a puddle, Mom. The paper's all got drenched.
MOTHER: Yipes! Well, it's really wet out today. You must have slipped, huh? Let's see if we can get these pages dry before tomorrow.

CHILD [spilling juice all over herself and the dining room table]: Oh nuts, I never do anything right!
FATHER: Hey, what are you blaming yourself for? The

glass was all slippery from the juice; I saw it. Accidents happen to everyone. They certainly happen to me.

Being polite to a child will gradually make the child become polite back to you. Children are mirrors for their parents. "When a young person swears," Martin Luther King, Jr., said once, "you should punish the parents, not the child."

5. *Explain the logic behind manners.* "Show courtesy to all people," Dag Hammarskjold remarked, "not because they are gentlemen, but because *you* are a gentleman." It's important for children to understand this principle, that manners are not arbitrary dicta but that they represent tried-and-true techniques derived over the years to help others and to increase one's own good karma.

When instructing the child to say *please,* for instance, explain that in ancient times the word *please* meant "for your pleasure." Then try playing the amusing game of putting this phrase into sentences: "For your pleasure, remember to turn the lights off in the bathroom." "For your pleasure, eat your string beans." The phrase begins to make more contextural sense when said this way.

When children place their feet on the table, explain that this part of the body brings germs and that germs can cause sickness for others. When children grab at their food, explain that greedy grabbing is a sign of disrespect for the cook who made the food and God who grew it. When children butt ahead in line make it clear that letting others go first is a way of remembering that we have a responsibility to treat our neighbors with concern. To greet someone with a warm hello is a sign of friendly feelings—and it gets the same back. The good thing about manners, parents can explain, is that they communicate feelings without need for words. What you may not be able to say about your feelings you can sometimes do instead.

6. *Teach manners politely.* In *Between Parent and Child* Dr. Haim Ginnot makes the important point that when parents teach manners they often do so in a remarkably impolite way.

William's father, for example, lunges out in an impolite growl: "William! Say 'Excuse me' when you burp!" Myra's mother screams at her daughter "For God's sake, Myra, how many times have I told you to say 'How do you do' when you shake a person's hand!" When Dick's etiquette slips his parents make a practice of publicly mouthing the age-old children's bugbear "Mind your manners!!"

Such confrontative commands serve to alienate, not encourage, and they set a negative example. "The best way of training the young," Plato explained, "is to train yourself at the same time; not to admonish them, but to never be seen doing the kind of things for which you *would* admonish them."

7. *Stress respect for grownups, particularly toward parents and grandparents.* A young person once approached the Prophet Muhammad and declared that he wished to follow the prophet's teaching. But he was very young, the boy explained, and his parents needed him at home. What should he do? The prophet replied that the boy should not follow him at this time. He should remain at home and serve his family. That would be a far better thing. "Why did the Prophet deny the young boy this idea?" asks the Sufi teacher Hazrat Inayat Khan, reflecting on the meaning of this story. "Because the Prophet thought that [remaining at home with one's parents] was the first ideal. If the young man did not reach the first ideal, how could he get to the second ideal? If he did not look up to his parents, did not appreciate them or feel grateful to them, how could he appreciate the Prophet?"

While respect for those older than oneself remains a foundational part of life in many Eastern countries, our own society has tended to reverse the process, worshiping youth and turning the elderly out of sight and mind. All the more reason then for instituting a policy of respect in your home. If children are taught to treat their parents as honored friends they will carry this attitude with them out into the world. Honor for the right, honor for good people, honor for wisdom, and honor for God all stem from the lessons children receive in respect for their elders.

What constitutes lack of respect in a child? Everyone knows

it when they see it. The tendency to argue, to hit, to talk back, lash out, to tease, to not listen, to be fresh and disobey, to give tit for tat without remorse. A parent's tendency is sometimes to laugh at such reactions and chalk them up to the child's immaturity. "She's only a little kid—what do you expect?" But to measure behavior in this way, Hazrat Inayat Khan responds, is to work against the child's better interests. "All disrespectful tendencies grow with the years in childhood," he writes. "One does not think that they are of any importance, but when they are allowed to grow they grow as enemies, bitter enemies of the child. . . . The lack of this tendency towards respect is a misfortune for man. And besides the man who has no respect for another has no respect for himself. He cannot have it, he has not that sense. Self-respect only comes to the man who has respect for another; you will always find in a disrespectful person a lack of self-respect."

A few more ideas for teaching respect:

• From infancy on young people should be taught to respect old age, scholarship, skill, religion, humility, good persons, industry, strength of character, and the Divine. Children will adopt heroes and role models no matter what. Better that parents encourage them to admire the proper heroes and the proper heroic acts. We become what we admire.

• If you see your child acting rudely toward an adult in a public place—with a waitress, say, or a janitor or an elderly neighbor—treat this breach of etiquette with the same severity you might if the child were acting fresh at home. Make it plain that people *must* be treated with good manners no matter what their race, job, or place in life. If an older person is standing on a bus, give that person your seat and urge your child to do the same for someone else. Prompt the child to get up when an older person walks into the room. Have the child hold the chair for adults, or hand older persons their cane. Really thoughtful behavior, bottom-line, is a form of Divine brotherly love.

• As a rule of thumb: A child should never—*never, ever*—be allowed to strike his or her parents. Such attacks must be severely discouraged and promptly punished—striking is the ultimate disrespectful act. One parent disciplined his son for hitting by making him do twenty-five sit-ups and twenty deep knee bends every day for a week—pain for pain. Another forbade the child to attend a much-coveted sleep-over party because she had raised her arm in anger to her grandmother. Never let this one go unrebuked.

· Encourage youngsters to refer to all grownups as "Mister" or "Miss." Ten-year-old children addressing ninety-year-old men and women as "Larry" or "Harriet" is strictly out of line in any household that wishes to instill esteem and respect. Stress the fact that these honorifics are terms of salute, and that we use them to honor the person we are speaking to. The honored adult is older, has seen more, done more, suffered more, and hence knows more and is, therefore, above the child on life's wisdom pyramid. For this fact alone he or she is owed basic courtesy. No matter what the other children do in this regard, insist that yours stick to the important formality of Mister and Miss.

· Stress the notion of respect for the environment and for all living beings in God's creation. The question "What beautiful things have you seen today?" cannot be asked too frequently. Tell children that every day is a holy day in nature, and that a divine spirit is present among growing things, showing itself silently through nature's signs. Encourage children to become involved in ecological clean-up campaigns and to learn more about the balance of nature, to participate in nature study groups and to go on overnight campouts.

One father, while taking walks with his son through the forest, would tell his son to stand perfectly still and listen to the sound of the moving leaves. He then explained that long ago in a country called Greece there were special wise persons who lived in the forests and who believed they could understand the language leaves speak as they rustle in the wind. People came from all over the world to confer with these wise persons and to ask them questions. Special temples were built in sacred groves of trees just for this purpose.

· Discourage random cruelty to any living thing. Stress that human beings have a duty to be courteous to all creation, not just to one another, and that we owe a special measure of kindness and respect to animals and insects, to fish, plants, trees, even to rocks and earth. When you see a child destroying an ant's nest or senselessly pulling the leaves off a plant, that is the time to introduce the notion of reverence for life and respect for Creation. "Until you can make a fly's wing," one mother told her child, "it's better not to destroy it."

"Crow Indian children are taught that everything you see has a purpose in this world and contributes something to life," explains Henry Old Coyote, recalling his Indian childhood on the Great Plains. "There is a purpose behind everything; there is a force out there and that same force is responsible for all that surrounds you. This applies even to hunting. We are taught that if we go hunting and get some meat, we leave a little for the flesh-eating animals and birds that are out there. We usually tell everything in general that we've left this meat so that all the flesh-eating animals can share it with us. . . . We are always taught to respect our surroundings."[3]

• Set an example with your own parents. If they are alive, make sure your children see you serving them. Speak to your parents with respect. Avoid criticizing them in front of a child. Don't contradict them in public, or argue with them, or condescend to them—this may signal to the child that it's all right for them to do the same with you.

• In general, realize that children will not be automatically respectful. Respect is a learned virtue, and parents must continue to insist on it until the time comes when, usually in the preadolescent years, it becomes a regular part of the child's worldview.

25.

Kindness

Many languages (including French) do not possess a word that corresponds precisely to the English word *kindness.* What this means from a sociopolitical perspective is open to interpretation, though from a spiritual view it suggests that kindness is by no means universally applauded and that, by extension, in many children's hearts this sublime feeling does not form naturally. It must be instilled by tender insistence.

Several years ago an elderly Buddhist monk visited New York City from Burma. Residing with a group of his followers in an uptown apartment for several weeks, the monk gave daily audiences. At one such event a woman in her thirties brought her two young boys, eight and eleven, to meet the esteemed visitor.

It was summer and the windows were open. In the middle of the interview, while the monk and the woman were conversing and the children were watching disinterestedly, a mosquito landed on the monk's arm and began to probe for blood. Someone was about to whisk it away when the monk shook his head. "It takes so little," he said quietly.

When the two boys witnessed this scene they stopped daydreaming and looked at the monk curiously. Apparently the thought of *not* killing a biting mosquito had never occurred to them. Picking up on their interest, the monk addressed them directly: "All living things wish to be happy," he said. "When you grow up you too will want such a thing. Do you know what you must do to become happy?"

The boys shook their heads.

"Learn to be kind to everyone," came the answer. "Even to boys who bully you. Teachers who are unkind to you. Every time such persons are mean and you are gracious back, you will get stronger. Stronger and stronger. Until one day you will sit alone and know that what makes everyone in the world happy is kindness." "Even mosquitos like it," he added with a twinkle. Then he recited this poem:

> *If you give no help*
> *To others . . .*
> *You are wasting*
> *Your prayers.*

"Kindness gives birth to kindness," wrote Sophocles, and this is surely part of the lesson the monk wished to instill into the children's hearts. Courage, patience, humility, politeness, all are necessary in life—but kindness is love, and love is the spiritual energy around which the other virtues rotate, like planets around a sun. By teaching children the importance of this luminous power parents will already have paved half the road to heaven for their child.

ESPECIALLY ENCOURAGE GENEROSITY

Even at the toddler age parents can encourage the sharing of toys with playmates. If youngsters are reluctant to lend their things, as they usually will be, parents should gently persist. Generosity is a wonderful first lesson in being kind.

Later, this training pays off when parents witness school-age children giving part of their allowance to poor people on the streets or spending their money to buy a toy for a sibling. As youngsters mature in insight and knowledge they discover that happiness can be derived from another person's pleasure as well as their own, and that being generous brings an indescribable rush of good inner feelings in its wake.

Teach your children the importance of sharing and help them distinguish it from random gift-giving. A group of Hindu families from India recently came to the United States, where they soon became acquainted with the American mania for gift-giving, especially during holiday seasons. Before long their own children were asking which toys they would be getting for Christmas or wondering why they were not being given lavish birthday parties.

Racking their brains for a way to offset what they considered an exercise in irreligious consumerism, the elders of this group decided that they would attempt to reverse the entire process and that on Western gift-giving holidays they would have the children *give* presents rather than receive them.

Thus on Christmas Day a party was duly thrown for the children in this community, and each was encouraged to bring a gift that would be given to a poor person. Traditional games were played, ice cream and cake were served, fun was had by all, and at the end the presents were packed into a fine box and delivered by the children themselves to a nearby orphanage. In this way the much-vaunted "spirit of Christmas giving" was truly put into practice, and in the process the children became imbued with a crucial message: it feels better to give than to get.

While give, give, give should be an ongoing theme in your family household, this does not mean that the take, take, take should be directly opposed. A child's tendency toward selfishness is not necessarily overcome by telling him or her to be more generous, or else! Instead of directly confronting lack of generosity, try ignoring it and accentuate its opposite. For example:

Young Jackie received a record player for Christmas. Jackie's older sister Meg wanted to play some of her own records on the machine but Jackie announced that no one in the world could touch it except herself and Mommy and Daddy. Rather than deliver a sermon on the importance of sharing, Mommy and Daddy decided to lay low. They told Meg (in front of Jackie) that Jackie was really an extremely generous girl, but that right now she was feeling possessive of her new toy. After she used it for a while, they assured Meg, Jackie would change her mind and share.

Each time the record question arose in the next few days, Jackie's parents went through the same routine, praising Jackie's charity and assuring Meg that her sister would soon soften. Which, in fact, she did, on her own, proudly announcing to her parents how generous she now was 'cause *she* had decided to share with her sister.

What happens if this method backfires, if the Jackies of the world never do change their minds? Parents have several options, all of which are more effective than forcing the issue.

For one, the next time Jackie makes a point of being stingy, her parents might tell her how sad this makes them feel and how bad it makes Meg feel as well. "I love both you and Meg very much," Mother explains. "But it makes my heart heavy to see ungenerousness in this house."

A guilt trip? Not really. The parents speak to *both* children about how sad they feel over the mutual lack of sharing. "You" messages are kept to a minimum. A true guilt trip, after all, makes children feel badly about things over which they have no understanding or control. Here Jackie really *is* in error, really *does* have control, and certainly does deserve *some* kind of emotional straightening out. So Jackie's parents opt to appeal to her conscience rather than give her a brow-beating. Not bad.

Then there is the cooperation and trade-off method. The

record machine belongs to Jackie, yes. But Meg has a wonderful toy stove Jackie has coveted for months. Jackie's parents arrange a deal. Jackie lets Meg play with her phonograph; Meg lets Jackie use her stove. "You're both such big-hearted girls," Jackie's mother now beams as the girls play happily with each other's toys.

"Once a youngster fully discovers the satisfaction of giving as well as getting," stresses the *Encyclopedia of Child Care and Guidance,* "his generosity at times is a delight to see. Giving is part of his growth too. It emphasizes the fact that certain things are really his, to do with as he pleases. It makes him feel good too. Occasionally a child may regret some hasty large heartedness—but this can help him learn to use better judgment about giving. Sometimes a parent has to step in and help him develop this judgment."[1]

LEARN KINDNESS BY CARING FOR ANIMALS

Children can be encouraged to keep pets, to feed them, play with them, most of all protect them. Youngsters usually need little encouragement in this area, and most seem to have a natural rapport with small, furry beings. At the same time, it is often surprising for parents to see how cruel children can be to pets. Natural curiosity mixed with the thrill of power and a tinge of childhood sadism is not unusual among animal-owning youngsters, and here again, an opportunity emerges. Note:

• When first purchasing a pet make it clear that nurturing the new family friend will be the child's responsibility, and that the most important thing he or she can do for the new pet is to treat it with *kindness.* "If you forget to feed Ricky or give him water," said a father to his child about their new cat, "that's fine. I forgive you. We all make mistakes. But if I see you mistreat him that's different. There are no excuses for cruelty."

• Lay out an easily followed pet-care schedule. Let there be a time for feeding, a time for exercise, a time for grooming.

Although the pleasure that comes from owning an animal can be considerably reduced if parents overstress the responsibility side of things, children should nonetheless realize that the creature's welfare depends upon their solicitude, and that it is their job to fill these needs selflessly.

· In the beginning some parents sit with their child during the "pet take-care" times, as one family called it, and demonstrate how to feed and groom in a loving way. Encourage the child to talk to the animal, even if it is just a fish or a turtle. Ask the animal questions, then ask the child how he or she thinks the animal might reply if it could speak. Empathy will develop as a result. Make clear that the animal is not like a human being, that it is lower on the creation scale than humanity, but that it is an intelligent creature with its own thoughts and feelings. Urge the child to become sensitive to them.

· After the novelty of owning a pet wears off children may ignore the once fussed-over dog or cat. This is a natural reaction. At the same time, complete abandonment should be disallowed and this inevitable lull of affections will provide a good opportunity to remind the child that caring for *anything* is a full-time job.

· The school-age child's stewardship of an animal can serve as a jumping-off point for indoctrination into the realities of human kindness and cruelty. Having hugged a warm puppy on a cold night, the fourth-grader now hears from a schoolmate that puppies are eaten in parts of the Philippines. Having purchased a kitten from the local animal shelter, the child discovers that the creature was abandoned by its former owners and that other cats are being put to death in the animal shelter every day. Having nursed a sick dog back to health, the child discovers that over 500 dogs and cats are killed in scientific laboratory experiments every hour of the day. Having finished a steak dinner the child learns that the meat came from a warm, big-eyed cow—and that pork is from piggies, mutton from lambs, and that an egg might have become a baby chick had it not been fried instead.

Many young children are appalled when they first hear the

facts of humankind's inhumanity to animals, and here parents can urge a virtue from a vice. Explain that since some people are cruel to animals, you and the child will make extra efforts to be kind to them. Since some persons kill animals, you will protect them. Many civic-minded, peace-loving, socially contributive adults have been steered toward public service by their decision as children not to eat meat, to adopt stray dogs and cats, to honor animal rights, and to compensate for the world's cruelty by being kind and considerate to all living creatures.

STRESS THE GOLDEN RULE

A student once asked Confucius what constituted true humanity. The master replied: "What the superior person does not want done to himself, he does not do to others. And so both in the state and in the home, people everywhere are made satisfied."

The Golden Rule: Write it in bold letters. Frame it. Hang it up on the child's bedroom wall. Have children write the words out. Suggest that they give copies to others. Encourage children to commit it to memory. Recite it before the child goes to sleep at night. Say it aloud to children from an early age; explain it in detail. Whenever you see or hear your children acting unkindly remind them that they don't like to be treated badly themselves—so why treat others this way? Remind them of the Golden Rule: "Therefore all things whatsoever ye would that men should do to you, do ye even so to them" (Mark 7:12).

USE THE WORD *KIND* AS OFTEN AS POSSIBLE

Instead of complimenting children on being "good" or acting "well behaved," tell them how "kind" they are. Or how caring, loving, giving.

EXAMPLE: *Robert shares his toy soldiers with a friend*
PARENT: I saw you sharing your soldiers. I know how much they mean to you. It must have taken a lot of effort to be so kind.

EXAMPLE: *Nancy and her mother are watching television*
PARENT: That's amazing, he knew that if he ran into the burning house to save the child he might die. I'd call that about the kindest thing I've seen in a long time.

EXAMPLE: *Paul's baby brother Mike knocks over a bottle of rubber cement on Paul's desk*
PARENT: I know how you're feeling, believe me, Paul. But Mike's only a baby and doesn't know any better. Be as kind as you can and don't get mad at him. Someday when he grows up he'll remember how loving you were, and he'll be the same way back to you.

CONGRATULATE ALL ATTEMPTS AT KINDNESS

When children behave tenderheartedly, let them know you approve. Don't hold back the applause. Make children feel decorated for their feats of caring. Let the world know that you approve. Announce the child's achievement proudly to his or her teacher, to parents or friends, to relatives, playmates, to anyone who counts.

Listeners won't be very much interested in all this, of course, but they will pretend that they are—and, anyway, it doesn't matter much what they think. It's the good associations the child forms that count.

DISCREDIT ALL CRUELTY

Make clear how hateful behavior hurts the doer as well as the receiver. When reading a fairy tale that features a miser or a villain, point out how the bad guy's behavior stops other people from liking him. Discuss it with the child. If it turns out that a friend has recently acted unkindly, mirror the way the child feels back: "I can guess you're pretty angry at X for yelling at you, aren't you? I don't blame you. When people behave unkindly to me I feel unkind back at them. I'm sure it's the same thing for you."

MAKE KINDNESS FUN

"An adventure is an inconvenience rightly considered," wrote G. K. Chesterton, and the same might be said about a gratuitous kindness: A kindness is an inconvenience turned into an adventure.

Make doing nice things for people fun enterprises, and let good deeds become a kind of entertainment. Ask children what they think will help X, what gifts Y would enjoy, what chores can be done make Z's burden lighter. Then do it. Ask children what they think will cheer up Uncle Joe. Ask them to guess what kind of flowers Mom would like to receive. Plan a surprise: Make your brother's bed and don't say who did it. Try to guess what Pop's favorite food is and then cook it. Give someone a surprise party. Let children pretend they are a certain friend or family member and feel what it is like to be this person. Then determine what makes that person happy and what makes him or her sad. Then let the child set about making them happy.

A mother and her daughter are sitting together having breakfast. It's Saturday and they are planning their day. "What nice thing can we do for someone this afternoon?" the mother asks."

"Visit Grandpa?" suggests the child.

"That's good for a start," Mother replies. "What can we do for him when we get there?"

"We could bring him flowers."

"Great, very kind. What else?"

"Help him clean out his basement. Like we did last year. He liked that a lot."

"Great again. How about if we sneak into his house while he's at work this afternoon and clean it up for him as a surprise?"

After a number of such interchanges children will start coming to you with suggestions; doing good deeds will become a joint venture. "Teach children," wrote Thomas Lickona, "that love usually doesn't take the form of grand gestures but small deeds. Setting the table without being asked. Reading a story to your little sister when you'd rather do something else. Obeying promptly. Controlling your anger when your brother calls you a name. Playing with a kid at school who doesn't have any friends."[2] "He who loves," Martin Buber remarked, "brings God and the world together."

ENCOURAGE FORGIVENESS

Few impulses are higher on the scale of human qualities than forgiveness, and few virtues are more important for children to learn. "Why, if God can forgive each person his or her nine thousand and ninety-nine sins every minute," asks the Christian mystic William Law, "can we not forgive other persons just *one* of theirs?" A certain general once said to the Protestant reformer John Wesley, "Sir, I never forgive. "Then I hope, sir," replied Wesley, "you never do anything wrong."

You may have difficulty getting this one across to children, of course. They will not be in a forgiving frame of mind after their best friend walks off with a favorite crash helmet or lets go of a wagon that ran over their toes. Nor can you force the issue. But you can create a forgiving climate by frequently forgiving others yourself.

Stress forgiveness as a model and as a goal. Highlight it in stories and scriptures: Christ forgave his enemies and his murderers. Muhammad forgave the Koresh who had so viciously persecuted him in Mecca. Buddha even forgave the devil. When the child does show signs of forgiving others, reward the attempt. Point out that holding a grudge is like swallowing poison. "Forgiveness," said William Blake, "is the greatest of all the virtues, because it humbly puts up with *all* the vices."

TEACH A CHILD THE IMPORTANCE OF COMPASSION AND LOVE

"Kindness is in our power," Samuel Johnson remarked, "but fondness is not. "Teach children the difference between love as a *virtue* and love as a *feeling,*" suggests Lickona, echoing Dr. Johnson's observation. In order to love your neighbors, he points out, you don't have to marry them, or enshrine them—or, in a certain sense, even like them. Especially if you think your neighbors are jerks. What children *can* do is to see each person's best side, however hard it may be to catch sight of. Also, to not speak of that person behind his or her back. To wish that person well. To do him or her no harm. And to help them should they be in pain. Though "Love thy neighbor" may be a bit too advanced for most of us, young and old, "Regard thy neighbor as a suffering, needful human being like yourself" is within our grasp.

And finally there is yet another kind of love, the love which human beings bear for for the Ineffable. Once again the real task of teaching the ultimate spiritual message—love for the Divine—falls to parents. Teach it with kindness and gentle persistence, with prayer and proper example. Teach it with all the ways and means that have been suggested in this book and in other books that speak of spiritual parenting.

But remember also: To raise a child who is courteous and humble, who wishes to serve others, who is not lazy and who believes in a higher power—this is big stuff, a big accomplishment, especially in our difficult, unspiritual times.

Parents who have done such a thing can take pride in their achievement. They can take pride in the fact that once the ground has been made fertile in a child the movement from human love to spiritual love, while not automatic and while definitely not easy, is now part of the young person's vision of possibilities.

The choice will ultimately be the child's. But the groundwork has been laid. And it has been laid by you. Consider your time well spent and your effort a noble one. Some would call it the *most* noble effort any parent can make.

PART 6

TEACHING
MEDITATION
TO CHILDREN

26.

Teaching Children Prayer and Meditation

Several years ago a young couple living in the suburbs of San Francisco, in Sonoma County, became interested in the study of Buddhism. Discovering that a center was located near their home, they began attending Buddhist meditation classes and sitting in on the center's binightly lectures. The head of the center was an elderly Chinese monk, a representative of one of the last surviving branches of Chinese Chan Buddhism. Under his guidance the couple learned several meditation methods and within a year felt themselves well on the way to spiritual progress.

One day during a private interview with the old monk the subject of children came up. The monk seemed surprised to learn that the couple had a six-year-old son at home. Why hadn't they told him about the child?

"We didn't think it mattered in terms of our own meditation practice," the father answered, "so we never mentioned it to anyone here."

The monk was adamant. Why hadn't the couple told him

about their son? Why wasn't he coming to the monastery for meditation instruction? Why wasn't he meditating at home along with his father and mother?

"But he's too young," the father protested. "He's only six."

"Young!" snorted the monk. "In China in old days we have him starting year earlier than this, maybe two. Because of you he is negligent and already wastes two years of life. Two years he could otherwise have used to come nearer to getting enlightenment!"

START CHILDREN MEDITATING NOW

Most children can be taught the fundamentals of meditation and prayer before they learn to read. In Tibet, where before the Chinese takeover, over half the male and female population were monks and nuns, children were sometimes brought by their families to monasteries when they were two and three years old. With the parents living nearby, these children were tutored in meditation techniques by the resident monks from an extremely early age, so that by the time they were in their teens they were extraordinarily well equipped for treading the pathway to nirvana.

Chogyam Trungpa, a Tibetan *tulku* (reincarnated lama) who eventually founded several Buddhist meditation centers and a college in America, has written penetratingly about his childhood training as a monk. At age five he was taught to memorize and recite various mantras; in the evening, after learning to read and write all day, chanting and concentration practice would follow. Later he was transported to a retreat center built above a cave called *Dorje Kyungdzong.* Here more than forty young monks were kept busy meditating in isolation day and night, Trungpa tells us, for four straight years.

At eight the young acolyte was taught to perform various temple rites and to use bells, drums, and other sacred instruments. "At eight years old," Trungpa writes, "a child is very sensitive, and it is the time to inculcate ideas which must last him his lifetime, so at the end of this year I went into retreat for a simple form of meditation. This was upon the *nyendrup* of Manjusri, the Bodhisattva of Wisdom: that is to say, I was instructed to visualize him with his various symbolical attributes and to contemplate his transcendental Wisdom, to repeat his *mantras* or sonorous embodiments, and to recite the verses which preceded and followed them. I took a vow that I would live in solitude for three months away from all contacts other than my tutor and my cook attendant."[1]

The point is not to tarry, for prayer and meditation are at the heart of all devotional practice. Children should be taught these techniques as soon as possible, with parents as their guides.

While the many spiritual ideas profiled throughout this book have their place in the education of young persons, most of these methods belong to the child's outer world. They are spiritual values and moral practices that, if adhered to, will preserve children's purity of heart and make them ripe for higher work as adults. With meditation, on the other hand, a different part of the child's being is exercised, the soul. Here is where the potential for higher consciousness is located, and here is where the heart can be awakened. Here, indeed, is where the *real* spiritual journey begins: all else is a preparation and support.

We find the importance of meditation confirmed in the world's great spiritual traditions. "In the life of the Indian," wrote Ohiyesa, a Sioux Indian and medicine man, "there was only one inevitable duty—the duty of prayer—the daily recognition of the Unseen and Eternal. His daily devotions were more necessary to him than daily food." The Hindu sage Swami Sivananda echoed these words: "You are in the world to concentrate your mind on God . . . it is your most important duty. You forget this duty because of illusion which takes the form of family, children, money, power, position, honor, name and fame." "Live in the world," warned the Hindu saint Ramakrishna, "but keep the pitcher steady on your head: that is to say, keep the mind firmly on God." "Meditation," remarked Al-Muhasibi, a Sufi saint from the ancient city of Baghdad, "is the chief possession of the gnostic."

WHAT IS MEDITATION?

Many pages have been filled through the years attempting to explain meditation. Rather than wander about too long in the labyrinthine halls of definition, a few descriptive statements will, hopefully, cut to the center of things and allow us to move on to the matter at hand—the technique of meditation itself and how it can be used by youngsters. A few essential facts and observations about meditation:

Meditation is a Method for Escaping the Everyday Concerns of Life and for Helping a Person Turn Inward

In Thailand it is still common practice for soldiers, businesspeople, shopkeepers, and professionals to take at least one month off each year, shave their heads, and enter a Buddhist monastery. While in retreat these part-time contemplatives pass their time shedding the cares of everyday life, studying religious texts, and attempting to advance themselves spiritually by means of daily meditations.

The point is that, given this time to contemplate, the meditation process will, as it were, take over the meditator and lead to the kind of inner knowledge and peace that could probably not be attained without it. This clearly is one of meditation's central assets. It helps practitioners leave the concerns of daily life and focus inward, onto parts of the self that are normally forgotten in the ordinary commotion of things.

Meditation is a Method for Quieting the Mind

What we in the West call our "ordinary" minds—our thinking and reasoning apparatus—is for the meditator a discursive thought-making machine that runs largely out of control; even at night it is restless and besieged with dreams; it is rarely still, even for a minute.

The mind is like a luminous screen onto which a film of

mental pictures is ceaselessly being projected. Witness the process from the projection booth: A thought image arises. It continues for a moment or so, then blends into a different thought image, then another and another, world without end. We don't really have much control over this stream of mental images. They are projected on their own by a process of mental momentum—one image evokes the next, which evokes the next, which evokes the next. The mind, if you will, a'thinks us.

Once again William James has pertinent things to tell us. He calls this process mental association:

> . . . *our musings pursue an erratic course, swerving continually into some new direction traced by the shifting play of interest as it ever falls on some partial item. . . . Thus, for instance, after looking at my clock just now (1879), I found myself thinking of a recent resolution in the Senate about our legal-tender notes. The clock called up the image of the man who had repaired its gong. He suggested the jeweller's shop where I had last seen him; that shop, some shirt-studs which I had bought there; they, the value of gold and its recent decline; the latter, the equal value of greenbacks, and this naturally, the question of how long they were to last. . . . This is the ordinary process of the association of ideas as it spontaneously goes on in average minds.* He may call it ORDINARY, or MIXED ASSOCIATIONS.[2]

Among modern psychologists this ever-flowing stream of thoughts, imaginings, memories, and desires is thought to be a normal phenomenon that need not—should not—be tampered with. Yet in many spiritual disciplines (in all, perhaps), this "normal" process is believed to cast an opaque veil between ourselves and our higher natures, and is thus frequently spoken of as a state of "spiritual sleep." George Gurdjieff refers to the subject through his disciple P. D. Ouspensky: "He [humankind] cannot stop the flow of his thoughts, he cannot control his imagination, his emotions, his attention. He lives in a subjective world of 'I love,' 'I do not love,' 'I like,' 'I do not like,' 'I want,' 'I do not want,' that is, of what he thinks he likes, of what he thinks he does not like. . . . The real world is hidden from him by a wall of imagination. *He lives in sleep.* He is asleep. What is called 'clear consciousness' is sleep and a far more dangerous sleep than sleep at night in bed."[3]

How does one go about breaking through this web of thought and imagination? By stilling the mind—through meditation.

Meditation Focuses the Mind on a Single Thought, Image, or Idea

When meditators concentrate their attention on a single mental point a stilling process takes place in the mind. This point of attention can take many forms. It may, for example, be a picture or statue (Hindu worshipers concentrate on the figure of Vishnu or Siva). It can be a mental image (Tibetan monks visualize deities in various forms, both benign and wrathful). It can be a spiritual idea (Christians may ponder the Stations of the Cross). It can be a sound or incantation (Sufis repeat certain names of God in a meditation known as *Zikr*). It can be a type of body movement (practitioners of Tai Chi focus awareness onto their arms, legs, and breath as they move through a series of floating, rhythmic movements). It can be one's own breath (some Buddhist meditators learn the fundamentals of meditation by counting their breaths). It can even be a puzzle or spiritual conundrum (Zen Buddhist masters give their disciples strange questions, or *koans,* to ponder, such as "What was your original face before you were born?" or "If you put a goose in a bottle and it grows larger every day, how will you get it out?").

The idea behind these different concentration techniques is always more or less the same in all disciplines: to stop the mind's incessant motion by fixing it onto a single point of attention.

If Meditators are Able to Remain in a State of One-Pointed Concentration for a Long Enough Period of Time a Breakthrough Can Take Place into Altered Consciousness

If the mind is kept thoughtless and one-pointed for a certain length of time higher states of awareness will follow. How long it takes is conjectural, though some claim that even two or three minutes without thoughts will produce spiritual rewards. In Hinduism this state is known as *samadhi.* In Christianity it is called *contemplation.*

Meditation and Prayer are Always Similar and Often the Same

When prayer is petitionary—when the supplicant asks the heavenly powers for help—a certain concentration is required to stop the mind from wandering. This practice is a form of one-pointed concentration, though a preliminary one, comparable to conversing in an absorbed way with a friend. When devotees move one step beyond simple petition and attempt to fix their prayer on an aspect of the Divine, to commune with it directly, or to empty themselves entirely so that higher energies can flow down into the heart, prayer and meditation become the same.

Meditation Exercises the Imaginative Faculties of the Mind and Improves the Powers of Concentration

One of the happy side effects of meditation is that it sharpens a young person's powers of attention and imagination. These powers can then be used to help improve many daily activities. Parents have often remarked that their children tend to concentrate better in school after they have been meditating or that they perform daily tasks with greater attention to detail.

The Best Way to Learn about Meditation Is to Try It

The many excellent books available on the subject of meditation include several on children's meditation. While these are worth perusing (see the bibliography following this chapter), the best and fastest way to understand what meditation is all about is to have children do it, and to have the parents do it with them. Here's how:

PREPARING TO MEDITATE

A set of ten meditation techniques follow, arranged in order of increasing sophistication and of age-appropriateness. The first few techniques are start-up exercises meant for preschoolers. The middle range is for children from approximately six to nine. The last is designed for youngsters from the ages of ten to preadolescent. Each exercise will list the age range most appropriate to its practice.

Before beginning these exercises, a few words about preparing yourself and your child for this exciting venture.

**Find a Quiet Place Away from
All Noise and Disturbance**

Once you start meditating you and your children will not wish to be disturbed. When meditation time rolls around each day, take the phone off the hook. Lock the door and put out the dog. Locate yourselves in an area removed from commotion and unwanted interruptions.

Some meditators keep a section of their house or apartment reserved exclusively for meditation. This space becomes inviolate for them, a special place of contemplation within the heart of home.

Sometimes meditating families decorate prayer areas with inspirational art appropriate to their spiritual interests: wall hangings and posters, art reproductions and images of sacred objects, statues, prayer rugs, poems, calligraphic prayers, incense burners, pictures of one's spiritual teacher. A shelf can be set aside for the display of icons, rosary beads, prayer wheels, beautiful objects from nature, whatever. Sacred books can be placed in a special niche. Muslims, for instance, make sure that any copy of the Koran is located in the highest spot in the room. Taoists keep copies of the *I Ching* in a high place and cover it with special silk wrappings.

When you walk into the prayer space, consider removing your shoes as a sign that you are entering sacred ground. When you leave, bow and give thanks. Children will enjoy taking part in these ceremonies and in decorating the prayer space. They may wish to contribute their art to its decor: paintings, clay figures, drawings of spiritual subjects. One family I know painted a large inspirational mural on the door to their meditation place. Another covered the floor with rugs and pillows made from recycled Persian carpets.

Plan on Meditating with Your Children

At first you will be needed as an instructor, then as a friendly co-meditator. Eventually, children will want to practice on their own, but this usually comes later. The sense of togetherness felt during meditation time is a very special emotion and should not be missed by any spiritually oriented family.

Be Consistent So That Children Will Not Forget and Lose Interest

Meditate with your children every day if possible. At first keep the sessions short. Five minutes seems a very lengthy stretch of time to a child of four or five. Older children can sit for longer periods, fifteen minutes to a half-hour, whatever is comfortable. The important thing is to make meditation part of the daily life-style. If it becomes a habit during the young years it will remain that way into adulthood.

Sit in a Comfortable Position

Children are limber and will enjoy meditating in the half-lotus sitting position (one leg resting on top of the other, tailor-style). Fine. If this suits them, go to it. But in the beginning don't force postures on children. You will have a difficult enough time getting them to sit still. Insisting that they assume a gymnastic position will only make double trouble. My own daughter likes to meditate while lying flat on her back, preferably in bed; not ideal, certainly, but better than nothing. Other children I know enjoy sitting on the bed next to a parent, kneeling, sitting on a chair or on a special meditation cushion. Play it by ear. After a while, when meditation becomes a daily observance, you can introduce more sophisticated positions.

Do a Few Minutes of Deep Breathing Before You Start

Deep breathing calms the mind. Why it works like this has never been thoroughly investigated by Western researchers, but anyone who has tried it quickly discovers it to be so. When you and the child are seated comfortably, breathe slowly and deeply through your nose several times, concentrating on each inhalation and exhalation as you breathe. In the beginning forget about alternate-nostril breathing techniques or other fancy yogic stuff. Elaborate breathing techniques are unnecessary at this stage and can even be harmful if not taught by a qualified instructor. Stick with simple deep in-breaths and long, slow out-breaths. Five to ten will do. Now you are ready to begin meditating.

TEN BASIC MEDITATION TECHNIQUES FOR CHILDREN

Meditation 1: *Sitting Quietly*

Age: Four to six

Purpose: To introduce children to relaxed sitting and inner silence

Technique:

While this meditation is for complete beginners, anyone, adults included, would do well to practice it occasionally.

Sit quietly next to the child and explain that you are going to enjoy a "quiet time" together. Explain that we are usually very noisy inside, talking, thinking, remembering, imagining. Now we are going to learn something different and very nice: becoming silent inside. You may wish to explain that some people are able to become so silent that they can hear the voice of God whispering to them. Or that during meditation some persons go to places, far away from this earth, where everything is calm and beautiful.

Tell children to relax, close their eyes, and then do the same. Release tensions and worries while you do the preliminary breathing. The more relaxed you are the more relaxed the child will be.

Now tell children to empty everything from their minds until they feel very, very peaceful inside. Tell them it is important to sit still and to concentrate only on the silence inside them. Ask if they can become so quiet that there is nothing left inside except them and God.

Sit together in this way for as long as the child lasts. Don't push it, but don't cut it short either. Two to three minutes is fine at first. As the child gets used to sitting you can extend the time.

Trouble-shooting:

Some children become giggly and self-conscious when they first practice this exercise. Don't scold them. You want the experience to be a totally positive one. Just remain silent and continue meditating. Usually the child will follow your lead. If not, wrap it up and try again tomorrow. There's plenty of time.

The idea of sitting totally still is new and odd to most

children and may make them feel silly or threatened. After you practice sitting for a week or two they will get the idea, and the giggling stage passes. Just keep at it.

Meditation 2: *Counting*

Age: Five to seven

Purpose: To teach one-pointed concentration

Technique:

Though years may be needed to master this particular technique, it appears easy and fun to most children. Kindergarteners and early-graders are already engrossed in learning their numbers at school, and if handled properly this method can become a complement to class learning as well as an aid to focusing the mind.

Sit comfortably. Take a few deep breaths, close your eyes, and relax. Explain to children that you are going to count out loud from one to ten and that they should count along with you. Tell them to visualize each number as you count. When you pronounce the number one, tell them to picture it. It might be fun to see this number dressed up like a clown, say, or to see it walking a tightrope over a crowd of other numbers. Whatever image comes to mind is fine, even if it's really crazy. On the other hand, they may wish to simply see the number itself. Fine. The important thing is to hold a mental picture of the number and to try not to think of anything else while you do.

Count slowly, and have the child count with you. Do two or three rounds of one to ten, then talk about how the different numbers look:

Which numbers do you like best?
What clothes does a six wear?
What color is a ten?

How tall is a seven?
Does a nine have a face? What does it look like?
Do threes tend to be young or old?
What makes Mr. Zero so fat?

This may also be a good place to take advantage of the spiritual implications hidden below the surface of the fun. Explain to a child how in the olden days religious groups in Greece called the Pythagoreans believed that the whole universe could be understood by studying numbers. They thought that each number has its own soul, and that if you make friends with numbers they can communicate spiritual messages to you.

Later on, when children are eight or nine years old, they can continue in this meditation with or without dressing the numbers up, whatever they prefer. Keeping the mind concentrated on a single number for a relatively extended period of time will build concentration and will help children sustain better attention in class.

Trouble-shooting:

Don't count too quickly. Allow children time to form their images. Sometimes parents describe what the number looks like in their own minds as they count. This is satisfying for some children, but for others it is diverting and sends them off on a tangent. They would rather do it themselves. Try it both ways.

Meditation 3: *Taking a Magical Journey*

Age: Five to ten

Purpose: To keep a child's thoughts fixed on a certain prolonged sequence of events and to exercise their visionary imagination

Technique:

Settle the child down, close eyes, and breathe deeply. Tell the child that you are now going to take a magical journey together in your minds. Explain what you will be doing: describing this journey step by step out loud. All he or she has to do is listen and then go along in their imagination. Here is a typical example of where you might go and what you might do on your magical journey. Eventually you will want to make up your own scenarios:

> *Let's take a walk out into an open field. Here we go. It's summertime and all the flowers are in bloom. There, bend over and smell one. What does it smell like?*

> *Do you see that tree over there? There's a big door at the base of it. Let's investigate.*

> *Here we are. Open the door for me, will you? It's too heavy for me to lift. Thanks. Ah ha! Look down here, a long staircase. Come on, let's go.*

> *It's dark in here. Make a wish for a light, will you? Just say to yourself "I wish for light in this darkness." There, that's better! Now we can see our way as we go down the stairs.*

> *Down we go, step by step. It's so quiet and beautiful in here! Down another step, and another.*

> *Do you hear that? It sounds like a rushing river. Keep walking down these stairs and let's investigate. There it is, a river. And my word, look, it's river of silver light. How beautiful! Where do you think it came from? There's a boat, too. Let's get in it and see where it takes us.*

> *Here we go, floating along the rushing silver river. Seems like we're entering a cavern of some sorts. Look at those rock walls, they have diamonds and rubies all over them—how beautiful!*

*Can you reach out of the boat and pluck one off? There, good
going. I got one, too. Looks like a diamond. We'll bring it back
with us when we return to our normal life.*

*Now our boat's going round a corner. Here's another beauti-
ful cavern. This one has strange drawings and words all over
the wall. What do they look like? Describe them to me. I think
it's a kind of secret language. I'll read a little to you. It says
"Welcome to The Gnome King's land. You are his welcome
visitors today. Tomorrow you must come to his palace. I want
to tell you a magical secret and give you a special object that you
can use whenever you are frightened. Till then it is time for you
to return to your normal life. See you tomorrow." Signed: The
Gnome King.*

Let your imagination take you from place to place. You can
introduce spiritual ideas into the context of the narrative
whenever you wish, just as long as they remain integral to the
story. Be sure to describe the visual details of each scene and
always keep them specific and vivid. Let children participate
in the action. Have them smell the flower, pluck the stone,
read the magical writing. After you have done this meditation
several times you might allow youngsters to take control and
let them dictate the action to you.

If appropriate, you can also use the magical-journey meditation as a way of addressing a child's problems. In this instance the child is afraid of being left alone at night. So tomorrow night the parent will have The Gnome King award the
child a special sword. The king will instruct the child to take
out this sword whenever he feels afraid and to cut his fear in
half with it. He will tell the child to keep this sword with him
in his mind for the rest of his life and to use it whenever the
need arises.

Trouble-shooting:

Unless you are a natural storyteller, give a little thought
ahead of time to the plot, purpose, and sequence of your

imaginary journey. Otherwise you run the risk of boring the child into restlessness. Some parents let their children physically act out certain passages of the story. They let them sword-fight with the sea serpent or carry the giant's treasure out while the giant is asleep. This is a great technique as far as games of imagination go, but it is not ideal for a meditation. Acting out scenes will excite children and activate their juices; the meditative and the introspective side of things will then be lost. Better to keep these sessions low-key and to confine them to the imagination alone.

Meditation 4: *Chanting a Sacred Sound*

Age: Five to adult

Purpose: To introduce children to the idea of sacred sounds and to help them sense this sound inside their own bodies

Technique:

Chanting is an ancient spiritual technique for stilling the mind and for invoking one's higher self. All spiritual ways have special prayers that are sung aloud, and all agree that the sound and vibration possess an individual power that can help put chanters into higher states of consciousness.

The particular chant you choose depends on your religious interest. Christians may wish their children to recite the prayer "Jesus Christ, Son of God, have mercy on me" over and over again. Some will want to chant "Jesu, Jesu, Jesu" or simply "God, God, God." Muslims often recite the sacred name of Allah many times, while people not connected with a particular religion can encourage children to chant such words as *love, happiness,* and *peace.*

For our purposes the Sanscrit word *Om* (pronounced Ah-ooooo-mmmmm) makes an excellent introductory chant. Considered by Hindus the primal sound containing all other sounds, Om is also believed to have mind-stilling qualities for adults and children alike. Kids savor its deeply rounded resonances, and many enjoy the way it seems to literally echo around a room when a group of chanters sings it together. Youngsters will also enjoy chanting the Sanscrit word *Shanti* (peace) along with the Om: "Om, Shanti; Om, Shanti; Om, Shanti."

Explain to children that this meditation requires that they concentrate on the Om word and become aware of the way it echoes and vibrates throughout their entire bodies. Tell them to sense its depth and resonance. To feel it in their chests, in their throats, and in their hearts. Tell them to listen to the Om with their "inner ear" and to try to hear its secret messages. Have them visualize the way it looks in their minds and to try to "see" its form as it leaves their mouths.

To begin chanting, sit in your meditation place with the child, take several deep breaths, relax, and close your eyes. Sit quietly for several minutes to clear your mind, then begin the chant.

After reciting Om together for several minutes, stop, take a breath or two, and maintain a moment or two of silence. Then start again. Repeat as many rounds of this starting and stopping as you and the child feel comfortable with.

Trouble-shooting:

Children may find the deep, cavernous Om sound funny at first and may have trouble staying serious when you introduce it. Once you get them into its deep, stilling rhythm, they usually become captivated by it despite themselves and soon get into the swing of things. This sound is, in fact, extremely powerful, and beginners should not chant it for more than several minutes at a time.

Meditation 5: *Hearing the Sounds Around You*

Age: Six to adult

Purpose: To learn concentration, expand awareness, and become more sensorily awake

Technique:

Explain to the child that you will now do a "listening" meditation together. Explain that the world is full of a multitude of sounds but that we are so distracted we often don't hear them. By focusing our awareness on the sounds in our immediate vicinity, however, we can become aware that the world is a much more active place than we ever imagined.

The meditation works like this. After taking a few deep breaths, close your eyes and relax. Sit very quietly together and tune into the various noises nearby. Try not to think about them, only listen to them. Use your ears, not your mind. It doesn't matter what impressions you focus on—a bird, a car, a plane, the wind in the trees, a truck horn, distant thunder, mixing sounds in the kitchen, an elevator going up and down next to your apartment. Just let the sounds enter you as they will without entertaining other thoughts. Keep at it for several minutes, then discuss the results together. Whenever you catch yourself drifting off into thought, bring your attention back to the external world and continue to listen.

Trouble-shooting:

This is not an easy meditation to sustain and children may find themselves slipping into daydreams relatively soon. If this occurs you may wish to have the child listen to one particular sound instead of several. Try setting up a metronome and tell the child to concentrate on its ticking. Or let a faucet drip and tune the listening concentration onto its pit-pat sound. Such a single pointed focus may prove easier for children than multiple points of concentration. Try it both ways.

Meditation 6: *Traveling to the Ends of the Sky*

Age: Six to twelve

Purpose: To concentrate, to enjoy a feeling of inner expansiveness, and to become aware of the notion of infinity

Technique:

Sit, relax, breathe, close your eyes. Tell the child you are going to explore the sky together today, and that you will visit the entire universe in a few minutes. Impossible? Let's try.

Pretend in your imagination that you can fly. Take an imaginary leap in the air and head straight up toward the stars.

Now we've arrived in outer space. We're up here together in the heavens where there are no walls, no ground, no top or bottom. No sides, no up, no down, no beginning, no end. Just infinite dimension with only the stars for company.

Look as far as you can directly in front of you and then fly in that direction. Explore as far as you can go. See what you can see. Don't stop until you've gone the limit. Then turn around and fly back as far as you can go in the other direction, checking things out as you do. Go to the end—wherever it happens to be.

Now return to your starting point. This time fly downward. When you've reached the limits turn around and go as far up as possible.

After you've plumbed the depths of up and down, return to your starting point. Then take a moment or two to reenter our world. Discuss what you have seen together in your brief tour of the universe.

Trouble-shooting:

This one takes imagination. Children may not know what to look for when they get into "outer space" and may ask you to tell them what they should be seeing. But if possible, let them do the imagining. The idea is to introduce children to the concept of infinity, of timelessness and spacelessness. Their own imaginations should be the guide, not yours.

Meditation 7: *The Expanding Point of Light*

Age: Six to twelve

Purpose: To concentrate and to directly involve the emotions in a meditative experience

Technique:

Sit quietly for a few moments and think of several people you love. Have only good thoughts about them. Now close your eyes and imagine a small dot of light situated in the center of your heart. This light is love. It is the affection you feel for those you care about.

Imagine that the light is getting bigger. It's growing and becoming brighter. Repeat to yourself: "Bigger and lighter, brighter and brighter." More and more love.

Now the light is as big as your whole chest. . . . Now your whole body. . . . Now it's as big as the room. . . . Now it's expanding to the size of house or apartment. Bigger and lighter, brighter and brighter. Feel the light flooding your entire body and filling every corner of the room. Feel it making you warm and happy. Everything around you has become part of this light. Everyone nearby is being touched by it and is being made happy by your love. It is like the light of the sun, which shines on every living thing no matter who or where. Bigger and lighter, brighter and brighter, more and more love.

Now imagine that the light is starting to get smaller again. Now it is shrinking down to the size of the room. . . . Now to the size of your body. . . . Now it is back in your chest again. Finally it returns to the tiny spot in your heart.

Tell the children that whenever they wish they can look in their hearts and see this light and remember that it is love. They can make the light grow in their chest whenever they sit quietly. They can experience what it's like to feel real love for their neighbors whenever they meditate.

Trouble-shooting:

Don't rush this exercise. Talk it through a step at a time without any sense of urgency. If the children have trouble making the light grow large, let them keep it at whatever size is convenient. This is an excellent meditation and if done properly can expand children's feeling abilities and introduce them to the notion of love as a dynamic, active force in the universe.

Meditation 8: *Sending Love to Others*

Agee: *Six to twelve*

Purpose: A continuation of Meditation 7 in which children attempt to generate love within themselves *and* send it into the world

Technique:

Sit quietly, breathe, relax. Have the child picture several favorite people. Have him or her think good thoughts about these people and wish them well.

Tell the young meditators to focus on the point of light in their hearts. Tell them to let this point of light grow large again, as in Meditation 7. When they feel it starting to expand have them think either of a person they care for very much, an unhappy person they know who needs love, or a sick person, a person in distress. Let them send this person light from their hearts. Tell them to visualize this light forming a bridge from their own hearts to the heart of the recipient. Let feelings of concern and compassion travel along this bridge and flood the person at the other end with good feelings, health, and strength of spirit.

After several minutes of directing the light flow outward concentrate on bringing it back. Imagine that the light has done its job and is now returning to your own heart, that the light is contracting, and finally that it becomes a simple small point in the heart once again. Take a few deep breaths and sit quietly for afterward, savoring the pleasant afterglow of this exercise.

Trouble-shooting:

A considerable outpouring of subtle energy will occur in this exercise if done properly, so keep meditation time down to several minutes in the beginning. Children will sometimes become deeply absorbed in this exercise. They may see lights, hear sounds, sense presences nearby. This can be good or bad, depending on the child. If he or she is especially sensitive and seems to become overly excited while practicing the exercise it may be better for a while to switch to more cerebral meditations such as 5, 6, and 9.

Meditation 9: *Concentrating on a Meditation Diagram*

Age: Six to adult

Purpose: To hone concentration skills and to involve the sense of sight in a meditation

Technique:

Meditation diagrams have been used by meditators for centuries. Some of these images, such as Tibetan mandala forms or Hindu yantras, are believed to contain occult power all their own. For our purposes, a simple home-made circle diagram will offer children all they need to engage their minds in a direct and challenging way.

Start by making a meditation chart. Draw a circle ten or twelve inches in circumference and place a large dot exactly in the center with a laundry marker. Children can use a compass and draw their own diagram. Pin the chart on a nearby wall and seat yourselves in front of it. Breathe and relax. The aim of this meditation is to concentrate on the dot in the center and to keep other thoughts subdued. Only the dot, nothing else.

Work at this feat of one-pointed concentration for, say, two or three minutes, then move your concentration effort to the circumference of the circle and keep it there for several minutes. You can eventually move back and forth between the two points of awareness, the dot and circumference, as often as you wish, returning to either quickly when other thoughts waft your attention away.

After you have made this effort for some time close your eyes and imagine the same dot or circumference in your mind's eye. Continue concentrating on these points for several more minutes, then open your eyes, breathe deeply, and relax. You can repeat this exercise as many times as you like.

Trouble-shooting:

Unlike most meditations, this one is done with the eyes open, which means that kids can become distracted especially easily. Make sure you are positioned in front of a wall or some similarly uninteresting place so that there will be a minimum of diversions to catch the eye.

Meditation 10: *Controlling Thought*

Age: Eight to adult

Purpose:

This exercise is a relatively advanced Southern Buddhist technique designed to help meditators enter deep states of concentration and to escape from the all-powerful grip of the ordinary thought-producing mind. It is best for older children who have shown an interest in meditation and who have logged at least a year of experience honing their concentration technique.

Technique:

Sit quietly, relax, breathe, and close your eyes. Parents will have to talk children through this one carefully the first few times.

Begin by focusing attention on the breath. It is unnecessary to alter your breathing in any way. Keep it natural and observe the steady in, out, in, out rhythms.

When your mind starts to stray from the breath:

1. Notice that you have stopped concentrating on the breath and that you are, in fact, thinking about something else.

2. Describe to yourself what you are thinking about. Do this in a concise single sentence. For example, assume that you have lost focus and are thinking instead about having a snack. Say to yourself: "thinking about a snack." Suppose you are thinking about going outside to get the mail. Identify this thought in a terse "thinking about getting the mail."

3. After making yourself aware of the break in concentration and then labeling the diverting thought, return to the breath again: in, out, in, out. When your concentration slips return to steps 1 and 2 above.

The goal of this meditation is not to violently tear your mind away from distractions but to disinterestedly note them, then quickly return back to the point of concentration. The more you can keep your mind on your breath the deeper the meditation will become.

Trouble-shooting:

As mentioned, this is a relatively advanced technique and children may find it difficult at first. It can become extremely frustrating to realize that one simply *can't* keep the mind on the breath for very long, and that thought insists on going off on tangents, sometimes long ones (meditators may sit for stretches of time, then suddenly realize their attention has been off in never-never land for the past five or ten minutes). But this realization itself is excellent—it will show children the true nature of their "monkey minds" (to borrow a Buddhist term), minds that are always jumping from one point to the next, minds that are never still. This is a necessary truth for any spiritually oriented person to comprehend, especially a child, and can help provide incentive for further spiritual work.

The breath, moreover, is an excellent point of focus in any meditation, and the gentle, non-self-judgmental quality of this particular exercise will give kids confidence and keep them coming back for more. Talk them through it at first, though. The principles of this exercise are a bit more complicated than in other meditations and they may take some getting used to. Once they are grasped and practiced regularly, this meditation can produce wonderful mind-calming results.

LAST THOUGHTS

A central notion to bear in mind when teaching children meditation—in fact, when practicing spiritual parenting of any kind—is that it is not a parent's job to enlighten children spiritually, only to introduce them to basic spiritual ideas and techniques. The point is to get youngsters into the *meditation habit,* to familiarize them the workings of their own consciousness and with the joys of silence and sitting still. Maria Montessori once described to Inayat Khan how in her class children were at first resistant to taking time out of the day to sit quietly and empty their minds. After practicing meditation for a while they began to look forward to these sessions, Montessori said, and eventually they begged for longer meditation periods.

This, essentially, is a parent's role in the situation: to acquaint young ones with the process and to encourage them to stick with it so that as they grow they will come to realize the value of inner attention on their own. Don't take on any further responsibilities in this department, and certainly don't burden yourself, as some parents do, with supposing it to be your duty to lead the child to divine enlightenment. That comes later on, hopefully, when young people choose their own spiritual way and their own spiritual teacher. Until then you are a ground breaker. Recall the Buddhist aphorism "Each person lives, dies, and meditates alone."

Finally, realize that while prayer and meditation are the true heart and soul of any spiritual practice, the types of exercise you choose for your child depend on your own personal belief system and on the type of spiritual input you wish your young ones to receive. The important thing above all is simply to do it, and to do it now, while the soil is tillable and the spirit receptive. And to do it with all your heart; if children know you are sincere about your beliefs they will become sincere about their own. But just do it—while the child is open and innocent and redolent of that divine place where we all come from and to which we are all returning, returning.

"The story of Adam's exile from the Garden of Eden," writes Inayat Khan in one of the most moving passages ever written about a child's spiritual life, "shows that there is a certain time in a man's life when he is in the Garden of Eden, and after that time he is exiled from there and no longer experiences that joy and happiness and freedom that once the soul possessed. There is not one soul in this world who has not experienced that Garden of Eden; and that Garden of Eden is babyhood."[4]

NOTES

CHAPTER 1
1. Bukkyo Dendo Kyokai, *L'Enseignement du Buddha*. Tokyo: Kosaido Printing Co., 1981, p.222
2. Unpublished notes of A. E. Orage.

CHAPTER 2
1. Carlos Casteneda. *Tales of Power*. New York: Simon & Schuster, 1974, pp. 201–3.
2. Norbert Glas, *Conception, Birth and Early Childhood*. Spring Valley, N.Y.: Anthroposophic Press, n.d., p. 37.
3. Deborah Jackson, *Three in a Bed: Why You Should Sleep with Your Baby*. London: Bloomsbury, 1989.
4. Frederick Leboyer, *Birth Without Violence*. New York: Knopf, 1975.
5. Charles Morris, *Psychology: An Introduction*. Englewood Cliffs: N.J.: Prentice-Hall, 1976, p. 75.
6. Joseph Chilton Pearce, *Magical Child*. New York: Dutton, 1986, p. 53.
7. W. S. Condon, "Neonatal Movement Is Synchronized with Adult Speech," *Science*, 183 (1974):99–101.
8. A. Meltzoff and M. K. Moore, "Newborn Infants Imitate Facial Gestures." *Child Development*, 54 (1983), pp. 702–9.
9. Eileen Shiff (ed.). *Experts Advise Parents: A Guide to Raising Loving, Responsible Children*. New York: Delacorte, 1987, p. 6.
10. Wilhelm zur Linden, *A Child Is Born: Pregnancy, Birth, and First Childhood*. London: Rudolf Steiner Press, 1973, p. 81.
11. Karlfried Durckheim, *Hara: The Vital Centre of Man*. London: Allen & Unwin, 1970, p. 31

12. Norman Garmezy and Michael Rutter (eds.), *Stress, Coping and Development in Children.* New York: McGraw-Hill, 1984, pp. 55, 140–52, 163.

13. Glas, p. 37.

14. zur Linden, p. 82.

15. A. Thomas, S. Chess, and H. G. Birth, "The Origin of Personality," *Scientific American,* August 1970, pp. 102–9.

16. Alison Clarke-Steward, *Child Care in the Family: A Review of Research and Some Propositions for Policy.* New York: Academic Press, 1977, p. 25.

17. Clarke-Steward, p. 15.

18. Margaret Ribble, *The Rights of Infants, Early Psychological Needs, and Their Satisfaction.* New York: Columbia University Press, 1947, pp. 4–7.

19. Ashley Montagu, *Touching.* New York: Harper, 1978, p. 114.

20. Montagu, pp. 112–13.

21. Montagu, p. 136.

22. Polly Berrien Berends, *Whole Child/Whole Parent.* New York: Harper, 1983, p. 169.

23. Glas, p. 84.

24. Hazrat Inayat Khan, *The Sufi Message,* Vol. 3. London: Barrie and Jenkins, 1971, pp. 13–14.

25. Zur Linden, p. 85.

26. Khan, p. 16.

27. Khan, p. 14.

CHAPTER 3

1. Norbert Glas, *Conception, Birth and Early Childhood,* p. 87.

2. Hazrat Inayat Khan, *The Sufi Message,* Vol. 3, p. 23

3. Elizabeth G. Hainstock, *Teaching Montessori in the House.* New York: Random House, 1968.

CHAPTER 4

1. Quoted in Elizabeth Manwell and Sophia Fahs, *Consider the Children: How They Grow.* Boston: Beacon, 1961, p. 111.

2. Allan Fromme, *The Parent's Handbook.* New York: Simon & Schuster, 1956, p. 90.

CHAPTER 5

1. Joseph Campbell, *Hero with a Thousand Faces.* Cleveland, Ohio: Meridian Books, 1970, pp. 3–4.

2. Sylvester M. Morey and Olivia L. Gilliam (eds.). *Respect for Life: The Traditional Upbringing of American Indian Children.* Spring Valley, N.Y.: Anthroposophic Press, p. 53.

3. Henning Nelms, *Magic and Showmanship: A Handbook for Conjurers.* New York: Dover, 1969.

CHAPTER 6

1. Sylvester M. Morey and Olivia L. Gilliam (eds.), *Respect for Life,* p. 54.

2. Peggy Jenkins, *A Child of God: Activities for Teaching Spiritual Values to Children of All Ages.* Englewood Cliffs, N. J.: Prentice-Hall, 1984.

3. Thomas Merton, *The Seven Storey Mountain.* New York: Harcourt, 1948, p. 53.

4. Peter Occhiogrosso, *Once a Catholic.* Boston: Houghton Mifflin, 1987, p. 104.

5. George Gurdjieff, *Meetings with Remarkable Men.* New York: Knopf, 1980, p. 39.

CHAPTER 7

1. Stella Chess and Alexander Thomas, *Know Your Child: An Authoritative Guide for Today's Parents.* New York: Basic Books, 1987, p. 41.

CHAPTER 8

1. Eileen Shiff (ed.), *Experts Advise Parents: A Guide to Raising Loving, Responsible Children.* New York: Delacorte, 1987, p. 18.

2. Shiff, p. 149.

3. Fitzhugh Dobson, "How to Discipline Effectively," in Shiff, p. 125.

4. Charles Shaefer, *How to Influence Children.* New York: Van Nostrand, Reinhold, 1978, p. 29.

5. Marie Shedlock, *The Art of the Story Teller.* New York: Dover, 1951, p. 102.
6. "Teaching Responsibility," in Shiff, p. 180.

CHAPTER 9
1. Gerald E. Nelson and Richard W. Lewark, *Who's the Boss? Love, Authority, and Parenting* Boston: Shambala, 1985.
2. Thomas Gordon, *P.E.T.—Parent Effectiveness Training.* New York: New American Library, 1975.

CHAPTER 13
1. Hazrat Inayat Khan, *The Sufi Message,* Vol. 3, p. 14.

CHAPTER 14
1. The Muslim Student's Association of the United States and Canada, "Parents' Manual: A Guide for Muslim Parents Living in North America." Indianapolis: American Trust Publications, 1976, pp. 132–35.
2. Polly Berrien Berends, *Whole Child/Whole Parent.* New York: Harper, 1983, pp. 124, 132.
3. C. N. Getman, *How to Develop Your Child's Intelligence.* Wayne, Pa.: Research Publications, 1971, p. 60.

CHAPTER 15
1. Sylvester M. Morey and Olivia L. Gilliam (eds.), *Respect for Life,* p. 117.

CHAPTER 20
1. Francis Ilg and Louise Bates Ames, *The Gessell Institute's Child Behavior Guide.* New York: Dell, 1979, p. 308.

CHAPTER 21
1. Thomas Lickona, *Raising Good Children.* New York: Bantam, 1985, p. 97.
2. Allen Fromme, *The Parent's Handbook,* p. 149.

CHAPTER 22

1. Haim Ginnot, *Between Parent and Child.* New York: Macmillan, 1980.

CHAPTER 23

1. Richard Wilhelm (trans.), *The I Ching or Book of Changes.* New York: Bollingen, 1966, p. xxv.

CHAPTER 24

1. A. R. Orage, *Psychological Exercises and Essays.* London: Janus Press, 1965, p. 76.

2. Michael Shulman and Eva Mekler, *Bringing up a Moral Child: A New Approach for Teaching Your Child to Be Kind, Just, and Responsible.* Reading, Mass.: Addison-Wesley, 1985, p. 227.

3. Sylvester M. Morey and Olivia L. Gilliam (eds.), *Respect for Life,* p. 117.

CHAPTER 25

1. Parents' Institute, *Encyclopedia of Child Care and Guidance.* New York: Doubleday & Co., 1959, p. 226.

2. Thomas Lickona, *Raising Good Children,* p. 334.

CHAPTER 26

1. Chogyam Trungpa, *Born in Tibet.* New York: Penguin, 1971, p. 50.

2. William James, *The Principles of Psychology.* New York: Holt, 1890, vol. 1, p. 573.

3. P. D. Ouspensky, *In Search of the Miraculous.* New York: Harcourt, 1977, p. 143.

4. Hazrat Inayat Khan, *The Sufi Message,* Vol. 3, p. 14.

Bibliography

BOOKS SPECIFICALLY ON SPIRITUAL PARENTING, VALUES, AND MORAL TRAINING

Armstrong, Thomas. *The Radiant Child*. Wheaton, Ill.: Theosophical Publishing House, 1985.

Berends, Polly Berrien. *Whole Child/Whole Parent*. New York: Harper, 1983.

Board of Trustees, Central Hindu College. *Sanatana Dharma: An Elementary Text Book of Hindu Religion and Ethics*. Benares: Freeman & Co., 1906.

Christenson, Larry. *The Christian Family*. Minneapolis: Bethany House, 1985.

Eyre, Linda and Richard Eyre. *Teaching Children Sensitivity*. New York: Ballantine, 1987.

Franzblau, Rose and Abraham Frauzblau. *A Sane and Happy Life: A Family Guide.* New York: Harcourt, 1963.

Gell, Heather. *Music, Movement, and the Young Child.* Sydney: Australasian Publishing Company, 1967.

Glas, Norbert. *Conception, Birth and Early Childhood.* Spring Valley, N.Y. Anthroposophic Press, n.d.

Grollman, Earl. *Talking About Death: A Dialogue Between Parent and Child.* Boston: Beacon, 1976.

Hainstock, Elizabeth G. *Teaching Montessori in the Home.* New York: Random House, 1968.

Heller, David. *Talking to Your Child About God.* New York: Bantam, 1988.

Hughes, Laurel. *How to Raise Good Children: Encouraging Moral Growth.* Nashville: Abingdon Press, 1988.

Jackson, Deborah. *Three In A Bed: Why You Should Sleep With Your Baby.* London: Bloomsbury, 1989.

Jenkins, Peggy. *A Child of God: Activities for Teaching Spiritual Values to Children of All Ages.* Englewood Cliffs, N.J.: Prentice-Hall, 1984.

Khan, Hazrat Inayat. *The Sufi Message,* Vol. 3, London: Barrie and Jenkins, 1971.

Klipper, Ilse. *My Magic Garden.* Palo Alto, Calif.: Pathways Press, 1980.

Konig, Karl. *The First Three Years of the Child.* New York: Anthroposophic Press, 1969.

Leboyer, Frederick. *Birth Without Violence.* New York: Knopf, 1975.

Lewis, Paul. *40 Ways to Teach Your Child Values.* Wheaton, Ill.: Tyndale House, 1987.

Lickona, Thomas. *Raising Good Children: From Birth Through the Teenage Years.* New York: Bantam Books, 1985.

Manwell, Elizabeth, and Sophia Fahs. *Consider the Children: How They Grow.* Boston: Beacon Press, 1961.

McGinnis, Kathleen and James McGinnis. *Parenting for Peace and Justice.* Maryknoll, N.Y.: Orbis Books, 1985.

Milicevic, Barbara. *Your Spiritual Child: Primer for Metaphysics and Yoga.* Marina del Rey, Calif.: DeVorss, 1984.

Morey, Sylvester M., and Olivia L. Gilliam (eds.). *Respect for Life: The Traditional Upbringing of American Indian Children.* Spring Valley, N.Y.: Anthroposophic Press, n.d.

The Muslim Student's Association of the United States and Canada. *"Parents' Manual: A Guide for Muslim Parents Living in North America."* Indianapolis: American Trust Publications, 1976.

Pearce, Joseph Chilton. *Magical Child.* New York: Bantam Books, 1986.

Rozman, Deborah. *Meditation for Children.* Millbrae, Calif.: Celestial Arts, 1977.

Rozman, Deborah. *Meditating with Children.* Boulder Creek, Ca.: University of the Trees Press, 1985.

Sharpe, Estelle Avery. *Character Building,* vols 1 and 2. Chicago: Howard-Severance Company, 1910.

Shedlock, Marie. *The Art of the Story-Teller.* New York: Dover, 1951.

Shulman, Michael, and Eva Mekler. *Bringing Up a Moral Child: A New Approach for Teaching Your Child to Be Kind, Just, and Responsible.* Reading, Mass.: Addison-Wesley, 1985

Zur Linden, Wilhelm. *A Child Is Born.* London: Rudolf Steiner Press, 1973.

HELPFUL BOOKS ON CHILD REARING IN GENERAL

Beck, Joan. *Effective Parenting.* New York: Simon & Schuster, 1976.

Chess, Stella, and Alexander Thomas. *Know Your Child: An Authoritative Guide for Today's Parents.* New York: Basic Books, 1987.

Dinkmeyer, Don and Gary McKay. *The Parent's Handbook.* Circle Pines, Minn.: American Guidance Service, 1982.

Dodson, Fitzhugh. *How to Parent.* New York: Signet, 1971.

Fleming, Don (with Linda Balahoutis). *How to Stop the Battle with Your Child.* Englewood Cliffs, N.J.: Prentice-Hall, 1987.

Fromme, Allan. *The Parent's Handbook.* New York: Simon & Schuster, 1956.

Ginott, Haim. *Between Parent and Child.* New York: Macmillan, 1978.

Gordon, Thomas. *P.E.T.—Parent Effectiveness Training.* New York: New American Library, 1975.

Ilg, Frances, and Louise Bates Ames, *The Gesell Institute's Child Behavior.* New York: Dell, 1979.

Larrick, Nancy, *A Parent's Guide to Children's Education.* New York: Trident Press, 1963.

Montagu, Ashley, *Touching.* New York: Harper, 1978.

Nelson, Gerald, and Richard Lewak. *Who's the Boss: Love, Authority, and Parenting.* Boston: Shambala, 1985.

Pratt, Caroline. *I Learn From Children.* New York: Cornerstone Library, 1970.

Shaefer, Charles. *How to Influence Children.* New York: Van Nostrand, Reinhold, 1978.

Shiff, Eileen (ed.). *Experts Advise Parents: A Guide to Raising Loving, Responsible Children.* New York: Delacorte, 1987.

Silver, Larry. *The Misunderstood Child.* New York: McGraw-Hill, 1984.

Smith, Gerald Walker. *Hidden Meanings.* New York: Celestial Arts, 1975.

White, Burton. *The First Three Years of Life.* Englewood Cliffs, N.J.: Prentice-Hall, 1985.

BOOKS OF GENERAL SPIRITUAL INTEREST FOR PARENTS

Blakney, Raymond (trans.). *Meister Eckhart.* New York: Harper Torchbooks, n.d.

Campbell, Joseph. *Hero with a Thousand Faces.* Cleveland, Ohio: Meridian Books, 1970.

Coomaraswamy, Ananda. *The Dance of Shiva.* New York: Noonday Press, n.d.

Durckheim, Karlfried. *Hara: The Vital Centre of Man.* London: Allen & Unwin, 1970.

Eaton, Gai. *The King of the Castle.* London: Bodley Head, 1977.

Eliade, Mircea. *The Two and the One.* New York: Harper Torchbooks, 1965.

Govinda, Lama Anagarika. *Foundations of Tibetan Mysticism.* New York: Dutton, 1960.

Guenon, René. *The Reign of Quantity and the Signs of the Times.* Baltimore: Penguin, 1973.

Gurdjieff, George. *Meetings with Remarkable Men.* New York: Knopf, 1980.

Jung, Carl. *Modern Man in Search of a Soul.* New York: Harvest Books, 1963.

Kadloubovsky, and Palmer (trans.). *Writings from the Philokalia on Prayer of the Heart.* London: Faber and Faber, 1962.

Kapleau, Philip. *The Three Pillars of Zen.* Boston: Beacon, 1965.

Lewis, C. S. *The Screwtape Letters.* New York: Collier Books, 1982.

Ouspensky, P. D. *In Search of the Miraculous.* New York: Harcourt, 1977.

Maharshi. *Talks with Ramana Maharshi.* Tiruvannamalai, India: Venkataraman Pub., n.d.

Merton, Thomas. *The Seven Storey Mountain.* New York: Harcourt, 1948.

Nasr, Seyyed Hossein. *Ideas and Realities in Islam.* Boston: Beacon Press, 1966.

Ryan, John (trans.). *St. Francis de Sales: Introduction to the Devout Life.* New York: Doubleday, 1959.

Schuon, Frithjof. *The Transcendent Unity of Religions.* London: Faber and Faber, n.d.

Smith, Huston. *Forgotten Truth.* New York: Harper Colophon, 1976.

Suzuki, D. T. *Studies in Zen.* New York: Delta, 1955.

Trungpa, Chogyam. *Cutting Through Spiritual Materialism.* Berkeley, Ca: Shambala, 1973.

Waley, Arthur. *The Way and Its Power: A Study of the Tao Te Ching.* New York: Grove Press, 1958.

Zimmer, Heinrich. *Myths and Symbols in Indian Art and Civilization.* New York: Harper Torchbooks, 1980.

Zimmer, Heinrich. *The Philosophies of India.* New York: Bollingen, 1953.

A USEFUL PERIODICAL

Holistic Education Review. Holistic Education Press, P.O. Box 1476, Greenfield, Mass. 01302.